Who Cares About

A Global View of the National Identity Debate

Vron Ware has been writing about anti-racism, feminism and national identity for many years, both as a journalist and an academic. Her first publication was 'Women and the National Front' (1978), and her books include *Beyond the Pale: white women, racism and history* (1992) and *Out of Whiteness: colour, politics and culture* (2002, with Les Back). She lives in London, and now works at the Open University as a Research Fellow in culture and citizenship.

The British Council is the United Kingdom's international organisation for educational opportunities and cultural relations. Its purpose is to build mutually beneficial relationships between people in the UK and other countries and to increase appreciation of the UK's creative ideas and achievements. It is registered in England as a charity.

Counterpoint is the cultural relations think tank of the British Council: www.counterpoint-online.org

VRON WARE

Who Cares About Britishness?

A Global View of the National Identity Debate

ARCADIA BOOKS

Arcadia Books Ltd
15–16 Nassau Street
London W1W 7AB

www.arcadiabooks.co.uk

First published in the United Kingdom by Arcadia Books 2007
Copyright © Vron Ware 2007
Foreword © Neil Kinnock 2007

A catalogue record for this book is available from the British Library

ISBN 1–905147–58–9

Typeset in Minion by Discript Limited, London WC2N 4BN
Printed in Finland by WS Bookwell

Arcadia Books supports English PEN, the fellowship of writers who work together
to promote literature and its understanding. English PEN upholds writers'
freedoms in Britain and around the world, challenging political and cultural
limits on free expression. To find out more, visit www.englishpen.org or contact
English PEN, 6–8 Amwell Street, London EC1R 1UQ

Arcadia Books distributors are as follows:

in the UK and elsewhere in Europe:
Turnaround Publishers Services
Unit 3, Olympia Trading Estate
Coburg Road
London N22 6TZ

in the US and Canada:
Independent Publishers Group
814 N. Franklin Street
Chicago, IL 60610

in Australia:
Tower Books
PO Box 213
Brookvale, NSW 2100

in New Zealand:
Addenda
PO Box 78224
Grey Lynn
Auckland

in South Africa:
Quartet Sales and Marketing
PO Box 1218
Northcliffe
Johannesburg 2115

Arcadia Books is the *Sunday Times* Small Publisher of the Year

To Marcus and Cora and their generation of world citizens.
And in memory of their grandmother, Beryl Gilroy.

I seek my country in a place where they appreciate people with complex identities, where there's no need to untangle different strands.

Fatou Diome, *The Belly of the Atlantic*

Contents

Foreword
by Neil Kinnock

Vron Ware's book is the result of her listening to and talking to young people in the UK and in India, Pakistan, Bangladesh, Kenya, Poland and Ireland. Many were taking part in a British Council project called *New National Identities* through which, with the help of our partners – the Ditchley Foundation – we were trying to achieve two important objectives. *Firstly*, we wanted to facilitate communication for voices that are not heard often enough in the prevalent discussions of Britishness – mainly young voices, which come from a range of cultural perspectives and from foreign countries as well as the UK. *Secondly*, we wanted participants in the project to examine a maxim of the cultural thinker, Stuart Hall: 'The re-invention of Britishness is just inescapably taking place on a global plane.'

On the face of it, that may seem to be a surprising claim, especially when some postulate an introverted nationalistic version of 'being British'. But since Britishness has, in so many ways, been produced by the gathering of Celtic and English nations, laced with Nordic, French and wider migrations, and shaped by World-striding centuries, it does seem to me to be appropriate to put the modern sense of identity into a realistically *global* context. As I have put it elsewhere: 'There is so much of the World in modern Britain because Britain has for so long been in so much of the World.' Certainly, in this generation when travel is easier than ever before, when much of popular culture is transnational, when labour markets are more liberalised and globalised, when English is the main global language, when barrier-free Europe has arrived and is enlarging, narrow views of 'Britishness' are myopic to the point of being economically as well as culturally disabling.

In short, if space is not made for a strong international dimension, and what it tells us about who we are, who we have been and – most importantly – who we can and will be, the attempt to understand or share Britishness will be beached in the shallows of national branding and opinion poll punditry.

Vron Ware was commissioned to write *Who Cares About*

Britishness? by the British Council's think tank, Counterpoint. We were not seeking a report on an international project; we sought a set of reflections that were assisted by the author's longstanding engagement with questions of national identity and race in Britain. Our requirements have certainly been met. This is a book which, above all, has been formed by *listening* to people and to cultures. More of that is needed as essential feedstock for national and local governmental policy planning, as raw material for projects and programmes of the British Council as the UK's leading international cultural relations organisation, and as an essential ingredient of media and public understanding of youthful perceptions of identity and loyalty. We thank Vron for the contribution which she is making to advances in all of those areas with this original and thought-provoking book.

Neil Kinnock
Chair of the British Council

Who Cares?

Britain may be a country but it is not really a place. When you emerge from the Channel Tunnel by train the steward welcomes you to England, not to some abstract notion of the United Kingdom or Grande Bretagne. Touching down in Heathrow or Gatwick the cabin crew wish you a pleasant stay in London. This simple point becomes clearer when your port of entry is in Scotland or Wales. Few people expect to be told that they have arrived in Britain when they disembark in Glasgow or Cardiff. The moment you realise that you have entered a different country is when you pass through immigration controls. As you line up in the appropriate queue to hold out your credentials, your relationship to Britain defines who you are and what right you have, or don't have, to be there at all. If you've got that dark-red passport, you're in. You may not be made welcome by the uniformed officer checking your papers and you may not be thrilled to be back, but as a citizen you have rights and expectations that belong to you by virtue of that document.

Britain is a composite nation, a patchwork of anomalies, mistakes and inconsistencies. It has a standing army but not a football team. It has an anthem, a flag and a queen, but there is no patron saint of the United Kingdom and no founding date of an original constitution to be celebrated with even token formality. Its population is ageing, its children unhappy and its leaders routinely mocked by a raucous media. Its budding youth comprises a nation of tribes, identifiable by facial piercings, skin colour, costume, hair style and musical tastes. They speak different languages, comprehensible to each other but which sound unfamiliar to their parents. The prisons are full, the schools lack discipline and the hospitals are overcrowded, over-managed and unclean. Young men plot to commit terrorist attacks on fellow citizens but the wrong suspects are arrested or even shot. The country is at war but it does not honour the soldiers who have died in its name. Its allegiances are split between opposing camps, bound equally to Europe and the United States by history and geography. The country that once boasted its own empire is now struggling to find a new role for itself in a vastly unequal global order that it once helped to shape. Welcome to modern Britain.

It is hard to write about the country with affection unless you start to feel sorry for the poor blighters who live there. Like any other nation, its history and culture has produced recognisable stereotypes but the national characteristics and flaws of the British are recognised the world over. By and large they drink too much, swear too much, blame the government for everything and laugh at themselves when things get rough. Or going to the other extreme, they keep a stiff upper lip and smile politely: no sex please, we're British. And it is easy to make it sound like a mess, a dysfunctional family masquerading as an imaginary nation, one that definitely has a past but which promises a rather uncertain future. The notion of pride in being British is best left to the Olympics where it intermittently makes sense. Until recently one of the most characteristically British things you could possibly do is not talk seriously about what it means to be British. Not unless you were a white supremacist with an axe to grind.

There is national identity and there is the identity of a nation. Britain is an old country, wherever you decide to date its origins. It has been around long enough to have survived layers of identity crises, regardless of who or what provoked them. But the old stories that kept it going no longer do the trick. The victory against fascism that masked the humiliation of giving up the empire is losing its unifying effect as the multinational generation that won the 1939–45 war is passing away. The future looks bleak with the prospect of climate change altering the distinctive ecology of the British Isles, let alone causing unpredictable and alarming changes on a planetary scale. Refugees from wars, famine and endemic poverty are straining to be allowed in. Talk of the clash of civilisations both within the country and the world at large, fuelled by a nuclear arms race, leads to apocalyptic visions of mutual destruction. The word *security* is supposed to make us feel safe, but in promising protection it undermines established liberties and tightens state control.

Lately we are told that something called Britishness is the solution to many of these problems. First and foremost it is not the country that is having the crisis. It's the people who live there who have lost their sense of perspective: they do not realise how lucky they are. Sometimes it can sound like a veiled threat: *Let's teach the immigrants what Britishness means and make them want to belong. If they don't like it they can shut up or get out.* Other times it can appear more benign: *Let's all sit down and talk about what our values really are, what distinguishes us as a nation and what makes us stick together.* There are many agendas at work: migration, racism, terrorism, security, privatisation, foreign policy, globalisation, multiculturalism, social justice, education, citizenship, democracy. All demand attention under the heading of national interests, and all are marked urgent.

So who does care about Britishness? Certainly not me, I thought, when I started this book. To be honest, the title wasn't even a question, it was more a reply. When something as important as national identity becomes a political football it is tempting to turn your back and refuse to play. But the history of thinking about national identity as a powerful political tool has a long and prestigious past of its own. Pride in nationality creates 'unreal loyalties', said Virginia Woolf in her analysis of fascism in 1938, along with 'religious pride, college pride, school pride, family pride and sex pride'. Her classic work *Three Guineas* demonstrated the continuities between inequalities of class, race and gender inside a country and the endemic conflict between nations that threatened to destroy the entire world.

At the start of the twenty-first century, arguments about the value of defining national identities must be adjusted to the unprecedented circumstances facing the planet as a whole. Globalisation undermines the very idea of national borders surrounding separate spaces that demand special allegiance. At the same time government measures to tighten security entail increasingly invasive technologies in order to control and protect citizens in the national interest. Faced with devastating climate change on a planetary scale and the dire effects of scarcity, genocide, inter-ethnic conflict and war in many regions, the emergence of collective identities that go beyond the nation state appears to be a solution as well as part of the problem.

It was in this context that I set out to explore the politics of redefining what it meant to be British. Was it a case of the government desperately trying to wedge the stable door shut after the horse had bolted, or, as George Orwell had memorably urged, another stage in the necessary process of becoming more ourselves? These were questions that already felt claustrophobic if they were confined to the UK itself, however internally divided and ethnically diverse it has come to be. I decided it would be much more useful to learn what national identity meant somewhere else, and set off on a journey to five countries that were once part of Britain's global empire: Bangladesh, India, Pakistan, Kenya and Ireland.

I started with two certainties that guided my inquiries throughout the book. First, the tortuous history of Britain's imperial ambitions, from the slave trade to the invasion of Iraq, means that Britishness is a concept that travels with heavy global baggage. Second, the views of Britishness from a distance, particularly among countries connected through post-colonial ties, were likely to be invaluable in the process of re-evaluating what it might mean now. What I could not predict was how much I would learn from my conversations with the people I met, and how relevant their dilemmas about their own identities would be to the problems that Britain faces at home.

My hypothesis was that national identity had decreasing relevance for the class of urban, educated and globally-oriented young women and men that I intended to canvas. But as this was to be a comparative exercise it was important not to neglect the same issues at home, and the further I travelled to find significant vantage points, the more I kept my sights firmly on the old country. However, my orientation to the outside world, guided by a host of extraordinary individuals I met before I left, inevitably meant a selective view of where I came from. This takes me back to my opening point about Britain not being a place. To explore Britishness without leaving the realm would mean travelling deep into Scotland, Wales, Northern Ireland and England. Others have taken that route and I felt it was time to take a different perspective.

My story begins and ends in London, not far from my front door. This was not just for my convenience though. The capital has a life of its own as an extraordinary organism kept alive by the efforts of people who can trace their origins all over the world. It is not an easy place to live, like so many cities in the over-developed world, but it offers countless opportunities to let people get on with their lives regardless of where they come from or what they look like. While its record of functioning multiculturalism represents what is best about the country as a whole, I do not for a moment want to imply that London can be substituted for Britain, or that this is the only – or even ideal – place to explore other aspects of British particularity.

The result is a post-colonial account of what the creaking centre of an old empire is gradually becoming. It represents an attempt to think with a new generation of young people whose marginalised voices are rarely heard in pronouncements about national identity delivered from on high. They speak for themselves although I have used their wisdom and insights to negotiate a range of different and difficult topics. I have endeavoured to place their concerns and arguments alongside each other where it feels appropriate, naming individuals whose generous contribution to this project enriched it exponentially as it progressed. In the process of meeting them, and all the other participants who gave me their time, I have rediscovered a country I was beginning to think we had lost.

Chapter One: London Calling

London calling to far away cities:
'Come quickly, I'll lend you [money] to get here.'
London calling to far away villages:
'Sure, I'll come; had enough of living like this.'

(Radio Bagdad, 2006)

The sign outside the Cafe La Rosh looked promising. 'Christmas special – Feast for Two: Eat as much as you like.' You couldn't guess what kind of food was on offer from the exterior of the restaurant, but there was an accompanying invitation with the Christmas offer: chicken tikka roll, chips and salad. It wasn't at all what I had imagined. Leyla had just rung me to say she had arrived early and I found her inside bundled up in her coat with dark rings under her eyes. Sadly she was not in the mood for eating as she had been up all night finishing an essay. She ordered a creamy cappuccino while I asked for samosas and dal. We sat in pale-yellow armchairs across a round table and waited for Shamser to join us.

We had all met in the summer, a few months earlier. Though I was introduced to them through separate routes, I had discovered that both had grown up in an area of north-east London that was completely unfamiliar to me, and I was intrigued by the way they had each talked about it. I wanted to know more about this part of the city and why Leyla and Shamser felt so attached to their respective neighbourhoods.

Shamser was born in Leytonstone to parents who had migrated from India. He had lived in plenty of other places since but had recently bought a flat there. Early on in our conversations he had described a vivid memory of something that happened when he was six. A visiting uncle had begun talking to his parents about their relationship to India and where they felt they belonged. Shamser remembered taking part, shocking his entire family by protesting that he was completely British. Later, of course, this had changed, so that he didn't want to identify himself as British at all.

'I never went through a crisis, though,' he told me. 'I never went round asking myself am I this or am I that? I was perfectly happy being from Leytonstone and having friends from school there. I just didn't feel the need to describe my identity in relation to the nation. Well, except in football. I have been an England fan since I was five and that doesn't cause me any traumas either – apart from when they lose.' I wondered if it was a coincidence that David Beckham was born and grew up in Leytonstone, and would have been roughly the same age as Shamser.

It had been Shamser's idea to meet in this particular cafe.

'This area has changed so much,' he said when he came in and took off his duffle coat. 'In the late eighties this part of the street was closed off. Everything was closing down. There was a big department store – that closed. Sainsbury's closed. There was a really nice little toyshop packed with things – that went too.' The way he spoke about it I could imagine him visiting the shop as a little boy with his pocket money.

'Then in about 1992 a different sort of people started moving in, young professionals. Coffee bars and new shops began to open.'

I had noticed on my way there that there were branches of Primark and Matalan, relatively new chain stores competing with each other to sell cheap but fashionable clothes. They had become enormously popular although one had to wonder what on earth the garment makers of the world got paid to supply them. There was nothing very gentrified-looking about the range of shops in the high street, but it had its own underground station and plenty of banks.

There was also the prospect of the 2012 Olympics development which promised the wholesale regeneration of east London, not to mention the rerouting of the cross-channel railway through Stratford which was just next door. Soon you'd be able to get from Leytonstone to Lisbon or Ljubljana without going anywhere near an airport. You could sense the property prices rising as we sat there eating our lunch. Shamser had been smart to buy his flat before young people in his situation were priced out of the market.

A large building round the corner which seemed to be called 'Zulus' had caught my attention. I asked what that was.

'That's a club for South Africans. It's really popular on

Friday nights – you see them queuing round the block. It gets busy round here at the weekends. There's an O'Neills up the street where all the people from Ilford go.'

O'Neills is another outlet popping up on every other high street. Its logo is written in Celtic script just to underline the point that it sells Irishness by the pint. Draft Guinness and mashed potatoes are high on the menu and customers know what they are getting because it's the same in every branch. I wondered if it was the underground that attracted people from further east.

'I used to live in Chingford, just north of here,' said Leyla, 'and I hated it. I am so happy to be back in Leyton. I feel like I belong.' Leyton was south-west of Leytonstone and although I wasn't sure how they differed from each other, I was learning that it was important not to confuse them. Leyla, who has a young daughter, had moved out of the area a few months earlier because her profile as a youth outreach worker within the Somali community had made her a little too visible on her home patch. But living further out of London was not to her taste. 'I didn't like it all, we were the only black people there and I reacted really badly to it.'

Shamser asked her where she lived now, and they were off. I couldn't follow a word of what they were saying as my knowledge of local geography was non-existent. It was all street names, council estates, junctions, landmarks, school rivalries, sixth-form colleges, gang territories, youth clubs and other dense details that were hard for an outsider to follow. I did pick up that Leyla felt very much at home in the estate where she lived now, even though it was the bitter rival of the one where she had grown up.

'Some people call me a traitor and won't come to visit,' she said, but I wasn't sure how serious she was being.

Both Leyla and Shamser had had plenty of experiences of life in other cities since they had left school. Leyla had married and moved briefly to the United States with her husband, while Shamser went to university in Manchester and lived up north for a few years, with a short spell in Germany. Both had returned to north-east London like homecoming pigeons.

'I didn't appreciate it until I moved away,' said Shamser. 'I went to live in Munich for a few months after I left school and that was the first time I realised that the world was not like Leytonstone. I feel safe here, and it's so much more friendly than anywhere else I've lived.'

Leyla was born in Somalia where her father managed a big construction company. She used to travel to other countries with him and spent a year in Saudi Arabia when she was younger. When the civil war broke out in 1992 her whole family moved to the UK. By that time she was twelve years old. They stayed with a relative for two weeks before being offered a flat in a high-rise block in Leyton. Her mother accepted it right away and they lived there for fifteen years. Leyla was quite aggrieved that the building had recently been demolished in order to improve the estate as it contained the memories of her teenage years. She admitted the gang culture had worsened in the last five years of living there, but before that she had loved it. I asked her what it was like when she first arrived.

'I was thrown straight into a secondary school without knowing how to speak English,' she replied. 'Imagine that – when you are supposed to be cool, too.' Her experience of travelling to other countries, and spending a year in an Italian primary school in Somalia where she and her sister were the only black children definitely gave her a taste of what it felt like to be different. In fact, she said that Leyton was the first place where she didn't feel that her skin colour was an issue. She was told it would take at least six months to settle in, but it took her about six weeks.

'I was lucky that I was put in a very friendly class and they looked after me. It was a mixture of Pakistani, white, Turkish and Caribbean kids, boys and girls. PE was the only class I hated, and that was because I had to let down my hair. There were a few problems with the black girls as my hair was different – it was very long and curly – and I felt pushed aside. After that I cut it off.'

Both agreed that the beauty of living around there was that you could be yourself, you could do anything and no one would mind. You could cover yourself up or dye your hair pink. No one gave you any trouble.

'You know, I realised that I've lived over half my life here now. When people ask me if I want to go back to Somalia I say yes, but deep down I know I'm not sure.'

The cafe had filled up by now and I called the waitress over to ask her if she minded turning the music down just a notch as I was having trouble hearing our conversation. She looked a little startled and it was plain that she didn't understand. 'Are you Polish?' I asked, forgetting that this was likely to be a routinely annoying question that she got asked wherever she went. 'No, Latvian,' she replied. I wondered if she got tired of being mistaken for one of her Baltic neighbours, and whether there was a growing Latvian presence in this part of London as well as the increasingly ubiquitous Polish one.

Leyla got up to leave as she had to fetch her five-year-old daughter from school. She looked tired as she put on her coat and scarf, and I felt for her having to keep going until bedtime. The two of them had found other connections through their youth work, and made arrangements to get their groups together to play football. It was only after Leyla had gone that I remembered I had wanted to ask her if she had any more information about the situation in Somalia following the invasion by Ethiopian forces.

I had mentioned it on the phone a few days earlier and she said she had been devastated. She had family and friends in the country and was telling me only a few months ago that normal life had improved dramatically since the Union of Islamic Courts had established control. I knew that her mother was hoping to go back and live there and that Leyla herself was contemplating the possibility of return. Now it looked as though Somalia would become completely polarised again, producing more refugees rather than allowing people to go back and help rebuild the country.

Just then Suja, the owner of the cafe, came over to greet Shamser who was a regular customer. We invited him to pull up a chair and join us. He was born in Tottenham, his parents having come from Bangladesh in the 1970s. He had run his own security company previously, but the cafe, which had been open for three years now, was the culmination of a dream. From the start he had had a very particular concept of how it should work.

'I wanted to create an eating place with Asian food,' he explained, 'but with nothing religious or ethnic about it. It doesn't look like an Indian restaurant, does it?'

The cut-price chicken tikka roll had certainly been a clue but it didn't prove anything. In April 2001 the late Robin Cook, then Foreign Secretary, gave a speech on the benefits of multi-culturalism to the country as a whole. 'Chicken Tikka Masala is now a true British national dish,' he said, 'not only because it is the most popular, but because it is a perfect illustration of the way Britain absorbs and adapts external influences. Chicken Tikka is an Indian dish. The Masala sauce was added to satisfy the desire of British people to have their meat served in gravy.'

Cook's speech raised plenty of eyebrows at the time but few people would quarrel with his underlying point. However, Suja's cafe symbolised more than a desire to cater for British tastes. He wanted a multicultural ambience that mixed styles and menus, and confounded people's expectations of what an 'Indian' should be like. There were no rows of tables neatly laid for meals. Instead there was a mixture of modern chairs, light in colour and varying in style. Round tables of different sizes, each had a vase with elegant lilies made of striking fabric and wire. The food was already prepared in steel dishes behind the counter, all labelled and ready to be warmed up. On one wall there was a large photograph of a red poppy next to a less prominent print of Arabic calligraphy, which, Suja explained later, was a blessing from the Koran.

'I wanted every type of person to come in and to break down barriers. Sometimes I have black Africans and white South Africans sitting across the table from each other. It's hard to get Asians in here, though I'm trying to get them to accept that you don't have to be typical of the culture to enjoy the food.'

'This cafe is like a story in itself,' he said. 'You see people coming and going.'

At that moment the door opened and an elderly woman came in. Suja greeted her as an old friend. It was clear she was a regular customer. There was an oriental-looking water pipe on one of the tables which I thought was a decoration. Little did I know that smoking shisha was the latest trend to hit London. When I pointed it out to Shamser earlier he said that if we stayed till three-thirty we would see a crowd of Indian and Pakistani schoolkids, all over sixteen, of course, crowd into the cafe and disappear downstairs to the designated shi-sha lounge.

Later, Suja took us down to show us the space. It was a much larger room furnished with sofas and armchairs. 'I'm going for the Bugsy Malone look,' he said. There was a piano in the corner, a bar for serving coffee, but no alcohol, and an old record player.

He was very happy that younger people had found this place to congregate and was doing everything to encourage them and make them feel at home. I was a little surprised to hear him say, 'Sometimes I get the police down here, to come and chat to the kids. They need to know the police are there for them, and they needn't be scared of them. It's good for the police, too, to have a chance to talk to the youth. I just believe that everything should be transparent, no barriers.'

Now in his early thirties, Suja had lived through phases of conflict between police and local groups. The practice of profiling Muslim youths was souring relations further, particularly since the Home Secretary's visit a few weeks earlier. Following the arrest of a number of suspects in connection with the notorious liquid bomb plot, a significant number of whom had east London addresses, John Reid had made a forceful speech filmed live by the media. Speaking directly to Muslim parents in the invited audience he told them: 'There is no nice way of saying this but fanatics are looking to groom and brainwash children, including your children, for suicide bombing.'

Citing a verse from the Koran that says that every parent is the herdsman of their family, he warned them to look for the telltale signs and to talk to their children before their hatred grew to a point where they risked losing them forever.

The speech was controversial at the time, partly because Reid was interrupted by two hecklers who turned the event into a media spectacle. A more considered response from some of those who had attended the meeting appeared in the local paper. A young woman who teaches at a pre-school in a local mosque was reported as saying: 'Why don't they listen to the root causes of what is going on, rather than coming and telling us how to raise our children?'

In spite of the Koranic blessing upstairs, Suja was keen to point out that he had no time for organised religion. He had been 'cured', he said, by teachers in his madrasa who were too quick with the cane when he was a boy. 'I don't believe in learning through pain. I decided to create my own beliefs: fear of God, and being honest with yourself.'

At the basis of his philosophy was the conviction that people everywhere were the same. 'Muslims in Iran, Iraq, wherever, they are all Muslims, they are all reading the same book. You can't say one nation is different from the others.'

He had moved into the area when he was seven after his parents divorced. The family's new neighbours, a woman from Cork whose husband, an Eastender, was also Irish, had a daughter the same age who went to the same school. For various reasons the family took Suja in and for the next ten years he spent most of his waking time within their household. He felt that this experience had allowed him to absorb important parts of Irish and British culture while he was growing up – the experience of Christmas among them.

It was almost time to go, although I was tempted to stay to watch the invasion of shisha-smoking sixth formers. Suja's friend called goodbye as he left the cafe, and Suja gave a warm reply. The comings and goings made you feel as though this was a popular meeting place for locals. He was in the midst of explaining why he felt so much more at ease in a multicultural part of the world, and why Leytonstone was special to him as well.

'When I was selling security systems I used to travel to different areas in London and outside. It opened my mind to how people are. I learned to be able to tell just by looking how friendly or open they would be, I could read the signs. When you go somewhere quiet, they are less likely to be open to strangers.'

'Do you mean somewhere that is mostly white?' I asked. There didn't seem to be any point in mincing words.

'Well yes, they were more wary. In a multicultural place you go into a shop and people are more friendly and ready to chat. More ready to act human to human.'

It was hard to imagine anyone not being charmed by Suja. He was someone who listened carefully to what you were saying as well as being open about his own opinions. One of his biggest complaints which emerged during our conversation was his sense that British people were losing their manners. 'Integration shouldn't mean that you should change,' he said. 'You don't compromise with who you are.'

Earlier Leyla had complained in a semi-serious aside that her manager, who was from the west of England and of an older generation, often scolded her for saying 'innit' as opposed to 'isn't it'. 'I tell her it's my language and I'll talk how I want,' she said. Since she ran a youth group I knew that she would be exposed to all of London's latest linguistic innovations – not that 'innit' was particularly new. It would be fascinating to see how Somali was changing locally as a result of so many young people growing up in the UK. Perhaps it was turning into Somenglish, keeping the Somali structure but increasingly infused with English words and phrases. What language did Leyla and her Somali friends use for texting, for example? I made a mental note to ask her next time we met.

The topic of manners had touched a chord in Shamser, too. He was telling Suja what it was like when he lived briefly in a small town in Yorkshire. People had time, they queued politely, they didn't get impatient. 'That must have been how things were before.' I began to wonder where I was, listening to two young men harking on about the old days.

The conversation turned back to London. Suja had grown up in Walthamstow, an area to the north of Leytonstone, and had gone to another rival school with which Shamser was familiar. 'Do you ever look at our generation and wonder where they are now? A good proportion of people I used to know went to jail,' he said. 'Did that happen at your school?'

'I don't know,' replied Suja, pausing to think. 'I suppose there are a lot of people I don't hear from.'

His mobile phone had rung several times during our conversation, but being a gentleman he had not taken any calls. The afternoon was getting on, however, and I felt bad for taking up his time. He did have a business to run, and I'd also discovered that he was responsible for the cooking as well. I knew that I would return as I wanted to talk to him about Bangladesh, for one thing. He had mentioned that his father was considered a hero after the 1971 war of liberation, and I wondered why he had brought his family to live here in the UK so soon after. What did he make of the current crisis unfolding in the country every day?

As I walked back along the main street I passed a number of shops with fading posters advertising Polish sausages and cheap beer in their windows. These signs of expatriate life reminded me that when I lived in the United States for a few years we used to go to an establishment called the British Shoppe to buy treats like mince pies and crackers at Christmas or chocolate digestive biscuits and fruit pastilles when we were homesick. This was a chintzy but lucrative outlet for imported goods where pictures of the royal family and the Union Jack helped sell the idea that Britishness could be bottled and packaged for export.

Whenever we paid through the nose for our purchases we would wonder what the local customers thought they were buying. Although we never sank low enough to fall for the exorbitantly-priced cream teas in the adjoining cafe, we did find that just being in a room with shelves of Birds custard, Mr Kipling cakes and Sharwoods curry sauce made us feel strangely attached to the old country in a way we couldn't really understand. Sometimes I found it quite overwhelming, and occasionally it brought tears to my eyes just to walk through the door and hear the jangling old-fashioned bell. There was something about the smell, too, that made me long to be back in England. I found this very disorienting because I have always thrived on living in unfamiliar places.

Now I tried to imagine what it would have been like growing up in Leytonstone. It was a damp blustery day and nobody looked particularly thrilled about anything. However, I knew from the way I felt about my own neighbourhood further west what it was like to feel at home in a small pocket of the city. It wasn't just about being born somewhere or the length of time you spent there. It was partly the way that your own history became enmeshed in the bricks and mortar. It was also the feeling that you could get on with your life unimpeded, finding the right balance between being anonymous and being recognised by familiar people. It was hard to quantify all the ingredients that made the right recipe for your own personal taste. Maybe it was, as Shamser put it, a question of being able to be yourself.

⤷

There were four of them altogether. Two older men were holding their wretched paper, the Union Jack emblazoned across the logo, and the two younger ones were kicking their heels against the pavement. Actually I don't really remember what they were doing. I just saw red, blue and white. Without even thinking I walked up and stood in front of their stall, holding my camera which I had brought along for this purpose. My mother had mentioned that the National Front had been spotted trying to sell their papers and I felt it was my duty to record their presence. Besides, this was a public place, the town square in fact, so I had every right to take their photograph. But on this occasion I was not just doing my job. I hated everything the fascists stood for and didn't think twice before showing them what I thought about them.

The idea that they thought they could do business in my town, of all places, made the throwaway phrase 'over my dead body' suddenly come alive. When I say 'my town' I mean the part of the country where I grew up, where I spent the first twenty years of my life when I wasn't at school. Where my family still lived, and so, I suppose, where I came from.

I was born in a tiny village about four miles away from the town centre, but those four miles of fields (more like three today) made a lot of difference. Andover had been a small market town but was designated an overspill area in the 1960s. People were moved en masse from the bombed areas of the East End of London to come and live in new housing estates and work in the modern factories. As a child I was aware of the transformation and learned very early that the people who lived in the town were of a different class than our family and friends. A visiting aunt once told me in a reproving voice: 'People like us don't go to Andover on Saturdays.' After that there was no stopping me.

This particular day was a Saturday too, and I was home for the weekend, visiting my parents. By then I had moved far, far away to Birmingham, finding refuge in this huge industrial city a million psychological miles away from the wastelands of the south. The enemies in my adopted hometown wouldn't expect to sell their propaganda in Balsall Heath, the suburb where I lived, although they had no problem driving through it at high speed and threatening anyone who didn't look white from the safety of their cars. But here they were in front of me, trying out new pastures, so to speak.

I adjusted my lens and very deliberately took pictures of the men standing in a group. By then they had noticed me, their expectant faces turning to frowns as they realised that I was not an eager Aryan recruit. Having taken my photographs I turned and strolled off with all the insouciance I could muster. My parents were standing a little way off with my boyfriend. I had not consulted them but I knew they were broadly supportive of my behaviour. As I joined them, my mother slipped her arm in mine to protect me despite the fact that she was smaller than me.

It was like poking a stick into a wasp nest. The two older men started towards us, and I could see that they weren't coming to introduce themselves politely. We turned and moved off towards the covered part of the shopping centre, talking intently as though we had no idea they were pursuing us. My heart was beating fast as I tried to think how we could shake them off.

My mother's maternal instincts rose to the fore. Adopting her 'you'll have to fight me first' demeanour she suggested we went into Boots, the chemist. This turned out to be an excellent idea as it was a large branch with many aisles where we could both spy on our pursuers and hide from them. We hovered about in the shampoos and hairsprays for what seemed like hours while one of the National Front men, wearing a brown leather jacket, stood scowling by the door.

After fifteen minutes or so, my father, who was a district councillor at that time, spotted a fellow member in the shop with whom he fell into conversation. I felt on firmer ground: democratic power was on our side and justice would prevail in the event of anything nasty happening. I began to imagine headlines in the local paper, and was even a little disappointed to see that the leather jacket had disappeared.

Eventually we went back to our car, looking over our shoulders, and they presumably packed up shop feeling a trifle rattled. I would like to say that they never dared try to sell their papers there again, but the truth was that in 1980 this was not a particularly ripe place for organised racist resentment. Margaret Thatcher had just been elected and Tory rhetoric was taking care of Great White Britain for the time being.

Because of industrial expansion, employment was exceptionally high in that town and the main social problem was lager-loutism and violence caused by drunken squaddies from nearby Salisbury Plain. In the late 1970s it was still unusual to see black people there, though there were a couple of stalls in the Saturday market run by Asians. This is not to say that there was no racism, but to suggest that the majority of residents did not, at that time, look to white supremacist organisations to make sense of their everyday conflicts and grievances.

The pictures that I took on that occasion were duly filed away and I continued to keep an eye on the National Front membership levels in south-west England. Although this slightly unpleasant incident happened over twenty-five years ago, the memory has remained with me so that I can almost feel the pressure of my finger on the camera shutter.

At the time I was working for *Searchlight* magazine, which was dedicated to monitoring and recording the activities of these kinds of groups. We kept tabs on the National Front, the British Movement and various other far-right organisations the breadth and length of the country, and made every attempt to expose their violently racist, anti-Semitic agenda. But I remember this incident so vividly because it propelled me to act almost without thinking, putting my family at risk of physical attack. I don't say this in order to claim any special sense of bravery, but to make the simple point that I felt a particularly visceral responsibility to keep fascism out of a place that held enormous personal significance.

The outrage I felt then has often given me reason to pause over those tangled questions of roots and origins, home and homeland. Dealing with racism in towns where immigrants had settled was one thing, but the very thought of my birthplace being sullied by these pinch-faced outsiders made the blood freeze in my veins. How dare they! But why should I care, given that I had long ago abandoned this neck of the woods? By the time that this happened I felt like a stranger there myself.

One reason I was puzzled to feel this selective responsibility towards Andover was that I had left the area as soon as I could. There was no question of living in a village near my parents, even if I had wanted to. There were few opportunities for employment, apart from the local industrial estate and I had already been fired from my first job there on the grounds that I was 'not cut out for factory work'. And, as for a sense of belonging, I don't think I ever thought about it. The bright lights definitely had a bit more going for them than the smell of silage.

Among the student population coming of age in the seventies, home was somewhere you left in order to make your own life. It was one's duty as a radical, or certainly political, person to recalibrate one's experience of childhood and class-bound upbringing in order to break free of one's capitalist conditioning. As for national identity, that was for dinosaurs.

I was confused then about these powerful feelings of propriety towards a town with which I certainly didn't identify except in a vague nostalgic way. In the intervening years I had travelled quite a long way to find more exciting places to live. Although Birmingham was perfect for my needs just then, my route there had already taken me to India and back in search of gainful employment. This was well before the era of NGOs, and gap years hadn't been invented so my journey was a bit haphazard. After three months of travelling throughout the country looking for a development project that might benefit from my unskilled labour, I returned a changed person. My sense of shame that the country of my birth had occupied and ruled India for almost two centuries was not so much misplaced, it was just irrelevant to the people I met who had plenty of other problems on their plates after twenty-five years of independence. I was told very politely but in no uncertain terms that it would be better if I applied my energies to the problems at the source. Although I had new direction in my life I was not sure if and when I would ever go back to India again. Travel had definitely broadened my mind but the most important thing I had learned was to look at what was most familiar through the eyes of strangers.

᠆᠆

In the grey light of dawn a tousled young woman falls out of the coach and into the arms of her waiting sister. They are soon joined by their mother, all three women rapturous to be reunited. Aga has been living in England for a year and has returned with her savings to start her own business back in Silesia, the western province of Poland, where the rest of her family lives. In spite of the evident joy at her homecoming, however, the signs are that not all is well. When Aga asks her mother why her father hadn't come to meet her, a shadow passes across the older woman's face. He couldn't come, she replies, without offering an explanation.

Aga goes straight to her room when they reach their apartment block. It is full of cardboard boxes, not at all the cosy little den that she had missed so intensely when she was away. 'What happened to my things, Mum?' she calls out, plainly upset that her childhood possessions had been moved out of sight. There is a feeling that no one wants to tell her what is going on.

Her father is a leading member of Solidarity at the local mine. They are striking to stop the management from closing down five pits and the dispute is taking its toll on the town. Aga accompanies her mother as she takes him some soup on the picket line, and it becomes clear that he has little time for and interest in anything but the strike. The young woman wants to tell her dad about her life in England. She reaches for a Solidarity banner and folds it over a barrel to make a cushion. 'Don't sit on that,' he barks, 'show some respect.' He is not impressed that she worked as a cleaner the whole time she was away, and that she stole money from a charity jar to feed the gas meter.

Things go from grim to ghastly. Aga's boyfriend, who has been waiting for her return, has had to take a job as a security guard working for the mine company. He tricks her into handing over her savings and blows it all on a new apartment for them behind her back. She finds out that her mother's hair salon has been closed down and that she now has to see customers in her old bedroom, hence the boxes. It becomes clear that her mother is having a breakdown and Aga uses the rest of her savings to refurbish her old salon and set her up in business.

The parents do not communicate and the father doesn't register what is happening to his wife as he spends all his time on the picket line. The younger sister attempts to leave home by marrying a young man she is physically repelled by. Rioting strikers destroy the new salon and the ex-boyfriend is out of a job.

This is the first of three interconnecting stories that make up the feature film *Ode to Joy*, written and directed by three young graduates from the prestigious Łódź Film School: Anna Kazejak-Dawid, Jan Komasa and Maciej Migas.

The second features a young man called Peras, an impoverished rap artist with a short fuse whose single makes it on to national radio. His last surviving relative, his grandmother, uses her dying breath to tell him to go to England to follow the girl he loves.

The final story centres on Wiktor, a disconsolate student who cannot recover from a failed relationship and who is in danger of spiralling into cynical nihilism. Throughout the film, the radio constantly plays Peras's rap as a connecting soundtrack: 'Throw your hands in the air – forget the bullshit the politicians tell you.' Having established that these three young lives are hardly worth living, the last scene shows them inside a silver coach hurtling along a motorway en route to England. Aga has since been joined by her sister, making the getaway complete.

I went to see the film in Hackney, not just London's poorest borough but along with neighbouring Tower Hamlets the 'sickest' place in Britain, according to the local newspaper's report on recent market research mapping health trends. The way that the UK functioned as a beacon of hope for a new generation of restless and frustrated Polish youth – in the film, at least – made me wonder if their British peers in the same sorts of situations would leave if they had a destination calling their names. But how realistic was it? I saw at least two Londoners turn to Polish friends and say something along the lines of 'Oh dear, it wasn't like that for you, was it?'

I wrote accusingly to my friend Michal who had tipped me off about the film: 'You didn't tell me it was so bleak.'

He replied within the hour: 'Bleak? C'mon, this is how Poles heal themselves, this is the national psychotherapy – to show reality as so grim, dark and sad that it makes you wonder how come you haven't committed suicide yet. And since you're alive the conclusion is that maybe you haven't got it as bad as it looks... at least you haven't got it as bad as your neighbour.'

Then he added: 'But it's true, in Poland if a movie has a happy end it usually is referred to as cheap, American-style. Unfortunately Poles have to import happiness or modes to express it.'

Michal's story does not reflect the experience of the disaffected young migrant who blew in after May 2004 when Poland became part of the European Union. His roots in London go back years – he even worked on a paper round once upon a time. He was born in Kraków to Polish parents, but his childhood was disrupted after they divorced. His mother subsequently married a Polish dissident who was granted political asylum in the UK after martial law was declared in Poland in 1981.

When he was in his early teens, Michal lived in London for two years and attended the same Catholic secondary school that Tony Blair's sons were to go to later. He hated it. The uniforms, the all-boy ethos, the strict Catholicism, the bullying, all came as a shock to a shy little boy coming from a small school in Poland where he knew everyone. Early on he found himself in a line to make his confession in a language he didn't speak and a religious ritual he had never encountered before. He stumbled into the booth and went through the motions in halting English but the experience has stayed with him to this day.

Being thrown into the deep end of London was a different story. Since his mother now had younger children to care for, Michal was obliged to make his own way between English language classes, school and speech therapy – he had developed a stammer in the meantime. As a result he got to grips with London's underground system at an early age and began his own relationship with the city. He returned to Poland to live with his father and finished school there before going on to university. Now in his early thirties he lives with his partner, who is from his home town, and their two children in southwest London, a stone's throw from where he first came to stay with his stepfather. With his ear to the ground in both countries he has become an expert witness at interpreting the traffic that flows between them.

It was Michal who also told me about the Polish version of the Clash song, 'London Calling'. He mentioned it in passing one day and offered to send it by email. I couldn't believe my ears when I listened to it later. Although I had heard the original many, many times before, it always took me back to the era of 1979 when it first came out. It was a weird experience now, listening to Radio Bagdad singing it in Polish, complete with the sound of Big Ben at the beginning and the same raw guitar chords. This time I felt the same instant recognition, but was mystified by its foreign lyrics. Later Michal was kind enough to send a translation. It was immediately clear that the song reflected the same explosion of frustration, anger, hope and humour that I saw in the film.

London calling to far away cities:
'Come quickly, I'll lend you [money] to get here.'
London calling to far away villages:
'Sure, I'll come; had enough of living like this.'

The group, Radio Bagdad, won the top prize for their performance at an alternative rock festival, which takes place in western Poland every year. Perhaps it was their punk style that swung it for them, helped by their anti-war stance in a country whose government also supported the invasion of Iraq. Another verse is a reminder that the experience of migration is a human one, not just confined to Eastern Europeans.

Despite the new era; the model is the same
Go, escape, better yourself.
When you dream too much or just lack any idea
London attracts like magnet an iron bar.

All over the world there are young women and men desperate to 'go, escape, better yourself', an ambition that is routinely viewed with suspicion and hostility in the destinations they head for, including London. But the song is right too that this is a new era.

When the EU admitted ten new countries in May 2004, the UK, along with Ireland and Sweden, held out for unrestricted work permits for the new members unlike other established members like France and Germany which decided to enforce a temporary quota system. Few analysts expected that the staggering estimate of 400,000 Poles would enter the UK in search of work within the first two years, setting in train a pattern of migration that is likely to transform both countries in ways that are not yet evident.

It's a new era too in that cheap travel allows people to shuttle to and fro, often keeping homes in two places. Later I was to meet Kasia who had been in London for five years after moving from Kraków with her partner. He came as the advance party three months earlier and quickly found work as a carpenter. When Kasia came she had no trouble settling into a job in a beauty salon as she had worked as a hair stylist for fourteen years in Poland. They were comfortable and content with their lives here, she told me. Everything is fine apart from the health service, and for that they simply go back to Poland.

Elzbieta, her sister, had a different story. Her husband works in London as a butcher but she prefers to stay in Kraków in a flat they had bought with their earnings. He comes to visit once a month but when I met her in London she told me she was on holiday with their two children, aged three and eight months. After the first child she had stayed in London with her husband and worked as a cleaner in a bank outside working hours so her partner could look after their daughter. She was quick to point out that she is employed on the other side of the counter in Kraków. When she had the second baby it got more complicated and expensive. Home for her was definitely Poland. 'I like to live in my own place there,' she said, 'and my mother can help with childcare.'

↶

Despite London's growing reputation as one of the great world cities, home of countless ethnic groups speaking many different languages, it was also the place where Britain's first fascist was successful at the polls. The election of the first BNP member to public office in September 1993 came as a seismic shock to the many people of my generation who had been active in the anti-racist movement of the 1970s and 1980s. I was standing in the checkout at my local branch of Sainsbury's when I heard the news that Derek Beackon had been elected as a local councillor with a majority of seven votes. The by-election, in a residential ward of the newly developed Docklands in east London, had been fought largely over the issue of housing for local residents. Beackon's election slogan 'Rights for Whites' had been unambiguous.

It appeared from the interviews carried out hastily in the streets that few people who voted for the BNP cared about their underlying policies and the ideologies on which this political faction was founded. The slogan had resonated among those who felt that their housing needs had been passed over in favour of the local Bangladeshi population. Their votes had been cast as a form of protest, reflecting their frustration and feelings of abandonment by their former representatives in the mainstream political parties.

The milestone that this election represented was the cause of demonstrative hand-wringing in the media. Much of the apparent anguish was along the lines of: 'This area suffered so much destruction at the hands of the Nazis – how could they vote for fascism today?' Pictures of jack-booted, Nazi-saluting thugs covered the front pages of newspapers with headlines such as, 'Votes, fists and boots for the BNP'; 'Sieg Heil... and now he's a British councillor'; and 'Day Cockney pride turned to shame: growing threat from Europe's evil boot boys.'

As the news sank in it became clear that this particular pattern of exploiting deeply held grievances by offering simplistic, racist rhetoric was more than just a protest vote. The dyke had been breeched, and the BNP had established, for the first time, that they could be a legitimate party of dissent among those who wanted to blame immigration for all their grievances. Research in the borough of Tower Hamlets subsequently revealed the complicated layers of local pride, deprivation, poverty and powerlessness that dovetailed with broader scripts of national decline and economic recession. Living in the shadow of the newly-built skyscraper at Canary Wharf, the voters who propelled the loathsome Beackon to power were having the full fruits of Thatcher's designer-suited financiers jammed in their faces.

Watching the brand new offices and luxury flats under construction, the local residents were daily reminded of their economic insignificance in a part of the city once known for its independent spirit. The small number of social-housing projects designed to keep the local politicians content were therefore destined to provoke competitiveness and jealousy among prospective beneficiaries, unless the transition to the new housing units was carried out in a scrupulously fair manner. The fact that the larger houses on one estate were ready for occupants sooner than the rest meant that Bangladeshi families who required four- and five-bedroom accommodation were allowed to move in first. This apparent act of favouritism was enough to illuminate the call for 'Rights for Whites' and beam it over the rooftops.

As it happened, Beackon was ousted at the subsequent election and replaced by a member of the Labour Party. Activists in the area devised various strategies to defeat the BNP at the polls and to counter the racism that flourished in this part of the city. There was a concerted campaign to register Bangladeshi women to vote, for example, and the main political parties were forced to admit their collusion with dubious housing allocations in order to placate traditional white voters.

By 2006 the BNP did not field a single candidate in the borough of Tower Hamlets. That was the good news. However, the same local election brought the headcount of councillors holding seats across the country to fifty. In the London Borough of Barking and Dagenham, just a few miles further east of Tower Hamlets, the BNP managed to get a record number of eleven candidates elected to the local council, making it the official opposition.

The BNP vote had been rising in this area of the city for a while. In the London Assembly elections of 2004, the party had polled nearly five per cent across London as a whole, with almost fifteen per cent in Barking and Dagenham. Shortly after, the BNP won a council by-election attracting over half the total vote. Although split into two constituencies for parliamentary candidates, the area did comparatively well in the general election of 2005, particularly in Barking where the BNP candidate gained seventeen per cent of the votes – almost 5,000 in all. In 2006 the party polled an average of forty-one per cent of votes in the wards they contested as opposed to Labour's thirty-four per cent.

The list of grievances propelling voters to support the BNP was long and complicated. It included a fierce resentment towards a new set of immigrants: Poles, Bosnians, Albanians, Kosovans, and Africans. Their presence was linked to problems in every area of life: employment, housing, health, schools and crime. These voters had not heard the news from on high that immigration was good for the economy, or if they had they weren't convinced. What mattered was that their home town was no longer recognisable as the place they remembered.

The racism and xenophobia expressed on the street was

not the only story. Further analysis showed that the anger was mixed with a sense of betrayal by a national Labour government that was supposed to represent working-class interests. The cumulative effects of the wars in Iraq and Afghanistan and the aftermath of the London bombings in July 2005 were impossible to measure, but the area had seen the closure of local industries with the loss of hundreds of jobs – the Ford Dagenham plant had cut its workforce by over a thousand jobs in 2002 – and a rapid increase in outsourcing.

In the months following the election of the eleven councillors the BNP have tried to consolidate their reputation as a viable political alternative to the main parties. Their significance lies not in their numbers or their ability to seize power. A post-election rally in Dagenham, for example, only attracted fifty supporters. Nor should their populist bigotry be allowed to detract attention from other modern conventions of racism and xenophobia that drag the idea of Britishness back into a more comforting past. There are two main reasons why the fate of the BNP and like-minded groups is important to this deciphering of national identity. First, their history reveals the causes and consequences of a narrow nationalism based on notions of purity, whiteness and destiny. Second, their increasing ability to garner votes in towns and suburbs across the country indicates that the grievances on which they feed cannot be dismissed as the racist paranoia of a demented minority. A YouGov poll carried out just before the elections that brought Barking and Dagenham to notoriety showed that the majority of people in the country supported the BNP's policies on immigration. The only redeeming news was that a significant number dissociated themselves from the organisation when they were asked if they would vote for them.

∽

'Guess how many languages are spoken in London schools?' Pratap knew the answer to his own question as he had just made a documentary about bilingual education. He still liked to ask people, though. Mostly they suggested a number under a hundred. It was actually 136 at the last count. His film *Found in Translation* followed students in three different schools who were taking their GCSEs in their second language. 'Speaking two languages helps you have different perspectives on things,' said Stefan, whose family language is Greek. 'And sometimes you can't say what you want in one language. We have two words in Greek for love, *agape* and *eros*. In English there's only one.'

We were in Mumbai and Pratap's knowledge of Punjabi was helping me extricate myself from a man selling the biggest balloons I had ever seen. They were about six foot long and as long and plump as bolsters. Being in a generous mood I did not try to resist the incessant sales pitch and thought it worth paying the couple of pounds to be left alone. But having bought one packet, I was immediately approached by a concerned rival balloon-seller who told me that I had been robbed, and that his were even bigger. I let Pratap deal with it and later discreetly put my packet of tainted balloons in a flowerpot for someone else to find.

He had travelled there from his home in east London to spend some time training young Indian filmmakers and our paths had crossed several times. From my point of view this was a lucky coincidence as it was useful to have a fellow Brit on hand who felt at home in both countries. We were down at the Gateway of India, the magnificent monument built in 1911 to commemorate the visit of King George V and Queen Mary. It was not finished until 1924 but it was the location of the withdrawal of the last British troops in February 1948. I had only seen pictures of it in daylight, but now it was beautifully lit in a way that illuminated the arches high above our heads. Pratap had offered to take me there to see how it had become a popular hangout place for locals as well as a tourist spot. Couples and families with young children were sitting on the wall that bounded the harbour, and a pleasure boat decorated with lights waited for passengers. As we strolled around in the balmy evening we talked about what was going on at home.

He grew up further east, not far from Barking and Dagenham, and knew all about fleeing from the suburbs. He was a few years younger than me but we belonged to the same generation in terms of the battle of Britishness. His family was Indian in origin and as a child he had heard his mother's stories about Gandhi in one ear while listening out for the sound of name-calling in the other.

'When I was growing up in Ilford, particularly in the late

seventies and early eighties there was a very strong polarisation between the Asian community and the white community. There was quite a lot of hostility and I found it a deeply unpleasant place in terms of relationships – a lot of racist graffiti and the sense that you weren't necessarily safe. You had to keep an eye open in case a situation could turn nasty. I couldn't wait to get out. I loved my home and all that, obviously, but couldn't wait to get out into the city. That was my idea of freedom.'

'What do you say when people ask where you're from?' I asked, on the understanding that this was a question Pratap faced everywhere he went, particularly outside the UK.

'It depends who they are. I usually say I'm a Londoner. If I need to, I explain that my grandparents are of Indian origin – they grew up in East Africa and then took different directions. On my mother's side my grandmother moved the whole family back to Delhi and was involved in the New Delhi Congress and independence movement and all that. My dad grew up in Zanzibar and got his degree at Durham University.'

We had left the Friday evening revellers at the Gateway and moved on to another tourist landmark, the world famous Taj hotel just next door. Like Pratap I too had family connections to India but they had been more remote. My father had been in the Indian Army during the 1940s and on my mother's side I had jute and tea in my blood. I had also been to Bombay before though the experience couldn't have been more different as I had been travelling on a shoestring that first time. The opulence of the Taj hotel was unlike anything I had seen in any country.

Feeling a bit peckish we decided to walk to Colaba, a more congenial district where the prices were likely to be more down-to-earth. We continued our conversation about what was going on in the headquarters of what used to be the British Raj. Pratap had long ago made his home in the East End, not far from London's financial district and the famous Brick Lane. After the devastation caused by the Blitz in the 1940s and the subsequent clearance of overcrowded and inadequate housing stock, many residents of this area were moved out of the city to more modern estates on the periphery or to new developments both north and south of the river. Some of them might well have ended up in Andover.

'Yeah,' said Pratap, 'and the next ripple of this argument is about the white flight to the suburbs. If you look at the dynamics of voting in the last local elections the BNP did quite well in places where there is no significant ethnic minority presence. The politics of racial division and even racial hatred are becoming rooted in other places, based on fear and refusal – that's where the argument needs to happen.'

Having spent all day listening to young Mumbaikers, as they called themselves, talking about prejudice, discrimination against minorities and the impact of the bombings on the trains there just a few months earlier, I found it slightly odd to be focusing attention on Britain again. But it was good to talk to someone who shared a more historical view of both countries, post-empire. I asked Pratap what he made of the BNP's success in east London.

'Some of those people, rightly or not, feel that they have been dispossessed.' He replied. 'A whole structural social change has been visited on them without any consultation. They feel as if they have lost their capital and parts of their country. We need to engage with this sort of fear in a straightforward and direct way.'

During the course of the evening I worked my way round to asking Pratap what he thought about Britishness now. I knew that he was a Buddhist and not interested in nationalism of any kind.

'In my case, for my generation of progressive people, it seemed really important to say that we were British and part of the British landscape. We were involved in a project of reinscribing, reinventing Britishness to make it reflect the realities as a place that is more open, more plural. Why should Britishness be hijacked by patriots, jingoists?'

In the 1970s the racists used to chant, 'Ain't no black in the Union Jack' as well as, 'If they're black, send them back.' The refusal to accept new communities of legal British citizens as permanent fixtures in the cities where they lived was not confined to the streets. Versions of the same sentiment could be heard from government ministers to sections of the media to schools, the police force and other important institutions. It took more than two decades to prove that being black and British, or Asian and British, was not a contradiction in terms.

Now young people in their twenties like Leyla were outraged at the idea that they couldn't be British or that they had to justify it.

'I don't think I could take a citizenship test now, though,' Pratap continued as we tucked into our masala dosas. 'Apparently you have to swear allegiance to the royal family. I couldn't do it. I don't agree with the hereditary principle and don't see why it has to be defined as Britishness. There's a very fine radical English tradition that does not follow the hereditary male principle. Why should that be excluded from the notion of Britishness?'

I asked him if he would ever say he was English. He was born in England, after all. Englishness was proving a harder nut to crack than Britishness because it had retained a more stubborn sense of exclusiveness based on outdated ideas of ethnicity and colour.

'I think British is easier – it's clearly a bit more plural as it includes the Celtic fringe: Northern Ireland, Wales, Scotland. It seems to accommodate regional difference. Beyond that, we have to let go of categories of nations and nationalism.'

ᔢ

'Where is your favourite place in the whole world?' I asked Muhamed, as we sat sipping carrot juice in my local patch. Without thinking for more than two seconds he replied, 'Do you know Grant and Cutlers, the foreign language bookshop in town?'

I pictured him browsing there for hours. He's one of those rare people who can learn any language if they set their mind to it and at the last count it was twenty-seven. He had got Welsh under his belt since the last time we had met. But I suspected that he felt at home in the bookshop because it didn't represent any one country. He was born in Tusla, Bosnia in 1985 and grew up in a council flat with Serb and Croat families next door. When the war started he remembers Catholic neighbours inviting them to share their food, and people were determined to stick together to keep each other safe. There was talk of declaring Tusla an independent republic in an effort to stay out of the war, but once the bombing started it became impossible. Muhamed's father disappeared first, and then his mother was killed soon after.

Muhamed does not talk much about his past although his prodigious memory emerges in other ways, like his love of languages and the way he observes small details. His stereotypical view of Britishness, as he puts it, had been formed some time ago as a result of meeting diplomats and seeing pictures of the queen. As a child he saw British people as eccentric, or in his words: 'Wacky, over-polite intellectuals who wore socks and sandals.' In Bosnia he was fascinated by the world beyond the war. He devoured travel guides and absorbed information about other countries by watching the Eurovision Song Contest year after year. 'Did you know,' he said, 'that the English were the first to sing a song with a green theme?'

The first time I met Muhamed he had only recently arrived in the country and he was amazed at all the fuss about the failure of multiculturalism. 'I wish Bosnia was like Britain,' he said, as he told me about his first impressions. 'You should be exporting your success stories, not beating yourselves up so much.' Passing through immigration control at Heathrow airport he observed that the officers appeared to be a great advertisement for the easy-going diversity he longed for at home. There were black, Asian, male and female, headscarved, turbaned, bearded and cleanshaven, and they were checking everyone else's right to be there.

A few months later I met up with him again when he came back to London for a job interview. This time he had been given the third degree. When he protested he was told that he was in the high-risk category: young, male, white, Muslim. The fact that the woman who led him off to the special interrogation room was a black Brit was little comfort on this occasion.

The journalist Gary Younge ended his book *No Place Like Home: A Black Briton's Journey Through the American South*, with an account of coming back through Heathrow's immigration controls. He dreaded the routine humiliation as much as he was excited to be home, knowing that it was an inevitable hazard of living in Europe. To his surprise, the man who scanned his passport made no comment, although he did look him up and down. Gary was expecting the usual 'Is this your only passport, sir?' or something else that would remind him that he did not match up to the bona fide image of a British citizen. He picked up his luggage and started to walk through customs, only to be stopped there and told to open his suit-case. It's hard to summarise the dialogue that follows, but the book ends with the words 'I was back home, to a bigotry I understand.'

The scene is a perfect mechanism for illustrating one of the most telling situations in the lives of the modern traveller. As soon as you get off the plane, train, bus or even boat, you are required to define yourself according to your passport. At this point you are officially reminded of who you are, where you belong and where you do not belong. This is partly dependent on your actual documents, but you are also at the mercy of the individual officers into whose hands you place them.

A recent British Home Office report, 'Exploring the Decision-Making of Immigration Officers', found that deci-sions are often based on stereotypes about those likely to be troublemakers. Officers at Britain's international airports said that they relied on 'instinct' and 'intuition' to identify those who 'looked the part'. Sometimes it was nationality that gave the game away. Some were considered 'devious', 'pushy' and 'arrogant'. But overall it was skin colour, ethnicity and reli-gion that tripped their security alerts. The report proved that over three months in 2005, non-white Americans were more than twice as likely to be stopped than light-skinned fellow US citizens. Non-white Canadians were nine times more likely to face prolonged questioning than whites. For South Africans the disparity was even higher. For every white South African who walked through unimpeded, ten non-white compatriots were stopped.

As Muhamed discovered, looking white is not necessarily a protection, particularly as security had been tightened fol-lowing the London bombings. Nor does possessing a British passport always guarantee a friendly 'welcome home' from fellow citizens in uniform. But that little dark-red book is not to be taken for granted, as almost everyone I spoke to testi-fied. The document constitutes Britishness in a pocket-sized form, and it is generally thought to be one of the best things about it. The ability to travel with legal documents that prove your right to citizenship in the UK remains a significant index of privilege in a world where the majority earn less than $2 a day. On the other hand, to those who proudly present their own national passports at Britain's airports, regardless of visas, return tickets, clean clothes and an impeccably polite manner, be prepared to feel small, unwanted, under suspicion and less than human.

⤸

Britain has borders, miles of them, and mostly they are not in dispute or even policed. The rugged coastline takes care of that. It's only in Northern Ireland that immigrants from further south are known as 'Mexicans' as they gradually pluck up the courage to take advantage of the economic growth next door. It's not just that house prices in Belfast compare favourably with those in Dublin. There is a sense that the wall in the head that separates the Republic from the North is becoming easier to scale than it used to be a decade ago. But the history of sectarianism has left deep habits of division that can get you down before you even open your mouth.

'I hate the 101 questions game,' said Gillian. 'I get so sick of it. Because my name could be either Catholic or Protestant, and my surname is neutral too, people don't know where I'm from. I'm not a sectarian person and I hate to be put in a box.'

Claire agreed. The Irish spelling of her name was 'Clare', so she had questions to answer about that, as well as about where she was from. She had grown up in Belfast with a Protestant background, but neither of her parents went to church. Now, when faced with the equal opportunities question on job forms, she routinely ticks 'None' when it comes to religion. 'Unless,' she added, 'it's relevant to the job or I really want it!'

I felt for her when she said this. When I fill out job applications I always balk at the ethnic identification panel. Ticking the 'white British' box feels like a defeat, or at least a concession. I tend to agree with James Baldwin who once wrote: 'As long as you think you're white there's no hope for you.' But at the same time there are occasions when institutions need to know if they are successfully changing entrenched patterns of prejudice. Asking people to check the box of their choice has to be better than strangers trying to work out what you look like or what your cultural background is from your name or place of birth.

We were in Dublin attending a conference on national identity and the media for journalism students from the north and south. The session that I was attending had begun conventionally enough with introductions but the discussion had immediately turned to the political and cultural freight carried by people's names. 'Names can open doors in one place and close them in others,' Piaras was saying. He was the oldest in the group and clearly benefited from a much longer experience. Everyone had an angle on this topic of conversation.

'My name is Robert McIntosh and I grew up in England. People always assumed I was Scottish, but as far as I am aware I don't have any Scottish family. My middle names are Patrick and James, so a lot of people think I must be Irish, too. I only moved to Belfast a few years ago to go to university. I basically identify as English because I grew up there, but moving to Ireland changes the way you think about yourself.'

'My name is Collette which I think was fashionable at the time I was born in Dublin. In our household nobody had strong political affinities or views.' Like many in her age group Collette left Dublin after finishing school but returned when she was in her thirties. 'I got out as soon as I could. I lived in Germany for eleven years and then in Egypt for five, and only came back a few years ago. Although I could say that at times I was struggling with my identity, I never felt differentiated as Irish.'

'Were you often mistaken as British?' she was asked.

'If people assume I'm British, I bristle!' she replied. 'I was watching football in Cairo once in the British Embassy with an Irish friend who is a diplomat, and we both reacted strongly to the giant Union Jack on the wall. It sent shivers down my spine.'

Earlier, several speakers had addressed the conference audience about how they saw their role as print journalists and editors. The theme of the debate was not the legacy of sectarianism that had dominated the first seventy years of the divided country, although this provided the often unspoken context for the day's discussions. The main topic was how Irish national identity was changing as a result of factors such as globalisation or membership of the European Union. Racism was high on the agenda as a problem that was eclipsing sectarian violence. Both the Republic of Ireland and Northern Ireland, which remained part of the UK, were experiencing unprecedented levels of immigration as well as returning Irish nationals attracted by economic and cultural developments in the country they had once fled.

I had walked into the historic library of the Royal Irish Academy when the conference was already under way. I was just in time to hear a young woman raise her hand and say, 'What is Irish identity anyway? How can we talk about new national identity when we don't even know what the old one was? It's impossible to define.'

Another student responded, 'I don't think we should be talking about national identity at this point. I would much rather feel like a global citizen.'

'But what does that mean?' asked another young woman. 'Identity has to work itself out from the bottom up. It is something that happens through interaction and on an everyday basis, too.'

Later when we explored some of these questions over a more congenial dinner, everyone agreed that Ireland had been changing rapidly since the 1980s. I learned that there was an emerging cricket league in Dublin, formed largely among South Asian workers in the city's expanding IT sector. Until recently cricket was unpopular in Ireland as it was always associated with England. There were stories about Polish workers settling into cheap accommodation in Belfast, only to find themselves surrounded by Protestant communities that were not exactly thrilled.

'But what about the Irish citizens who are coming back?' I asked. 'How are they regarded by the people who stayed?'

Piaras had mentioned the fact that the number of former emigrants returning was the highest it had ever been. 'They don't have to apologise or justify themselves,' he said. 'There is a sense that everyone is reframing their identity because there is so much freedom to move around.'

Some of this freedom has adversely affected hundreds of those who have recently returned. New laws aimed at migrants from the newly expanded Europe have challenged the entitlements of lifelong Irish citizens who happen to have lived outside the country. In an attempt to stop 'welfare tourism' whereby anyone holding an EU passport would be able to claim benefits such as unemployment assistance and old-age pensions, the law was changed in May 2004 when ten new members, including Poland, joined. From that point, eligibility now depends on proof of two years residency. This has affected almost a thousand Irish citizens who are unable to show 'habitual status'. But apart from the shock of not being able to claim benefits that were taken for granted, many returning Irish find that the country has changed in other ways while they were away.

'A lot of people in Ireland come from rural areas, and they identify strongly with certain landscapes. They know a lot about where they're from,' said Eric. 'But increasingly people don't recognise the places of their childhood. The culture is changing all the time.'

⌒

'*What, in England they wear veils?* – that's what my friends in Pakistan say when I tell them about what goes on here. You'd be lucky to see one in Lahore.'

Tariq and I were sitting in the buffet car on the train to Leeds one Monday morning. Although we had just met, I had dragged him out of the quiet carriage after my companion had been reprimanded for answering his phone. Tariq was from Lahore, but currently living in Leeds studying for his PhD in politics. I invited him to come and get a cup of tea so we could actually talk above a whisper without enduring frowns from our neighbours across the aisle.

'I studied English literature for my first and second degrees,' he told me. 'When I got a place at Leeds University I thought I was coming to live in Brontë country, you know, the Yorkshire Moors and all that. I was so shocked when I got here. It couldn't have been more different from what I imagined. I was used to the Gothic architecture that the British left behind in Pakistan, and was so surprised at the modern buildings here, especially the council estates.'

Tariq had imagined the people in Leeds to be different, too. He had arrived expecting a rather Victorian sense of Britishness. For him the country was associated with imperial qualities such as being innovative, rational, hard-working, seeing a job through to the end. This was overlaid with martial values too, such as discipline and self-control. He was bound to get a shock in the clubbing capital of England. But it wasn't just the hedonism.

'I think the Victorians were more focused, less lazy. Now there is more of a benefit culture.'

He also had strong views about the Muslim communities he had met in Yorkshire. 'You would be surprised how crazy the imams are who come here,' he said. 'They are from rural areas of Pakistan and would never get a job over there.'

He told me a story about his barber, an immigrant from rural Pakistan. His wife was having trouble conceiving and asked customers to pray for them. '"Why don't you just go to the doctor?" I asked. He told me that prayers had worked for his brother-in-law and he was sure it would help them.'

Tariq was scandalised. 'They are living in the Stone Age,' he told me. 'This country really has a problem on its hands.'

I told him that I was due to visit Lahore, where he had studied at the prestigious Government College University. I asked his advice on where to go and what to see.

'It's a beautiful city, you'll love it. Go to the Mall, the main street, it's right in the centre. The station looks like Kings Cross, and the streets have names like Albert Road, Victoria Road. That's partly why we associate England with Victorian qualities, especially architecture.'

I asked him about his plans after he had finished his course. 'Everyone says I should stay, but my heart is in Pakistan. People are so modern there, and it seems so primitive here.'

I remembered my encounter with Tariq wherever I went, and not just in Lahore. Education provides one very compelling reason for young people to leave home and come to countries like Britain, though the costs for international students make it an option only for those on scholarships or from wealthy backgrounds. Spending a few years abroad can make it hard to return, particularly if employment opportunities there are limited. The experience of living among people of your own age from different cultural and social backgrounds allows a certain freedom to remake oneself. New relationships formed as a young adult become more significant and ties to family can easily become fractured over time. Falling in or out of love can radically affect a decision to stay or move on somewhere else.

Maki and her partner came to London together to do their PhDs. After they completed their studies, he went back to take a job in Japan but Maki was reluctant to return. In the meantime she had found opportunities in London where she had made good friends and had become used to a particular way of life. After her mother died, and then her grandmother a few years later, she realised that she felt less drawn to Japan, and less inclined to think about returning. But no matter how long she stays she still finds that people ask her constantly, not just, 'Where are you from?' but also, 'How often do you go back?'

Going 'back' for her means delicate negotiations about where to stay and being increasingly aware that she doesn't have anywhere she can call home in Japan. While she doesn't want to presume to call herself a Londoner, she is tired of having to answer that particular pattern of questions and assumptions. 'Obviously with friends I can explain my situation,' she says, 'but now that I have a new job I keep having these encounters and I'm beginning to resent the idea that I am not allowed to think of London as my home.'

Things were very different for Roxana, a young Colombian woman whose plans to do a PhD in London didn't work out. When she first came she was in a long-term relationship that finished soon after the couple arrived. She was not prepared for the loneliness that followed. 'London is a place for lonely people,' she said. 'I am an only child. I had the notion of being alone very clearly. For a person like me it feels such a relief that I am actually going back to Colombia and that I don't have to struggle any more trying to make myself alive here.'

When Roxana arrived at the London School of Economics she was astonished to meet large numbers of Colombians working as cleaners and security officials at the university. She became involved in the life of the community and planned to do ethnographic work on women's experiences of living in London. She told me she had learned a great deal about how people managed to make meaningful lives for themselves, especially in such difficult economic and social conditions.

'Language is a huge cultural barrier,' she said, 'especially when people have health problems and don't have language tools to explain to the doctor how they feel. Or they are scared of going to the doctor because they are afraid they will send them away or even report them. It's very good for doctors who come here from Colombia, though – they make a lot of money!'

Roxana knew this from her own experience. Jeannette, her mother, was visiting and had symptoms of a possible blood clot in her leg. When I met up with them they had gone to a doctor in the Colombian community, but Jeannette was desperate for a second opinion. I just assumed that they were entitled to go to the casualty clinic at the local hospital, thinking that in this respect, the NHS was something British that was worth boasting about. Roxana was doubtful if they were entitled to use NHS services for free. I began to wonder if I was right and asked Shamser, who is a sociologist working in public health. 'Just tell them to go along and explain what the problem is,' he said when I rang him. 'If there is an emergency they will see her.'

As it turned out there was no problem being seen in the hospital due to the possible seriousness of the symptoms, and Jeannette was relieved to have had a check-up. Shamser explained to me later that they were right to be cautious because the law had changed. Until 2004 you were entitled to free primary and secondary health care, he told me, that is, if you could show you had lived in the UK for twelve months, regardless of your status. Now you have to prove that you are lawfully resident (or agree to be returned home if your residence claim has been rejected) to be entitled to see a doctor unless you are suffering from certain infectious diseases, have a severe mental illness or, like Roxana's mother, need emergency treatment. Although, he added, health workers had made it clear that they did not want to be responsible for policing those eligible for care.

Being unfamiliar with the system and not knowing how to access health centres only adds to the stress of living in a strange country, especially if your residential status is in doubt or you are young and have arrived in difficult and traumatic circumstances. Shamser had been working with young asylum seekers in east London who had become separated from their families but were too old to be classed as children. The situation of many of these young people, fleeing from countries like Somalia, Burundi, Guinea and Vietnam, would have been more desperate had it not been for an initiative set up by a medical humanitarian organisation normally associated with emergency relief in war zones and the developing world.

'Did you know,' Shamser asked me, 'that Médecins du Monde has set up a project in east London to work with vulnerable migrants, homeless people, and female street sex workers?'

The organisation was started in France in order to provide health care to marginalised groups in developing countries, but as volunteers returned from overseas they began to realise that a significant number of people in Europe had no access to health care either. Trained medical staff work on a voluntary basis to make sure that individuals know how to make appointments and more importantly find out their rights if they are waiting for asylum decisions.

Among the young separated migrants interviewed by Shamser, the overriding problem was the sense of having no control over their lives. Those who spoke English with an accent, regardless of physical appearance, found that they were constantly suspected of doing something illegal. Their entitlement to live in the country as refugees was constantly being questioned and very few allowances were made for the traumatic experiences that had led to their precarious and vulnerable situation. Those who came from countries associated with terrorism, war or other destabilising forces – such as Afghanistan or Sierra Leone – often faced particular hostility, according to Shamser's research.

'Global political processes create the conditions that cause people to flee,' he concluded, 'and then penalise them when they end up in east London.'

✌

'Where do you feel more at home?' I asked Farhana as we sat down for our enormous breakfast in Karachi. She had recently married but since her job was in Oxford she was temporarily commuting from her parents' house in Banbury to Nottingham where her husband was based. 'I like Nottingham,' she said, 'I am already beginning to make new friends there.' Breakfast in a fancy hotel in Pakistan was like having all three meals rolled into one. It was hard not to be greedy and take everything on offer. There was even that abomination, the continental breakfast with the requisite croissant and assorted pastries.

I was asking Farhana what it was like growing up in Banbury, a smallish town in Oxfordshire with a surprisingly large community of residents who had come from Pakistan. Her father worked for British Rail, and was originally based in Oxford where Farhana was born. When she was ten, his job was transferred to Banbury so he moved the whole family there. It was also where his sister lived. Now as we travelled together in Pakistan I was forced to draw a family tree to make sure I followed Farhana's intricate web of relatives that stretched from Banbury to Bradford to Kashmir. Not that they were all strictly related, as the designation of aunt, uncle and cousin also applied to old family friends.

We had arrived at different times the night before as I was travelling from India. The first thing I saw as I came out of Karachi airport was a giant illuminated branch of McDonald's with a huge banner across the building that read: 'Where fun lands, worries take off!' I checked into the hotel and walked into my room to find the TV switched on and showing a football match between Newcastle and Manchester City in midplay. I was aware that there was something about the noise of fans shouting, and the atmosphere of the game that produced a wave of affection for boozy, disreputable Britishness. I left it on and contemplated the idea that I was sort of near home, or I would have been if a north-London club was playing.

I had asked Farhana to accompany me on my trip to Pakistan so that she could act as my guide there too, as well as talking me through her experience of growing up in the UK. She was born in 1977, the year I went to work at *Searchlight*, equipped only with an introduction by a mutual friend and a burning ambition to be the next John Pilger. When I lived in Birmingham at that time I taught English to many women of her mother's age, also from rural areas of Pakistan, but their daughters had been small then and I only knew them as children.

As we travelled together, we had plenty of time to find out about each other's pasts. She had a habit of carrying a large bucket of Maltesers in her luggage, which, she explained, was a precaution against being stranded somewhere without refreshments. Whenever we went anywhere near an airport, out they would come and we would eat handfuls to restore our flagging energy. I had never eaten so many in one sitting in my life.

Over a more nutritious breakfast, however, I had asked her to tell me about her family history. I told her about the student I met on the train, and she agreed that his impression of primitive and backward-looking Pakistani immigrants was typical of an urbanite from Lahore. The stereotype appeals to anyone looking for easy explanations of why multiculturalism had failed because it feeds into preconceptions about life in rural Pakistan as well as in the segregated northern towns of England. On the other hand, Farhana pointed out, one of her cousins lived in Bradford with her husband who was an imam in a local mosque. 'He knew the right people so didn't have to go through an interview process,' she said. 'And it's easier to live inside the community there because the teachers can all speak Urdu and half the kids in school are Pakistani.'

Farhana's father came to Britain in the mid-sixties, from Kashmir, one of the first substantial waves of migrants to come to work in Britain's factories and foundries. At that time, visas for those who wanted to come and work in the UK were open to people from the poorest parts of Pakistan, and her father was able to pay for his ticket by selling some land. As he was the oldest son it fell to him to go off and earn enough money to help support the entire family. Within ten years he had built a house for the family in Kashmir, provided for his parents, married off four brothers and two sisters and bought a house in Oxford. In 1975 he married Farhana's mother who came to join him from Pakistan proper.

'They didn't know each other before. She didn't speak English, although by then my dad did.'

I asked her if she was ever aware of her mother being homesick. 'I don't know, I don't remember. Dad now tells me she found it hard. A couple of times she took us back to Pakistan for about six months. The first time I must have been about two or three, then six or seven.'

Farhana looked radiant that morning. I had met her several times in London through work, and she was always wearing a combination of jeans, long tops and sometimes a dress. I don't really remember. Today she looked like she was going to a party and she was making me feel distinctly under-dressed. Her outfit, she told me, was from a shop in Leicester, and she was thrilled to be able to break it out at last. It was not the sort of thing you'd wear to work in England. It was a pale-green, flowing shalwar kameez suit, but unlike the brilliantly coloured outfits in Bangladesh the shirt was more like a dress as it came down almost to her ankles. She wore her long hair down and had bangles and earrings to match.

In the same way that Farhana spoke openly and affectionately about her parents' commitments in both countries, so she was happy to elaborate on the different paths that her siblings had taken. Both of her brothers were agreeable to marrying brides from Pakistan. The older one was paired with their father's step-brother's daughter. I asked her how he had felt about that.

'Our parents had agreed on the marriage when he was younger, and he didn't want to upset them. He was only twenty-two, and he went along with it. She found it really hard – there was a huge personality clash between her and mum, and me, too. In Pakistan you are desperate to come to the UK so you agree to marriage without checking. Then it all goes wrong and you wonder why. The girl was supposed to finish her education, but her brothers made her stay at home and learn to cook. For the next five years she sat around and didn't do anything until they were married, which really annoyed my parents. After that they said they were not going to do it again, but my younger brother married a girl from Pakistan. He wanted to – he had met her a few times before, though.'

Farhana had made it clear in previous conversations that her parents were considered very liberal by others in their circle. They had encouraged her to go to university and to travel to the Middle East as a volunteer peacenik. But even after the problems in her brothers' relationships with Pakistani brides, they still let her know that they would prefer to be involved in their daughters' choice of partners.

'With us girls, they tried for years, but we said no. They really do put pressure on you. If we had said yes they would have brought men over. Men are the breadwinners in Pakistan, but when they come over to marry British Pakistani girls they often end up doing demoralising jobs. This makes the cultural differences so much harder to deal with.'

↬

On 11 September 2001 Leyla woke up to find her life had

changed irrevocably. The day before she had left her family home in Leyton to fly to Minneapolis to join her new husband, a fellow Somali refugee who had settled in the United States. She had originally booked a flight that allowed her to change in New York, a city she had long wanted to visit. If her husband hadn't insisted on flying non-stop to Minneapolis she would possibly never have arrived as she was due to have landed on the morning of 11 September. As it was, she arrived in a different part of the country the evening before to be welcomed with warm smiles and a sense of possibility in a city that was to be her new home.

During the two-month period that she stayed in Minnesota, Leyla had plenty of time to contemplate what she wanted from life. She had trained as a dental nurse and by the age of nineteen she was the senior nurse in a practice in east London. As the oldest child in her family she felt her responsibilities keenly and was motivated to succeed, although it has to be said that marrying this young man, whom she met while he was on holiday in London, was something of an act of rebellion as well.

Marooned in the suburbs with no access to a car and feeling the instant hostility to Muslims after the attacks, Leyla began to wish she had never come. After two months she returned home to Leyton but by this time she was expecting a child. It was this that gave her a new direction in life as she discovered over the next few months.

Later I was to meet others whose lives had changed on that day. For Bano, a young woman born in the UK to Indian and Pakistani parents, the transformation came from outside at first, poisoning her relationship to the country she had thought of as home. She was a northerner, born in Sheffield and brought up in Blackburn. She was the kind of girl who wound up her parents by living in jeans through her teenage years. She never dreamed of wearing a hijab.

It was the way that non-Muslim friends reacted to the attacks on New York that upset her to the core. 'How does it make you feel?' they asked, as though the fact that she nominally shared the same faith as the hijackers might make her more sympathetic to their mission, and less shocked by the deaths of thousands of people. Her response was to urge her parents to buy a house in Pakistan where they could escape if necessary. In the process of deciding where they might feel more at home, the family began to explore new connections in a country that had also changed.

Chapter Two: Majority Report

The squatter settlement ran alongside two train tracks but seemed to be entirely incorporated into a market area on the other side. It was Friday morning, and there were many people selling bowls of fresh fish, some of it still alive and thrashing about. From time to time a train would come through and everyone would step away from the tracks, but they would take little notice and stand as near as eighteen inches to the moving train. The train tracks provide a thoroughfare to walk around, and make a bit of space to do business. There were several groups of women and children gathered round huge piles of yellow pods, taking the seeds out to sell to merchants.

Mahmud, my guide, lives just by there and is recognised by many people. He occasionally stops when he sees a good photographic image, but often too many people gather and pose for him so he misses his chance. He notices a dead body laid out in front of a family home, discreetly covered with a sheet and barely noticeable. 'They must have died in the night,' he observes quietly as he begins to focus his camera. A relative emerges from the hut, angrily remonstrating because she thinks he is taking pictures to sell them. He assures her he isn't.

It's interesting to watch someone like that working. My pictures of people are usually sneaky because I feel guilty and self-conscious, and I don't like them to see me do it, wherever I am. It must be all those years of spying on fascists. I can see from Mahmud's style that it's better if people know and are comfortable with that. He is planning a big project, and looking for a writer who can work with him to tell people's stories.

Apparently twenty per cent of Dhaka's population live in squatter communities like this. They buy water very cheaply from someone who can tap into an illegal supply nearby, and they take electricity from local shops, mostly without paying. I didn't ask about sewage and sanitation. The dwellings are made with pieces of wood, canes, and sacking made from plastic, as far as I can see. Cooking pots sit on fires in clay bowls. There is no shade, except for inside the structures which are mostly made of corrugated tin and plastic sheeting.

We walk along slowly, picking our way over the rails, and then cut through to the markets. Huge quantities of seafood, vegetables, pineapples, bananas, poultry – each kind of produce has its own corner. It is still quite early in the morning so not too crowded. The area with the trucks waiting to take goods away is very polluted. The market acts like a wholesaler's, and some people are evidently buying for their shops and restaurants. We choose a green coconut over a pineapple for breakfast. On the way back to the flat we see a man stripping old electrical cables to remove the copper wiring.

Later, in the privacy of my hotel room, I took a good look at my pictures. They had turned out quite well, and because I was shadowing Mahmud, some were even artistic. I sent a selection to a friend in London. 'Why did you do that?' he asked. 'What gave you the right to go and gawp at those people? Did you learn anything? Do you feel a better person?'

I had wrestled with this before I went, and after I came back, too. What did I expect to learn that I couldn't get from a book or the Internet? A Google search of 'Dhaka slums' will reveal that the number of slum dwellers has doubled in a decade, reaching 3.4 million people. Slum density in Dhaka is 891 people per acre, and ninety per cent live below Bangladesh's poverty line. Most of the people who live there have jobs too, as transport workers, domestic cleaners, day labourers, factory workers and hawkers. You can find that information in less than ten seconds.

I defended my visit because I wanted to look beyond the appalling statistics to witness something else. I am not talking about the romance of the slum-dwellers, the heroic resilience of the people or the creativity with which they carry on with their daily lives in such abysmal conditions. I had asked myself many times the night before, if it is voyeuristic to go and look at poverty. Is it morally better to look away when you have the chance to see? The benefit to my own education was clear, and my only doubt was what I was bringing away.

It was not the image of helpless poverty and want associated with the word *slum*, but rather an imprint of a different scale of inequality that I wanted seared on to my brain. In my mind's eye I saw London's untidy skyline etched against a different horizon. The wealth created there and in other powerful financial centres was being generated by a vast network of neo-liberal mechanisms that were increasing the yawning gulf between global rich and local poor on a daily basis. The relatively new country of Bangladesh existed in a region that had been profoundly changed by British occupation ever since the East India Company – the first joint-stock company in the world – set up shop in Bengal in the seventeenth century. The livelihood, and therefore the well-being, of the women I saw cooking breakfast on wood fires depended to a large extent on the price of labour in a global market and the endless expansion of consumer needs among people drowning in affluence thousands of miles away. What did it mean to talk about Britishness or 'national values' when the health of all societies was determined by powerful economic forces that favoured the wealthy and kept the vast majority of the poor out of sight?

As angry and disturbed as I was, however, I was glad to have Mahmud's serenity to counter my despair. Back at his flat he showed me the books of photography he had published, one on women at work and another a study of the communities that make a living on the country's extensive network of rivers. His extraordinary pictures of rural Bangladesh brought me back to earth. They reminded me of what many of Dhaka's new citizens had left behind in their flight to the city, pointing to different dimensions of hardship that demand urgent attention. His documentary project helped me focus on the dynamics that cause conflict and inequality within nations, as well as the economic and geo-political lines of division that run between them.

'Why are you interested in my pictures of indigenous peoples?' Mahmud had asked me two days earlier. That was a good question, but I was taken aback to find myself having to answer rather than being the one doing the asking. I told him that I hoped that my explorations of national identity in different countries would prompt open discussions about who belonged and who got left out of the collective equation. Everyone has their minorities whether they are regarded as aliens, settlers or natives, but I wanted to find out how questions of racism, bigotry and majority indifference were negotiated in different places. I also told him that we don't often hear about these things in countries like Bangladesh unless they affect the UK directly.

It was my second evening in Dhaka, and we were sitting in a pizza restaurant in Gulshan, one of the city's more middle-class suburbs. We had begun our conversation earlier, when I met Mahmud in the gallery that was showing his photographs documenting a small community called the Mru, living deep in the Chittagong Hill Tracts. After the gallery closed we went for a stroll to take advantage of the lifting of the emergency security restrictions that had been in place the previous day. I had arrived at the start of the constitutional crisis precipitated by the ruling party's choice of caretaker prime minister, and the atmosphere in the capital was still tense. We decided to go and get something to eat as it was still relatively early in the evening and there were a few restaurants staying open despite the crisis. I must say I was not expecting to eat pizza two days after leaving London, but rebuked myself for being surprised that a capital city like Dhaka would offer such a familiar range of cosmopolitan food.

A group of five young women had just sat down nearby, and proceeded to share several courses of pizza and different pasta dishes as they caught up with each other's news.

Mahmud's response to my answer was to rant about the highly-educated layer of society that lived, as he said, in air-conditioned rooms, oblivious to what was going on around them. 'Earlier today I took an American student, who I am training, to the biggest drug-taking place in Dhaka. I don't think that one per cent of these people here know that this place exists.' He had gestured to the people in the restaurant. 'Those in my generation who have money think it's best to educate their children in English-medium schools rather than Bengali. This leaves a big gap. The educated class do not know their own people.'

Born in the neighbouring Indian state of Assam, he moved with his whole family to Bangladesh in 1965. His father, who ran a madrasa, had him schooled there in order to acquire basic literacy and maths skills. He learned English along the way, and took some courses at Dhaka University where he studied public administration when he wasn't being an activist. He was proud that he spoke and wrote better Bangla than many of his 'better-educated' friends who all went to English-medium schools.

As we waited for our order, I asked Mahmud to talk about what motivated him. 'So what is your aim with these pictures of the Mru people?' I now countered. 'Is it to make people across the country visible to each other? To get people to recognise each other as human beings?' I asked.

'No,' he replied sternly, 'not as human beings, as equal citizens. That would be saying we are superior. Everyone born in the same country should have the same status. But I also want to emphasise that there are indigenous peoples here in Bangladesh. They were here before us, but because we have power we think that we were here first. Not many people know about them.'

The area known as the Chittagong Hill Tracts is the only mountainous part of the country. It is just one section of a vast expanse of rainforest that stretches from the hills above the city of Chittagong right across the north-eastern states of India and the northern part of Burma to the south. Always impossible to police, let alone contain within borders that run through impenetrable jungle, the area has proved a nightmare for successive waves of invaders seeking to subdue its inhabitants.

Comprised of thirteen distinct groups with different social customs, languages, and religious traditions including Buddhism, Christianity, Hinduism and animism, the Adivasis, or aboriginals as they were known throughout the region, began to occupy the region in the fifteenth century having travelled from Burma. In 1947 they were incorporated into the newly formed Muslim-majority East Pakistan, bordered by the Indian states of Tripura and Mizoram to the north-east, and by Burma on the other side. In 1964 the region's special status was revoked, partly as a result of the building of a large dam that flooded a vast section of the area, displacing more than 100,000 Chakmas, the largest group within the region. Bengali settlers were encouraged to settle there in order to open up the land for economic exploitation which interfered with Adivasi patterns of cultivation and provoked more conflict. After the war of liberation in 1971, successive Bangladeshi governments used military force to counter the self-defence organisation that was formed in 1972.

The insurgency added to the country's destabilisation in the 1970s and 1980s and resulted in the deaths of more than 25,000 people. In 1997 an international peace deal was brokered which brought the tribal peoples into the democratic structure of Bangladesh. The agreement provided them with a degree of autonomy by giving them responsibility for issues such as law and order, public administration, tribal law and social justice, environmental preservation, youth welfare and local tourism. Although it was broadly acceptable, it left many difficult issues unresolved. One was the migration of settlers who continue to this day to encroach on the area. Another was the presence of troops, which the government, most recently led by the Bangladeshi National Party, was reluctant to withdraw.

I asked Mahmud whether he had difficulty getting through to the region where the Mru lived. 'The army will stop me, even though I have permission. It's because of the history of resistance there, particularly since 1982 when they started placing Bengali people in the hills. There are far fewer killings than there were, but it does still happen. Basically it's a land issue.'

Mahmud was very aware of the power that photographers had as they marched into these secluded areas with huge camera lenses swinging from their necks. He had decided some time ago to approach his work differently, building up trust with the community he was filming. He had also pledged to donate a proportion of his book sales to support a school in a remote area. In theory there were a number of schools serving different indigenous groups but there were so few teachers that many were not functioning.

'I told them that if you're educated you can raise your voice, and that is the best reason to send your kids to school.'

Despite their marginal status in Bangladeshi civil society and their geographically remote location, the Mru people featuring in Mahmud's pictures are connected to the rest of the world via satellite TV. When he showed them the photographs that he had selected for publication, one of the older men commented, 'You have made us look like those people on the National Geographic channel. I didn't know we looked like that!'

Viewing the exhibition was an unsettling experience partly because this was indeed how the Mru people appeared – there was no disguising that. The captions to the photos did not read like detached ethnographic descriptions but instead used extracts from interviews with members of the community. There were many stories relating to medical practices and spiritual beliefs – the Mru practice a form of animism – and one is left to wonder about incidents of disease and mortality rates. The work raises a challenge to younger generations of Bangladeshis as they inherit their parents' struggle to sustain a modern secular state that can accommodate the demands of religious and ethnic minorities for autonomy.

Several days later I took a stack of newspapers that I had saved from my hotel and scoured them for clues about how Bangladeshis talked about the different problems facing their country. I found many insightful columns discussing the current crisis, and some interesting news items that filled in details. But there was one article, entitled 'To the polls, unless your name be Das, Tripura, or Roy' that seemed most relevant to the questions I was asking. It directly addressed the marginalisation of minorities within Bangladesh, both within the project of building national identity and through the failure to recognise – and respond to – the electoral power of non-Muslim voters.

The writer, Naeem Mohaiemen, a human-rights activist working with the Paharis, was particularly angry about the way that the idealism of his student days had dissipated, leaving a national project that was both diminished and divisive. He had attended a school that had an affirmative action policy, with the result that almost half of the students were Hindu or Christian. Later, when he and his fellow students crowded round the noticeboard looking at their exam results, the spread of qualifications and indicators of future success gave no indication of any discrimination based on faith or ethnicity. Their graduating class was sometimes known as Generation 71, providing the first wave of bankers, industrialists, television directors and other executive members of the young country's elite.

It was only when he took a closer look at the careers of his non-Muslim friends, two decades later, that he realised that Hindus, Christians, Buddhists, Paharis, Adivasis and all other minority communities constituted an invisible second class within Bangladesh.

'Our numerical majority,' he wrote, 'has chosen methods of predatory nationalism that include racist tactics that echo the Pakistan period, reify Bengali Muslims, and render all other identities invisible.'

He warned: 'When these small groups assert their presence and refuse to be assimilated within a Bengali Muslim identity, spectacular and extreme violence is our tool for producing a homogenised national map.'

Quoting Hannah Arendt's argument in 1968 that the idea of a national peoplehood was a fatal flaw in developed societies, he castigated the Awami League, the party that led the liberation movement, for not being prepared to come out forcefully in favour of a secular country in which all minorities, including Hindus and indigenous peoples, were represented.

Naeem's appeal for a secular country that does not fall for a genocidal version of nationalism ends: 'I shout at all of you with rage, because I refuse to accept a haven for me that is a nightmare for others.'

The article made an impression on me at the time because of the way the writer made the connection between nationalism and the persecution of minorities. A few weeks later I heard from him indirectly through an online petition circulated through the human-rights organisation, Awaaz. Writing in another Bangladeshi national paper, Naeem called attention to a new atrocity that had taken place in the Chittagong Hill Tracts. Choles Ritchil, a Garo Adivasi activist opposing the construction of an eco-park in the habitat of Garo tribals, was tortured and killed while in the custody of the joint army and police forces. Choles was leading the campaign to prevent the development which would take over 3,000 acres of land, causing the eviction of nearly 25,000 Garo people from their homes besides causing a wholesale loss of livelihood.

This time Naeem's anger was communicated in more sarcastic tones directed at the liberal establishment:

'I'm sorry, Choles Ritchil. I didn't believe the evidence of your body. I kept thinking the torture report was a hysterical invention. So much damage to one corpse, it seemed impossible. No, it is impossible. Isn't it? It must all be lies. Those human-rights groups, we know they always exaggerate – just to get foreign funding and create a bad image for Bangladesh.

I'm sorry because I couldn't find tears. How easy it was to dismiss your face on that poster. You look nothing like me. You have what my classmates so crudely called "chinky eyes". No one in my family has ever married anyone who looks like you, and even if we did we would make sure you converted to our religion. You see, you don't really exist. This is a country for Bengalis, not anyone else. Now you realise that, slowly, surely.'

⁓

When England was chock-full of factories, the skies covered in smoke and the cities groaning with slums, it used to be known as the workshop of the world. A century and a half later most would agree that this dubious honour now falls to China. However, a lot of people in Kenya would claim it too, although without the smoke or the factories unless you count the industrial flower and vegetable production poisoning the lakes. 'This is the land of workshops,' someone said, rather wearily, on my first day in Nairobi. 'As long as we have a self-proliferating army of NGOs, poverty will never be history.'

I was sitting in a room full of young people listening to the early stages of a discussion about identity. The conversation was becoming increasingly heated as individuals shared their reactions to a reading performed by one of the participants. David, originally from Rwanda and now a student at a local university, had come prepared for intense engagement with Kenyan peers.

'Identity crisis,' he said, 'is defined in the Webster dictionary as "losing purpose for existence".'

'What we are doing here,' he continued, 'is a kind of therapy. It's all very well being angry but if you get stuck there, it can make you feel like a victim, and this doesn't lead anywhere.'

Everyone was quiet. They knew what he was talking about without his having to describe the things he had witnessed as a child.

Murad, a Kenyan filmmaker of South Asian heritage, had just read us an extract from a recently published novel called *Londonstani* by British author Gautam Malkani. He started at the beginning with an account of a group of British-born Indian boys in west London in the act of kicking a white boy who had allegedly called them 'Pakis'. It was framed by the perspective of the narrator, himself British and Indian, who was in awe of the gang leader administering the punishment to the young man, the 'Gora', lying on the ground with blood on his face. He was in awe of his dress, his boots, his way of talking and his authority. The dialogue was written in colloquial English, a mixture of black and Asian slang with a local inflection.

No one in the room had read the book or knew what happened next, apart from Murad. The discussion began with an implicit understanding that the white boy on the ground had been caught expressing typically British and racist sentiments and was getting his just desserts. One or two observed that he showed how British people, meaning whites, were unsure of their own identity. You could see this, they said, because the boy clearly longed to be like those who were kicking his head in. He was attracted to their power and confidence in some pathological way.

Some expressed dismay that these young people – emblematic of many in their generation – looked up to each other based on the branded goods they wore on their bodies. They recognised the syndrome that style and image, and an ability to act macho, mattered more on the street than any sense of ethical behaviour. This came across clearly in the section read out by Murad.

When it came to Wahida's turn, she said in her quiet voice, 'I identify with the boy being kicked on the ground. I think it is important to look at the victim's point of view, to listen to the experience of minorities.'

Wahida was from the port city of Mombasa, centre of Kenya's coastal area. Like the Swahili language, the population in that part of the country had long been composed of influences and contributions from different ethnic and cultural groups. While she herself was a Muslim, the discussion about identity in Kenya was not so much about faith differences – although the previous president Daniel Arap Moi had encouraged the proliferation of Christian churches – but about the balance of power between ethnic groups in other areas where there was a greater link between territory, land ownership and identity.

After just two hours of discussion, I had heard many times

that in a country where your name identifies your ethnic background, it is difficult to avoid the stereotypes and resentments based on what happened in Kenya both during and since British rule. One of the strategies of colonial government – apart from defining territories as nations by arbitrarily declaring boundaries to divide one colony from another – was to manipulate divisions between the ethnic groups, or tribes, by intervening in local disputes, and by allocating land and political privilege accordingly. As a result, ethnic identity could connote anything from proximity to power, relationship to the land, entitlement to certain rights, physical and even intellectual characteristics, and other, more subtle, minor differences that were not obvious to an outsider.

After spending ten years in South Africa, Binyavanga, who was chairing the discussion, told us how he had thought differently about ethnicity as a result of living somewhere else that was divided along ethnic, as well as racial lines. On his return to Kenya he decided to test the theory that you could tell just by looking at a person's features and appearance if they were Kikuyu, or Lua or Masai, for example. For several days he sat in Nairobi's main bus station observing the crowds coming and going. When he felt certain that he could identify an individual as a member of a particular group, he would find a way of asking them.

Time and time again he got it wrong, much to his initial surprise. His research took him to a different conclusion however. 'Although you can never tell what tribe someone belongs to, you can always tell their class.' In a country where just one per cent of people had bank accounts, their socio-economic status was much more obvious than their ethnic heritage.

Katenga, another Rwandan student taking part in the discussion, spoke about the fatal assumptions made between Hutus and Tutsis on the basis of characteristics such as skin colour, height and build. 'Which group are you from?' someone asked sympathetically. 'I don't answer that question,' he replied. 'I am Rwandan.'

↬

The air space outside my window is rose-tinted, and its beauty adds to my sense of relief at the enforced solitude of my flight. The cabin steward hands me an English-language newspaper and I take it eagerly. It takes me a few minutes to realise that *The Statesman* is from India which is where I'm headed. I am overwhelmed at the thought of returning after such a long absence, thirty-one years to be precise. I had always wondered if I would ever go back and under what circumstances.

The front page of the newspaper carries the headline: 'PM Plays Minority Card.' Describing pluralism and socio-religious diversity as the defining features of India, Prime Minister Dr. Manmohan Singh made a strong pitch for 'creating an environment where all Indians can strive for equitable prosperity transcending religious frictions'. He was addressing a conference organised by the National Commission for Minorities, and the occasion was the publication of the Sachar Report on Minorities that set an agenda for the next five years.

Inside the paper I see a cartoon showing the same two men in two different conversations. In the first, one of the men is holding the Sachar Report and looking worried. His companion is saying, 'Tsk, Tsk, how terrible! Muslims now have a status lower than Dalits!' Next the two men are drawn in different positions. 'Hooray,' says the other, looking exuberant, 'Dalits have progressed. They have already overtaken Muslims!'

Investigating this report I found out later that it was the first systematic study of the social, economic and educational status of Indian Muslims and that it paid particular attention to the Dalits, a sector of society sometimes referred to as 'Untouchables' within Muslim communities. In another article I read that the Minorities Affairs Minister, A. R. Antulay, launched an attack on the previous government, the fundamentalist Bharatiya Janata Party, for its neglect of minority issues. He maintained that it was the government's key responsibility to ensure welfare of minorities, both linguistic and religious, who made up more than thirty per cent of the country's population.

'If minorityism does not have to be in India where else should it be in the world?' he asked.

↬

Sitting in the cafe area of one of Kolkata's largest bookshops, I sipped my scalding peppermint tea and reflected on the idea that I could be anywhere. If I hadn't just walked along the crowded street to get there, but arrived blindfolded from the airport, I would not even know what country I was in. There was European music playing, Mozart, and we were surrounded by books that were mostly in English. My companions around the table were discussing a seminar we had all attended earlier, the topic of which was, 'Me, Myself, I: Indian or Global?'

Julius, a Slovakian exchange student, was talking about something that had puzzled him ever since he arrived in Kolkata to study political science as an undergraduate. A citizen of a former socialist state, he admitted that his under-standing of organised religion was understandably shaped by very different attitudes to faith. What was the basis of com-munalism in India, he wanted to know. The subject had come up because Rafat, a young lecturer, had just remarked, semi-seriously, that 'being careful about what you say about religion is part of our identity as Indians'.

Julius explained now that he had approached one of his lecturers with this question and wanted a second opinion on her response. She had explained that the reason that religion was such a divisive force in society was because both Islam and Hinduism structured everyday life in different ways, and it was this that led to conflict.

Nila, a professor in the same institution, was intrigued as she knew the person concerned and was surprised at this rather conservative and simplistic answer. 'It's true, religion does play a role in the construction of place,' she argued. 'But after Partition all the major conflicts have been language-based. OK, there have been separatist issues that were based on reli-gious differences, but look at the newspapers of the 1950s – it was all about language as the chief index of cultural difference. No one talked about other factors.'

Rafat, however, disagreed with her and began to talk about his own background as evidence. Earlier I had heard him say by way of introducing himself: 'I don't believe in being rooted, I believe in being detached.' He described his family as being part of a traditional Muslim community, living in what he referred to as a ghetto in a town called Kalimpong. He had been given a strict madrasa education and it was only when he went to university that he began to read the text of the Koran. 'The culture didn't encourage understanding,' he said. 'It was actually very painful for me to realise that I could question what I had been taught, and that there were many other versions of Islam.'

Rafat attended St Xavier's College in Kolkata, a university founded by Jesuits in the early nineteenth century. Although nominally a Christian institution, its stated aims today, according to its website, are to nurture young men and women to become:

> [...] agents of social change in the country, thus aiming at making its own contribution towards transformation of all the present day social condition so that principles of social justice, equality of opportunity, genuine freedom and respect for religious and moral values, enshrined in the Constitution of India, may prevail and the possibility of living a fully human existence may be open before all.

There Rafat found himself being asked to read 'The Song of Roland', and remembers feeling humiliated by the way that Muslims were being portrayed from a Christian perspective. 'But then I read Edward Said and others, and realised that I could read this text in different ways – that basically this was a construction of Muslim identity that made sense in medieval Europe.' His understanding that any kind of monolithic identity was utterly faulty – and false – opened his eyes to the study of literature as a vehicle to explore historical and cultural change. He now teaches English at the same university as Nila.

Nila laughed as she remembered how she and her colleagues had reacted when, soon after he first arrived, this serious young man enquired whether their departmental dinner included halal meat. 'This threw us into confusion,' she said. 'Should we be pluralist and respect his customs, or should we try to persuade him to eat everything, like we all did. We sat and discussed it for two days!' Meanwhile Rafat brought his own sandwiches, oblivious to the way he had challenged the limits of their liberal secularism.

Nila gave another example of how people learned from each other through interacting in ways that confounded stereotypes and made them question their own behaviour. 'We were doing research on madrasa education in Bengal, and drove out to a very poor district where more than half of the population was

Muslim. We were invited into the home of a middle-class family, and to our surprise they also invited the driver to come and eat with us at the table. This would never happen in a Hindu house – they would offer the driver lunch but he would be expected to eat on his own or with the servants. But this behaviour was progressive in so many ways, it really made us think.'

This readiness to question our own ethics and norms when faced with people doing things differently in our midst is the foundation of a functional multi-faith society. But it can only flourish if that society does not encourage a hierarchy of faith-based practices. Later I began reading the book I bought from the shop, *The Argumentative Indian* by Amartya Sen.

It was a Buddhist emperor, Ashoka, in the third century BCE, he writes, who recognised the importance of celebrating the co-existence of different religions, and who first laid down the principles of open, mutually respectful debate in situations of conflict. 'That political principle figures a great deal in later discussions in India, but the most powerful defence of toleration and of the need for the state to be equidistant from different religions came from a Muslim Indian emperor, Akbar.'

This position, he adds, was argued in the 1590s when Europe was groaning under the Inquisition.

∽

Sange is a second-generation Tibetan refugee living in Kolkata. She doesn't speak Tibetan or identify with any country other than India, but because of the way she looks, she says she is often mistaken for Japanese or Chinese. How does she know? 'Because people speak to me in English.' Sometimes they assume she is from the north-eastern states, one of those people often referred to as 'chinkees'. 'I am instantly tagged as an outsider,' she complains with a sigh. 'But I think I share this with many of my fellow Indians, this confusion about who we really are.' Later she admits: 'People in the north-east resort to stereotypes too – we all do it.'

Sandeesha's family is from Uttar Pradesh, a northern state sharing a border with Nepal. For some reason an error was made in her passport. Her name Raypa was changed to Rayapa – and this is enough to identify her as south Indian. But she doesn't look south Indian, so this puzzles people. She once missed a plane because her appearance did not match the name on her passport, much to her annoyance. Based on her looks, a friend's mother gave her squid to eat, thought to be a delicacy in the north-east along with snakes and other 'squirmy, rubbery things'. Sandeesha was mortified at being assumed to be something she was not, but touched at the same time by her friends' thoughtfulness.

'India is a land of contradictions,' said Pranav. 'We don't have a concept of Indianness because this is a divided society, not a multicultural one. There is no common citizenship and people are divided by communalism and caste – it's all economic. India's "diversity" is entirely due to accidents of history.'

'India was diverse before diversity was defined,' said Rhagiv. 'But your identity only becomes important when you are in a minority.'

'Or,' added Altaf, 'when you choose an identity that you are not born with. We are born into a religion but we are free to reject it.'

'My name – Atya Khan – identifies me as a Muslim but people often say, "You don't look like a Muslim", as I wear jeans rather than a burka. Sometimes I feel lonely in my own homeland. When the bombs went off in Mumbai my friend's husband was killed. I actually had to think – should I go and be with her and console her? In the end I went to give blood. I feel disillusioned with religion. Sometimes we don't want to express how we feel with our friends, it's too painful. Recently I was talking to someone and she said as a joke: "You should go and live in Pakistan." I was so hurt I went away and wrote an article about it for our student paper. I often give my name as Atiya just so that people can't make assumptions about me.'

'I was meeting my friend in a restaurant soon after the bombs,' said Ipshita. 'She got there before me, but when I told the waiters I was looking for someone they couldn't believe it was this woman in a burka. They asked, "How can she be your friend?"'

Sanghay reflected: 'I am not a Muslim but I have a beard, and I was a witness to the bomb blasts on 11 July. Afterwards I have been stopped so many times and made to go through the metal detectors. I know that it's because of my beard, but I am not angry, I don't know why.'

'For a country to function as a truly pluralist society, people have to feel free to choose their identities in the belief that social and cultural equity is possible,' suggested Rita. 'But when you have a national narrative about "unity in diversity" this promotes a certain level of hypocrisy. People can kid themselves that they are really being tolerant and open-minded about what other Indians believe in when deep social inequalities are perpetuated through differential access to resources, jobs and education.'

～

I had spent the first part of the day travelling by train and was feeling pretty far from home. It was hard not to get confused travelling north of Birmingham. England is a small country but there are a lot of famous towns crammed together and it's hard to visualise where they all sit on the map. It was only when I alighted from the train at Blackburn, my final destination, that I realised I had forgotten to print out the directions to where I was going, and that I didn't have the telephone number of my hosts, either.

Blackburn had become notorious in the previous months because of the controversy over women wearing the niqab. It was the constituency of Jack Straw MP and a region that had long become habituated to conflict over issues of segregation and inter-community conflict. As a result of Straw's opinion piece in the local *Lancashire Evening Telegraph*, the town had been besieged by the media for several weeks doing their best to remind the rest of the country of things they didn't really want to know about. But the niqab debate wasn't my reason for going there today and the only problem I faced was that I was in danger of losing my way.

I needn't have worried though as a few phone calls got me through to the offices of Youth Action and Amar, my contact, offered to come and meet me. I refused, confident that I could remember his directions, only to discover that their location was barely five minutes' walk from the station. But the complexion of the town itself had disoriented me. There was no indication that this was a town that was dominated, in the public's mind at least, by an overwhelmingly Asian population. From my brief experience of the regenerated centre I passed through on my route, the town bore few traces of anything but a northern English cathedral town that had once boasted an elegant veneer of Victorian prosperity.

Youth Action is a national, publicly-funded organisation that harnesses the energy of young people looking for useful things to do, and I had come to find out what Amar's branch was doing. I had met him a few months earlier and spoken to him several times on the phone. This was more difficult than it sounds as he was constantly on the move. I discovered later that he was one of those people who communicated through his BlackBerry, which explained at least why his emails were on the curt side. In person he wasn't like that at all, and greeted me warmly as soon as I arrived. He ushered me into a bright but sparsely decorated meeting room and I realised from the plate of biscuits on the table that we were going to talk business rather than have lunch. As we waited for others to join us Amar told me about some of the projects he had been working on. He had recently returned from a trip to Brussels where he accompanied a group of young Muslims on a tour of the European Parliament. It was part of a citizenship project designed to explore the issue of Muslim European identity, and they were making the most of the fact that the Member of the European Parliament for the north-west was also head of the Labour Party in Europe.

I was eager to hear more about Amar's work, but first I was struggling with a more abstract, theoretical question. When Bano, a young woman researching social development, joined us, I jumped straight in, knowing from my brief contact with her before this meeting that she had a very astute reading of current debates about Britishness.

'Tell me, do you think that a strongly defined national identity is a useful device for protecting and supporting minorities?' I asked them both. Ten minutes after I had first spoken to her by phone, having received her contact details from a mutual friend, I had heard Bano's authoritative voice coming out of the radio in a documentary about the niqab controversy.

'Not if you keep calling them minorities,' she replied without missing a beat. I asked her to explain.

'The moment you identify groups as "minorities" you identify them as different,' she said. 'If you are different from the majority then you can't be British like the rest, you're always an "other". It underlines the idea that your race or ethnicity or faith has to have a box of its own as opposed to being mainstream.'

Bano was very firm on this point. Leaving aside her professional views which reflected her engagement with Asian and Muslim communities in the north-west, she had also learned from her life experience what it felt like to be made to identify as a member of a minority group whether you wanted to or not.

'I've always known I was Asian or Muslim, but I always felt British when I was growing up in Sheffield. I went to a mixed school where I was literally a minority, but I didn't really think about it. It was only when I came here to Blackburn at the age of fourteen and went to a school that was ninety-five per cent Asian – that's when I stopped feeling British. That, and 9/11, of course.'

I was surprised when she first told me that being in a predominantly Asian school made her feel more aware of being different.

'But why did you feel less British when you went to the mainly Asian school?' I asked. It didn't immediately make sense.

'Because the teachers kept telling us, you're Asian. They were all white – I remember my history teacher told me: "Just chill out, you'll be barefoot and pregnant by the time you're sixteen." He just assumed that I would be married off and there was no point in doing any work at school.'

As Bano reminisced about the differences between the two schools, Amar joined in:

'People live in an Asian ghetto, they go to the state school which is mostly Asian, they have their mosques. They live their whole life in an Asian area. The system is designed like that. In my day there were no "minority" teachers, but I had a better experience. One of my teachers suggested I become the school librarian and through that I found I was good at organising things. It gave me skills that have been really useful. I think there are lots of Asian teachers now who feel a stigma after 9/11 and 7/7, and they try to keep a low profile. If you have to give up your identity as British, you will never belong.'

⌒

Shocked by the blazing lights of McDonald's on landing in Karachi, I jumped at the chance of going out on the town. I was eager, too, to follow Tariq's advice and explore the modern side of life in Pakistan. Seema, the young woman who met me at the hotel, offered to take me to supper with a little shopping thrown in. I asked to go to somewhere new and she was more than happy to oblige by taking me to one of her favourite malls. It was like being back in the US again – there was even a popcorn kiosk whose fragrance filled the entire building and left me feeling giddy. The building was full of families – it being Saturday night – and hordes of young girls. Young men in groups are not allowed in, Seema told me, but as she spoke a gaggle of older boys passed us on the stairs. She says that they find ways – the usual one is that someone's sister works on security. The shops ranged from familiar brands to local designer outlets with beautiful fabrics, handbags, clothes and jewellery. It was all terribly expensive. I didn't buy anything. Seema showed me a store with non-alcoholic perfume and we tried lots of different brands.

She took me to the food court on the top floor and asked if I'd like to eat there. The choice was overwhelming and it was mostly chicken. Dishes ranged from Pakistani to Mexican via Italy and China. I ordered some fish and rice of indeterminate ethnicity, and I wished I had held out for a Pakistani option. But it all looked pretty plastic. We sat chatting amid the hubbub of families all around us, although I had to make an effort to talk and not just sit there watching people.

∽

European imperialism cut a swathe of desserts across the world to prove that gastronomic exchange was not a one-way street. As tapioca, sago, semolina and rice pudding were brought back to fill the stomachs of British schoolchildren, Anglo-French recipes for trifle, blancmange, apple pie, soufflé and crème caramel found new after-dinner life long after the colonial households that once insisted on such niceties had been sent packing. After trifle in Islamabad, minus the sherry, on my last day in Pakistan, I reflected on the unpredictability of cultural mixture and the versatility of custard.

I had spoken to Bano shortly before I travelled to Pakistan. I wanted to ask her advice on what sort of questions to ask the young people I had planned to meet there. 'So do you feel more comfortable in Pakistan, then?' I asked her. 'How do you think that they see you, as a British person?'

'Well,' she replied. 'It's odd. I find that people are very Westernised there, especially in big cities. They stare if I eat rice with my hand. Even in villages, rural areas where you have to use a shovel to go to the loo, sometimes they look at me strangely if I don't use a spoon to eat rice.'

'So what would you want to ask them, if you were in my shoes?' I asked. She thought for a few minutes.

'I'd want to know what they thought about Pakistan, of course. But do they sometimes wonder: Would my life have been different if my parents had emigrated to the UK before I was born? If they were planning to go, I'd ask them what they would hang their cap on and what they would let go of?'

I took Bano's questions with me to Karachi, Lahore and Islamabad as I tried to find out if there was something that might be called 'Pakistaniness'. My experience there was different from anywhere else I went. On the road leading up to the airport in the capital, Islamabad, there is a monument bearing the profile of Muhammed Ali Jinnah, one of the founders of Pakistan and its first president, with the giant words: Faith, Unity, Discipline. You can't miss it. Both times I passed it I thought more deeply about my conversations with the young people I had met. A significant number had been quick to express a rather formal patriotism and to say things like, 'My country's flag is a symbol of my identity.' I knew this wasn't the whole story, but it made me curious about what it must be like to live in a new country.

This degree of loyalty to a national project was connected, in my mind, to the shortest answer I received to Bano's question: What would you take with you if you were to emigrate to the UK? For many, being Pakistani was inseparable from being Muslim, and the reply 'my faith' came almost without thinking. Their understanding of Islam as a tolerant religion that accommodated those of other faiths was a firm component of their patriotism.

'This changes from city to city and from province to province,' said Iftikhar in Lahore. 'In urban centres like Lahore and Karachi you will find people talking about being Muslim first and then Pakistani. That's the majority of the population. But if you go to Peshawar or a city in the north-west frontier province, people would talk about their ethnic origin. They would say, for example, "I'm a Pashtun first, Muslim second, and then Pakistani." It's not a question that will be the same all over.'

The words 'faith, unity, discipline' were a stark reminder of the country's traumatic origins, forged from conflicting ideals about the role of faith in questions of citizenship and belonging, government and the rule of law. But just yards away there are plenty of signs that the economic forces of neo-liberalism are driving the higher and lower echelons of society further apart as they are everywhere else in the world. Huge billboards show ecstatic women with mobile phones pressed to their ears, adorning the streets and public places with a cheerful sense of optimism and affluence that reminded me of my visit to the mall in Karachi. Banners advertising new Mediterranean-style villas fly from lamp posts down the middle of the modern capital's dual carriageways.

Despite the sometimes defensive note about how the country was viewed from the outside, few people denied the economic problems that divided the population within cities as well as across regions. Beneath the instinctive loyalty to Pakistan and the lack of public discussion about life for non-Muslims, there was a readiness to admit that feelings about national identity, in the big cities at least, were directly related to social class and income. I wished that Bano had been there with me as I sat and watched these ideas dramatically unfold in a short play improvised by a group of students in Islamabad.

Scene: TV Studio, live broadcast of a panel discussion.

Cast:

Presenter	Wali
University graduate (MA)	Mohammed
Middle-class housewife, (Mrs I)	Shirin
British-born, confused Desi (BBCD)	Farhana
Poor farmer (PF)	Hamza
Member of Parliament (MP)	Mariam

Presenter: Welcome to *Fifteen Minutes*. Please welcome my guests who have given their valuable time to come into the studio to discuss our topic of the week. First, Mr

Mohammed, do you feel that the media has a large role to play in defining national identity?

MA: I just want a job. I am not in the least interested in national identity. I just need a job. My mum is sick and I have to pay bills, rent and lots of other things. My sister is still unmarried. I don't care about any identity.

Mrs I: What media, what national language, what culture? I don't like this media.

BBCD: I have problem with the media. I don't feel they represent my views at all. I hate them.

PF: What media? I don't even have a TV. You talk about media, satellite TV. I don't have a TV – you give me TV and then I'll talk to you about it.

MP: I think the media provides a very important representation of what a nation thinks about its country. This gentleman is complaining about the media – I'm sorry if you don't have TV because if you had one you'd see how much positive work they are doing…

PF: You the government, right? What are you doing for me?

MP: We give you loans…

PF: What loans? They don't even let me enter the bank!

MP: There is so much foreign aid coming for you. Members of Parliament like us are going about begging the super nations for loans for you…

PF: You are in for five years… before five years I earn 500 rupees a day. After five years I earn 120. Where are the rupees? That's what you do…

MP: You are worried about supporting your children! Look at me – we as parliamentarians have a responsibility to support the whole nation!

PF: The whole nation! Put food on my table – how much I ask? I have a donkey cart.

Presenter: I think we are running out of time now and we should move on to the next question…

MA: (Hands the MP a folder): Please have a look at my CV.

MP: Sure. This is what we are doing. We are giving people jobs. Ungrateful people like you (turns to PF). Make your CV!

PF: How can I make my CV? I don't even know how to read and write!

Presenter: Next question, please, please. Do you believe that ordinary citizens should have more say in their country's foreign policy?

MA: I think the public does participate in making foreign policy. Our members are elected through our votes, so indirectly we are making foreign policy.

Mrs I: I don't know. Ask my husband, he is very involved... shall I call him? (Gets out mobile)

Presenter: Do you have any opinions of your own?

Mrs I: No...

BBCD: I am a firm believer in protesting. I hate the foreign policy of this country. We should get rid of the leader – what's his name? Pervez Mushharr, Musharraf? Get rid of him!

PF: What foreign policy! What you do with foreign policy! I say make domestic policy, put food on my table, educate my children.

MP: We are a democratically elected government. We represent every single person sitting here.

PF: You represent me? You have a donkey cart?

MP: We are a Third World developing country. It's easy to complain but it's difficult to make foreign policy...

PF: I say forget foreign policy! Make domestic policy to put food on my table!

MP: We are talking about foreign policy with a person who only cares about a piece of bread. He does not care about the policies of this whole nation.

Presenter: Next question... Do you think governments should be actively involved in promoting national identity?

MP: Yes, we do. On every 14 August and 23 March we play national anthem, we play national songs...

PF: She plays national songs! You know what I do? I work. With this (holds up shovel).

MP: Think about those who sacrificed so much for this free air that you breathe.

PF: Sacrificed for what? There is no nation – who cares for us?

MA: (To presenter) I'll give you an updated CV. I work weekends and holidays. Do you have any job opportunities?

Presenter: Next question: How does migration out of the country affect Pakistan?

MP: It is very wrong and I am totally against it. People should be responsible enough to...

PF: Forget about migration!

MP: You keep interrupting! Migration – look at him! I appreciate you, son. (Turns to audience) He is working in his own country, mixing his sweat and blood in this country. (Turns to farmer) If I give you a visa will you migrate to England?

PF: I want food. Give me food in England, I will go. Give me food in Alaska, I will go to bloody Alaska.

Presenter: What about you Mr Mohammed?

MA: I am ready to go anywhere – on Mars, on the moon, anywhere. Just give me a job. For heaven's sake, give me a job.

Mrs I: I want to go to England, they have good shops over there.

Presenter: Good decision to go, Farhana?

BBCD: Hmm, I know a lot of people find it difficult when they migrate to the UK. I think if they are willing to accept, to integrate into British culture, then yes.

Presenter: Last question: If any of you had to migrate to the UK what would you take with you and what would you leave?

PF: What would I take? My donkey cart? I have nothing.

MP: He'll stay here and I promise we will provide youths like him with everything. This is our country, our national identity, we can make it better.

PF: These people, they have corrupted our country. Riding in their black mirrored Mercedes cars... while I pass by on my donkey cart.

Mrs I: I would take nothing. I would buy everything from there.

MA: I would take nothing, just myself.

Presenter: We can all see that our views on national identity depend on our position in society. All of you have different backgrounds and come from different places – but at least we can all agree to differ.

&

'Britain is paradise on earth,' said Muhamed, as we sat down to eat our Italian gelato in the middle of winter. 'From the point of view of a white, educated, homosexual young man in his mid-twenties, Britain is a far better place than Bosnia. Or Austria, for that matter, where my boyfriend lives. Although it's more accepting there, the only way I can visit him is with a student visa. As a Bosnian citizen I can't work without a permit. And there's no way we could live together in Bosnia. If he could get a job here, under EU rules he could import me and we could have a civil partnership. That would be ideal.'

I never know where Muhamed is and I always worry if I don't hear from him. Once he wrote me an email from a bus travelling from Austria to somewhere in Bosnia which, as he said, used to be home a long time ago. A few weeks later, when I was in Delhi, I remembered his predicament about where to live.

Akhil was talking about the rights of sexual minorities in India. 'We all watched Elton John's wedding,' he said laughing, although he was not trying to make a joke. Akhil's point was that it was the British who donated Section 377 to the Indian Penal Code in 1860, making it an offence to 'have carnal intercourse against the order of nature'. Known as the 'Anti-sodomy law' the act in theory applied to heterosexuals as well, but in effect it has criminalised all same-sex behaviour irrespective of consent.

'You can buy copies of the Kama Sutra on any street corner in India,' he said, 'and you can see men and women doing all sorts of activities with each other. But the chapter on homoeroticism will have been deleted.'

The inherited and anachronistic law is being challenged in the courts as a result of a concerted campaign orchestrated by the Indian section of the international organisation, the Naz Foundation, and supported by public figures across the diaspora. One powerful argument is that it blocks effective ways to prevent HIV/Aids by forcing sexual minorities to conceal their behaviour and lifestyles. The law has made it possible for police to blackmail and harass suspects, which often leads to imprisonment, corruption and suicide. But Akhil was doubtful that decriminalisation would lead to civil partnerships in the near future. 'Things are changing, though, and if Britain can do away with repressive laws, so can India.'

Akhil's point about the Kama Sutra was not a throwaway remark. The story of exotic Indian sexuality has long fascinated travellers and tourists, becoming part of the colonial view of what it meant to be Indian. The legacy of this has influenced public health agendas in India, not just by outdated measures like Section 377 but also by prohibiting all sexual behaviour judged to be deviant. Erasing the diversity of sexual identities that have developed within particular cultural contexts over a long period of time forces people to adopt headings used in North America and Europe such as gay, lesbian, bisexual and so on. These labels do not always reflect the reality of people's lives. In many parts of the world, a married man who chooses to have sex with another male does not necessarily identify as someone who is gay, for example. There might be many more categories of minority sexual behaviour that are tolerated – or prohibited – within different communities. For this reason the Naz Foundation International is careful to emphasise its belief in 'the innate capacity of local peoples to develop their own appropriate sexual health services, where the beneficiaries of a service are also the providers of that service.'

Akhil was adamant that gender and sexuality had to be tackled together. 'All marginalities intersect, and it's important not to fight oppression in an isolated manner. You just have to look at the matrimonial ads in the paper to see the problems there.'

He showed me a poem by Sonali from a collection of writing on queer politics in India, entitled *Because I Have a Voice*. It was called 'Sum Total – a matrimonial':

> *One Indian woman*
> *Plus*
> *a lesbian*
> *Minus*
> *a dutiful obedient wife*
> *Minus*
> *a tall, thin, slender, eligible girl*
> *Minus*
> *long, beautiful hair*
> *Minus*
> *a doctor, an engineer, or even a businesswoman*
> *Minus*
> *timid and speechless*
> *Plus*
> *determined and opinionated*
> *Divided by*
> *abusive demons*

*Multiplied by
a will to survive
Sums me up*

⌐

Muhamed's past had made him extra sensitive to the role that
ethnic and religious bigotry plays in daily life. But rather than
assign all faiths to the history of human error he is curious
about the roles they continue to play in modern times. One
minute he was telling me that he was fascinated by the history of the Church of England, and next he admitted that he
supported Liverpool, both because and in spite of the fact that
they were associated with Catholics. 'Did you know that the
last pope was a fan of Liverpool FC?' he asked me. This was
because one of their goalkeepers, Jerzy Dudek, was Polish. The
late Pope John Paul II who had played football in his youth in
Poland met the Polish national team in 2004. He told Dudek
that he was a fan, and that he followed Liverpool wherever they
played for that reason.

'Being Catholic is part of Polish national identity,' said
Gosia the first time I met her. 'Telling us that we can't call
ourselves Christian is like saying we are not allowed to speak
our language.' Gosia had been in trouble because the community group she had set up in Haringey with the council's support had elected to call itself the Polish and Eastern European
Christian Family Centre. 'You can't do that,' said a manager
disapprovingly, 'we will stop your funding if you insist on calling yourselves a Christian group.'

'I was so upset,' recalled Gosia, 'and the group couldn't
believe it. It's like we came from communism to live in a free
country and they tell us we are not allowed to be ourselves. All
we want to do is stand for our values and bring our children
up in our faith.'

Gosia had founded the group four years earlier and never
had any problems until this point. She came to the UK in 1991,
an earlier generation of youth drawn magnetically to life outside the Communist bloc, and had ended up staying when
she met and married her Irish partner. Shortly before 2004
she had noticed the number of young women moving into
the area of north London where she had lived for over ten
years, and decided to start a centre where she could help the

newcomers find out about services like health, education and English classes.

'Christianity is part of who we are,' she told the council when they threatened to withdraw funding. One of the accusations was that as a Christian group they were likely to discriminate against gays and lesbians. It was not an isolated incident of a local council picking on a politically incorrect organisation. At the time the government was discussing legislation to make it illegal to discriminate against homosexuals and transsexuals when providing goods and services, and both the Catholic and Anglican communities were up in arms.

Gosia won the argument by insisting that the council's anxieties were misplaced. 'We don't promote homosexuality but we welcome homosexuals if they want to join our group,' she told them. 'All we are trying to do is make sure that our children learn to love and respect each other. One of the ways we do this is by singing nursery rhymes together as a group. Some of these songs are Christian but no one is forced to sing them.'

Remembering the fuss when the press got hold of a spurious story about the 'loony leftie' councils banning the nursery rhyme 'Baa Baa Black Sheep' on the grounds that it was racist, I decided to go and investigate for myself. I found the play session in full swing in the Salvation Army chapel in north London, just as Gosia's mothers were moving their chairs into a circle and sitting with their children on their laps. We all introduced ourselves by name and Gosia started us off. Within minutes everyone was holding their hands up as if they were paws. I didn't know the words to that one, but the most surprising thing was that they had 'Twinkle, Twinkle, Little Star' in English. I had expected something a bit more controversial, like 'Onwards Christian Soldiers' or even 'All Things Bright and Beautiful'.

At the end of the singsong a woman stood in the middle of the circle and talked to the group about a meeting to call for a Polish language Mass in a Catholic church not far away. In west London where the Polish community has been established since the 1940s there are churches running services every hour to accommodate swelling congregations. Most of the new Catholic churchgoers are from Eastern Europe, but it is a phenomenon growing across the country wherever there are migrant groups. But just as church attendance can serve to remind people who they are and what is important, so the freedom to opt out offers the chance to find new identities less bound by the idea of national culture.

Earlier that morning before the singing began I had got talking to Kasia who was minding her sister's baby. I asked her how important her faith was to her. 'I think religion is a private matter,' she told me. 'I believe in God but I hate priests – I can speak to Him at home.'

I asked her whether it was true that most Poles attended church as a matter of habit.

'People here don't go so much as they do at home. At home the older people all go to Mass, but younger people not so much. When they have kids they start to go again.'

Later I asked my friend Rebecca to canvas the young people who worked in a bar with her. She soon came back with an answer. They don't go to church very much here, they told her, but they didn't want their mothers to find out.

Michal added another detail to an increasingly familiar story.

'In fact,' he said, when we were talking about religious identity among young Poles, 'a lot of people come here because there's more freedom to be what you want to be. There's quite a network of gays and lesbians helping each other find jobs and places to live. It's been important to be able to protest against the homophobia of the Polish government, too.'

～

'Christianity makes a poor state religion, especially for an empire,' said Nelson, a Mennonite friend. 'The central figure in Christianity is a man who loved his enemies, identified with the marginalised, and started a movement whose adherents would not fight in the army or worship the emperor.'

We were walking our daughters to their primary school in north London in the mid 1990s, falling into spontaneous and wide-ranging conversation as we habitually did when our paths crossed. When he and his family moved back to the United States we often reflected on our encounters with their radical Christianity as we missed their friendship and quaint mid-Western ways.

I remember being slightly shocked when visiting a cemetery

with a child who had been schooled in the fiercely secular French system by atheist parents. As she ran around the graves, fascinated by the different shapes, statues and symbols she seemed to lack any reference point for understanding how people thought about death. The words on the tombstones were utterly foreign to her, and I wondered what the effect might be of raising a new generation who had no comprehension, not just of Christianity, but of what faith and religious practices meant to other people.

But are faith schools the best way to foster a sense of curiosity and respect for other people's beliefs? Philosopher Amartya Sen vehemently disagrees. In his book, *Identity and Violence: The Illusion of Destiny*, he insists that it is hard to over-estimate the importance of non-sectarian education that treats children as human beings, for whom religious and faith-based distinctions make up only one part of their identities. He writes:

> Rather than reducing existing state-financed, faith-based schools, actually *adding* others to them – Muslim schools, Hindu schools, and Sikh schools to preexisting Christian ones – can have the effect of reducing the role of reasoning which the children may have the opportunity to cultivate and use. [...] It is unfair to children who have not yet had much opportunity of reasoning and choice to be put into rigid boxes guided by one specific criterion of categorisation, and to be told, 'That is your identity and this is all you are going to get.'

There are further problems with faith schools that emerge from other dimensions of social division in the UK. Many church schools, whether Catholic or Church of England, have become magnets for middle-class parents who are attracted by their more selective entry requirements. This is often because they associate the greater mix of ethnicities in ordinary state schools with lower academic standards. At a time when the blame for segregation is being laid at the door of minorities, this phenomenon suggests that some of the wrong people are being targeted for anti-social behaviour. The academic standards of a school are one thing, narrowly measured in league tables and SAT scores. They fail to reveal much about the ethos of a school and its policies against bullying, for example. Many parents struggle to balance a million and one factors in order to decide which state school to send their children to, although for the majority there is virtually no choice as it is tied to where they live.

The freedom to move a child from a school that enjoys a diverse intake of children to one that is predominantly (or, as the Minister for Education inadvisedly phrased it on the radio just this morning, 'purely') white, simply because of social stigma, is further evidence of how entangled class, wealth and racism have become. The word 'multicultural' is used as a smokescreen to designate something far worse than cultural diversity in the imaginations of those who imagine themselves to be 'purely' white. Used in conjunction with schools it increasingly operates as a euphemism for a possibly convivial but unruly mix of under-achieving and economically unambitious riff-raff.

Private schools all over the country are full of wealthier children from elite families that are not white, but white parents seldom use their presence as an excuse to move their offspring to a more exclusive, segregated institution. The news that Second Lieutenant Folarin Adeyemi Olatokunbo Olugbemiga Kuku has been appointed as the first black officer in the Grenadier Guards in the regiment's 350-year-old history, must be tempered by the fact that he went to Harrow and plays polo with Prince William whom he met at Sandhurst. This is not to say that he did not, or will not in the future, experience racism either on a personal or institutional level, but that his parents were able to buy the most exclusive education available in this country, and it is unlikely that anyone withdrew their child as a result.

Amar was in the process of buying a house in Blackburn so he knew all about the phenomenon known as 'white flight'. His estate agent had told him about it. They were looking at properties in a particular area that Amar liked, and he noticed that there were a suspicious number of For Sale signs. When he made inquiries, the agent, a young white man, told him that he had been shocked to hear people say they were moving out because they didn't want to smell curry in the next door house. They were also worried about falling property values as more Asians moved in.

We were talking about how the levels of segregation had worsened in towns like Blackburn, and how this might be reversed. In Amar's view it was mostly the fault of social policy, and a short-sighted approach to investing in schools during the preceding decades. The riots in nearby Oldham, Burnley and Bradford in 2001 had helped to get things moving as well. Apart from revealing to the rest of the country how deeply white and Asians were divided in some of the northern post-industrial towns, the disturbances had drawn attention to the chronic under-funding of institutions that brought the communities together. Amar was optimistic though about the government's latest plans to build schools that functioned more as community centres. 'We need to get schools to open up in the evenings and at weekends so that they can become places where local people meet on a more normal or routine basis. Education shouldn't just be about the formal things – though they are important. There are some schools here that have fantastic extracurricular activities, but they don't get such good academic results. The academic schools don't care about anything else.'

Schools could only do so much in breaking down barriers, he thought, and it's often the attitudes of the parents that are responsible for narrow-minded behaviour. It is natural for children to reflect the views of their families, but this becomes a potential problem when they are not encouraged to think for themselves in school. Research in Lancashire shows that half of the pupils at an all-white school in Burnley felt it was unimportant to respect people regardless of gender or religion, and a quarter felt that they did not see the need to show tolerance towards those with different views. The study also found that only one in ten white students showed an interest in learning about other religions, compared with four in ten Muslims who were interviewed at a mixed school in Blackburn.

One of the authors of the report, Andrew Holden, from the University of Lancaster, suggested that the research done so far challenged the assumptions that it was Muslims who were having trouble integrating. 'White children seem to benefit more from mixed schooling,' he commented, 'in encouraging positive attitudes to other ethnic groups.'

Now only twenty-four, Amar had long ago decided to take

matters into his own hands. He joined Youth Action as a volunteer, becoming a full-time worker almost four years ago. The most valuable thing you could do with young people, it seemed to him, was to take them out of their familiar surroundings and expose them to different ideas and experiences. When we met he was just about to take a group to Belfast to bring together kids from different faiths, including none at all, and he was excited about the prospect.

'Belfast is just thirty minutes from here by plane,' he said, 'but it's a different world. One of the many things that everyone has to contend with, wherever they come from, is stereotyping and labelling. If we engage as human beings we can talk about common things and move beyond that sort of thing. This is absolutely not about teaching tolerance, it's about teaching mutual respect. It's priceless – bringing people together to talk, even if they are of different faiths and have different points of view. If they learn mutual respect there's no value you can put on that.'

The afternoon was wearing on and I was aware that both Amar and Bano had jobs to do. I was mindful too that I had to find my way back to Manchester before nightfall. But I still didn't have a clear answer to my question: How does national identity look from the perspective of minorities? In fact I was developing new lines of inquiry that led me further away from any sense of a solution or ready-made answer. Where, for example, does the concept of national identity become relevant or constructive in righting wrongs inherited from the past?

Again Bano had an answer: 'The problem with defining national identity in terms of who belongs now is that it effectively excludes those new groups who might come here in the future. But we have to recognise too that there is a specific agenda to this so-called debate. These questions,' she continued, 'are you British, or what is Britishness, are clearly targeted at Muslims. It's not about Asians in general. You can see how Sikhs or Hindus are distancing themselves from Muslims. And with the Home Secretary, Ruth Kelly, you don't hear her asking the Chinese community if they are Chinese first or British? Or accusing Chinatown of being a separate culture.'

Both she and Amar had been talking about the concept of community as a double-edged sword. 'My inbox is full,' said

Bano, 'and it shows that if you can speak a full sentence you get called a community leader. But I decline. I don't speak for anybody and I don't want to be put into a position that I can't fulfill.'

'I think community can be a useful idea if you want to get things done,' observed Amar, 'but I agree that the notion of leadership sets up a fake construct. A lot of us do similar things and we want to reflect voices rather than tell people what to do.'

'You know,' he continued, 'a Chinese friend said to me the other day that a lot of Chinese people think it's unfair that Muslims get so much attention. The Chinese community is almost invisible. I told him they should just be thankful. They are welcome to change places any time.'

↝

'Food saved our family,' said Helen, who had learned to talk in sound bites as a way of remedying the national indifference towards the British-born Chinese population. She had been putting the finishing touches to her book, *Sweet Mandarin: the courageous true story of three generations of Chinese women and their journey from East to West.* Sweet Mandarin was also the name of the restaurant she runs with two sisters, Lisa and Janet, in Manchester.

Unfortunately I had chosen to visit Helen in mid-morning so I had to be content with elevenses rather than 'Mabel's vegetarian claypot' which I would have ordered, had I come at lunchtime. This was no ordinary Chinese restaurant and takeaway. I knew enough about urban regeneration to know that anything called the 'northern quarter', where the restaurant was situated, constitutes what is known in property terms as a 'good address'. The location was definitely not Chinatown although I had spotted that destination on the front of a bus on my way there.

At first I didn't notice Sweet Mandarin as it was daytime and it was not lit up. The exterior design was completely in keeping with the mixture of narrow Victorian lanes and red brick, industrial buildings that characterised the area. Situated on a corner, it had windows on two sides and a commanding view of the outside world. From the corner you could see the Arndale Centre, a feature of the new shopping area which had been completely rebuilt after the area was destroyed by an IRA bomb in 1996. The interior was light and modern too, with a prominent bar and an array of slender black tables with chrome chairs. Colin, a Malaysian student at Manchester University, was busy getting the restaurant ready for business.

Helen was upset that I couldn't stay for lunch, and I promised to come back at a later date. But it wasn't strictly necessary to eat there to appreciate the spirit of this place. It reminded me of Suja's boldness in asserting his own version of his ideal eating and meeting place. There was no attempt to follow a standard script as far as making the place look ethnic or exotic, as though the more authentic the wallpaper the more appealing the menu. But there were no compromises on the food. In both cases recipes had emanated from family kitchens where cooks knew where to find the right spices, however far from their origins. Integration meant hanging on to the important things in life, allowing change to happen through experience and taste rather than as a result of trying to please other people.

It was Helen's grandmother who had given Helen and her sisters the idea to open their own place. Lily Kwok had been a maid to a British family in Hong Kong. She was brought to England in the 1950s as a favourite servant, and when the family died she was left a substantial legacy. She used this to start her own restaurant, called Lung Fung – which means dragon and phoenix – and became the first Chinese woman to run her own establishment.

'She brought my mother and an uncle when my mum was seven and they grew up here from 1963. At that time there were very few people of colour here. It was before Chinatown – there was no food, or language or Chinese culture. Through her restaurant, and her cooking which became really well known, she helped to integrate our family into British society. Her story is a bit of social history.'

Helen's decision to write a book about her grandmother was also a way to explore the position of BBCs, as she referred to British-born Chinese, and to assert their right to be included in national debates about identity and belonging.

'I grew up in a modest working-class takeaway in a predominantly white area,' she said. 'I soon learned that we were different – there were no other Chinese living there. Hooligans would say things to my mum, call us chinks, for example. When you get these negative reactions from people, your identity as a British person is challenged. You learn to see yourself as not 100 per cent British. But then when we went back to Hong Kong it really was an eye-opener, it was like a foreign land to me. I felt much more British than Chinese. There were language differences for a start – I definitely felt British. Sometimes if you go away from home you feel clearer, it brings it home to you. The generational change is very significant. My mum and my grandmother didn't have the opportunity to have education – although my mother went to high school. The three of us all did Masters, and have professional careers. Education sets us free.'

'What do you see as the future for the next generation?' I asked.

'I hope they still feel Chinese and want to be part of the wider community.'

I remembered Bano's remark about Ruth Kelly. 'So what's your impression of the Chinese community as a whole,' I asked. 'Do you think it's possible to generalise?'

'I've noticed that some people try to deny their Chinese identity in order to integrate. They don't want Chinese identity as they think it would hold them back. The other group still maintains the language but is not interested in integrating. They stay within the Chinese community, and only use legal services in Chinatown for example. It's the same with banking – they deal with cash only, or use loan sharks, and when it comes to health they only visit Chinese doctors. Being BBC is the best of both worlds. I've never seen it as a barrier. I only experienced my "identity" when I talked to my grandmother, when I found out the sacrifices that my mother and grandmother made for us.'

When Helen went off to take a phone call I started chatting to Colin. 'Are you British?' I asked, not knowing if he was a relative or a visitor. 'No, no,' he replied hastily, 'I am from Malaysia. I am a student here.' I asked him how he found it living in Manchester and he shook his head rather sadly. 'I don't really like it. It's not friendly. But I can earn much better money here. I think I will stay on as long as I can.'

The previous day I had learned that significant numbers of British Pakistanis were moving to retire in Malaysia. Not only was it warmer and cheaper, but as a Muslim-majority society it seemed to offer a more congenial experience of everyday life. I shared this with Colin and he looked as surprised as I had been when I heard about it, though possibly for different reasons.

∽

'Back home is wonderful,' said Peray. 'Lots of people go back once a year. There is a huge scene there – raves, our own radio station, club nights, the beaches...'

Peray was making it sound as though British-born Turks had the best of both worlds: one foot in the UK and the other in the Mediterranean. But that wasn't what she meant at all. While the Chinese were often cited as an invisible but relatively successful ethnic group in Britain, Turkish-speaking communities exist below the radar completely.

'The trouble is that we haven't developed our own identity here, though. Nobody really pays us much attention. Outside the UK, Turks have a strong culture and history. Community leaders – and don't get me started on them,' said Peray pointedly, 'get involved in politics around Turkey and Cyprus, not about Turks here. For someone like myself – I am British with Turkish origins – it's frustrating that we don't have a stronger voice in national debates.'

Since we both lived in the same part of north London, I suggested we meet in Finsbury Park. A brand new cafe had just opened, part of the facelift given to the area around the lake. The new playground was bustling with parents and children, everyone enjoying the new space in a welcome reappearance of warm weather in early September. As I watched the children running squealing through the water jets put there for that very purpose, I was aware that there was the usual mix of costumes, languages and appearances making the most of the park, and that it had been like this since we first brought our own children here in the early 1980s. There were a few details that had changed in addition to the brand new climbing frames.

You could always hire rowing boats in the summer to potter round the lake, but today I noticed a slight difference. The little hut where you paid your money was covered with a display of mini flags from all over the world. I wondered how many people actually bought one to fly from their bows. The sterns of the boats also had brightly painted motifs. I could see that one had a red St George's cross, another a skull and crossbones.

Because the cafe area was crowded we had to speak up, but it was clear that Peray rarely had a problem making her voice heard locally. She was currently advising the local council on their drugs and substance abuse policy for young people, and was wired into Turkish-speaking youth groups through her voluntary work. She was just telling me a story about something that had happened at a Safer Schools Conference. One of the female contributors suggested that some young men needed to be told that it was not appropriate to harass women – even though it might be acceptable in their own culture. It was obvious what she meant.

'I wasn't having that so I stood up and said, "Excuse me, can you tell me in which culture it is acceptable to harass women? It's certainly not in Muslim culture."'

It was education that gave her the confidence to intervene in situations like that, she explained, although it was her actual experience in school that motivated her to pursue a career as an advocate for Turkish youth. Peray had an MA in Human Rights, but it was not as a result of excelling at school where she had left with inauspicious qualifications. At the age of eleven she entered secondary school as a bright and talented girl. It was during the Thatcher years, long before the concept of teaching citizenship was a twinkle in anyone's eyes.

'I started off with straight A's and ended up with F's and U's and no qualifications. It was the school ethos... that's why it winds me up when I hear people talking about families and the community being to blame. The teachers had no expectations and they made assumptions based on things like race, ethnicity and gender. It was a very mixed school as there was a large estate where a lot of white working-class families lived. There were a lot of black kids, Asians, and a few Cypriots. There were waves of refugees – Bangladeshis at one point, and then Somalis and Kurdish. The school was quite progressive in the way that they made everyone feel welcome. The trouble was that no one was expected do well. And the lack of discipline was taken too far. There was a lot of sexual harassment, especially directed towards the younger girls. My family didn't understand what I was going through. For them it was a British school and the Brits were good at everything. They just didn't get it.'

Peray's father had come to the UK from Turkish Cyprus in the 1950s, and her mother a little later. He owned two shops, one of which was in Kings Cross. Often he would come to work on Monday to find his windows smashed. Sometimes men would come in late at night and abuse him for being Turkish, but he never complained, to his family at least. He told his children that he was happy enough to have moved to London, and to be paying towards his state pension which would give him security in later years.

As Peray told me this she acknowledged that it must have been different for the first generation settling in Britain. But these stories about her parents' humiliation had made her more determined to stand up for herself and to defend others, too. But she still felt that the Turkish Cypriot community was partly to blame for allowing itself both to be treated badly and to be ignored.

'The community has failed to respond to racism in an organised fashion. They could have learned from what black groups have been doing in the last forty years. But many wouldn't align themselves with blacks and Asians. They would say they were white Europeans, and their focus has been on politics back home.'

Peray was incensed that after all this time Turkish and Kurdish youth were evidently failing in the school system. 'Turkish kids have been consistently invisible,' she said, 'though figures show that they are predominantly at the bottom of lists in areas where they are concentrated. There is a lost generation. Because of the focus on our history, and the political situation in Cyprus, there is still a strong sense of yearning to be authentically Turkish. It's a big problem. A lot of young people are turning to the far right. I've noticed that younger Turks have started with Muslim identity. Even my cousins have started to go to mosque.'

↫

While Peray and Helen talked of the humiliation that their parents had to endure from racist bigots, I could tell from their voices where their steel had come from. Their stories were not atypical even if they were seldom heard. But there are always other accounts of how much easier it was for those who came before, as though the current climate of asylum-seeker bashing and paranoia about Muslims is a very recent phenomenon. Sometimes this rosy view of the past is used to counter equally unhelpful caricatures of unbridgeable difference.

Take the life histories of the peasant farmers in rural Pakistan, men like Farhana's father who took up the offer of free visas to work in Britain from the 1950s onwards, helping rebuild the country after the devastation of six years of war. This generation has been increasingly written into a powerful narrative about why Muslim communities have become isolated from the rest of the country, victims of their own refusal to belong. Unwholesome cultural practices have been blamed, from arranged marriages to illiterate imams and poor language skills. Their chosen separation from mainstream British society, so the script goes, has burdened their children with an uneasy and unhealthy relationship to their own parents, to the wider public sphere, and above all to themselves. No wonder then that their communities have set themselves apart and are living in the past.

It makes a convincing picture for those seeking a ready answer to the question of what motivated the bombers on 7 July. And it is one that rests on a fundamental misconception. It presumes that the backward 'peasant farmers' encountered a nation of highly educated, sophisticated citizens with uniformly modern habits and forward-thinking ways. It is a fantasy version of history designed to provide cheap explanations for problems that many European countries are grappling with today. The second half of the twentieth century saw enormous changes in British society which were experienced, albeit unevenly, across all classes, ethnicities and faiths, and in all industries, institutions and professions. In the 1950s there were people throughout the British Isles, from the capital city to the smallest hamlet, living without electricity and running water, with rudimentary sanitation, and meagre diets limited by post-war rationing and scarcity. Working-class boys were expected to leave school at fifteen and get a job, and the only careers open to girls apart from home-making and motherhood were secretarial work and nursing. It was a different age.

The immigrants who came from all over the crumbling empire, from Asia, Africa and the Caribbean, were affected by, grumbled about, welcomed and got used to the uneven changes brought by modernisation along with everybody else. Their presence, along with new generations born in the UK, was also responsible for transforming the country too, again in many different ways. But just as it is important to counter the version of history that makes these settlers, or particular categories of them, perpetual outsiders, so it is wrong to erase the record of just how hard it was because they were not allowed to forget that they came from elsewhere.

Several times on my travels I heard a rather youthful refrain which sounded dangerously like, 'Our parents came to Britain and worked their fingers to the bone. They were quite happy to talk to their neighbours, but they were also allowed to be who they wanted to be. No one questioned their allegiance.'

The more I heard these kinds of comments the more worried I became. I heard a note of defiance that implied that Muslims were the first minority to assert their rights to live here on their own terms. Had they not heard of Enoch Powell, for goodness sake, or Margaret Thatcher's populist remark about British people feeling 'swamped' by different cultures? The amnesia that comes with youth is not helped by a lack of curiosity about the past. The difficult histories of minorities demanding not just equal treatment before the law, but also a recognition of religious and cultural difference, has had an impact on what it means to be British for everyone who lives here. But it is not just young people who are unaware of previous generations' struggles to make the country a more just and inclusive place, wherever they came from. When Jack Straw wrote his column in Blackburn's local paper protesting about the full face veil worn by some of his constituents, he too should have remembered the battles over what other religious minorities wore on their heads and how they marked their particular identities on their bodies.

In August 1967 a young Sikh named T. S. Sandhu turned up for work at Wolverhampton bus garage after being away on sick leave for three weeks. In the intervening period he had grown a beard. Although he was aware that it was not permitted under the rules of the bus company, Sandhu claimed that he had had a religious conversion as a result of his illness and that the beard was an indispensable mark of his faith. He was sent home and told to shave it off.

Two years later, in April 1969, a year after Enoch Powell had made his notorious 'Rivers of Blood' speech in Birmingham, a Sikh activist called Mr Jolly announced that he was preparing to set himself on fire outside the council offices. His threat, which was being closely followed across the Punjab as well as in the national British media, was the culmination of a bitter campaign to force the city council to overturn a ban on turbans for bus drivers and conductors. Just days before he was due to carry out his plan, the council caved in and passed a resolution that permitted Sikh busmen to wear turbans in place of the regulation caps.

Wolverhampton was the last borough council in Britain to resist the demands of this minority to wear the outward signs of their faith. In Manchester where there had been great resistance on the part of the union, the campaign had run from 1959 until 1967 when it was finally successful. So why was Wolverhampton so bothered about what its bus conductors wore on their heads? It was well known that few wore their caps anyway on the grounds that they were uncomfortable. And what did its ordinary citizens feel about their elected leaders' recalcitrance as well as their retreat under pressure?

Judging from the letters to the local press, many of the good people of Wolverhampton felt extremely aggrieved by Jolly's behaviour. 'What a pitiful climbdown by the Transport Committee,' wrote one. 'How the coloured folk must be laughing at the way the whites give way.' The Transport Committee chairman who was clearly not convinced that this decision was the right outcome was reported as saying, 'The ordinary man in the street feels that this is an encroachment on his way of life.' Many Sikhs too felt that the tactics of the campaign organisers had alienated public opinion in their zeal to get their own way.

Throughout the campaign there had been talk of outside agitators, motivations that were not strictly religious in character, and power struggles within the local organisation leading the charge. This was not one particular Sikh temple, nor even a consortium of temples, but a militant political party called the

Sharomani Akali Dal (Army of the Immortals) which was centrally concerned with the politics of Sikh self-government in India. Having campaigned for a Sikh homeland in the Punjab, where Sikh religion and history would be compulsory in schools and Punjabi the official language, they were included in the coalition government of the state when the region was restructured in 1966.

As the hostilities intensified between the authorities and Mr Pannchi, who started out as the leader of the campaign and who was in fact the founder of the British-based branch of Akali Dal, it was clear that they were being closely monitored back in India where there was a great deal of solidarity towards the Sikh community. Demonstrations were held, the local Indian media kept readers informed, and Mr Pannchi made frequent trips back to the Punjab where he claimed he was in consultation with party leaders.

There were further reasons why these political links were significant. Shortly before the young Sandhu made his stand at Wolverhampton bus garage, his father had been involved in a similar dispute at the Goodyear Tyre factory where he worked. In an effort to challenge the management's position on the turban issue, which seems to have been ambiguous, Sandhu Senior and his colleagues who were also members of the Akali Dal, called on Mr Pannchi to represent them. His opening gambit was to issue a threat. He told them that if the company did not back down he would urge for industrial action in Goodyear factories in the Punjab where many party members were employees. The management protested that it did not have a problem with turbans per se, but that they should merely conform to safety regulations. Further dispute was avoided by agreeing on requisite details.

Pannchi's style of leadership had thus been tested before with satisfactory results, setting the tone for what was to follow. However, his first discussions with the bus drivers' union on behalf of the young Sandhu began with an explanation of his desire to grow his hair, and a plea to respect Sikh religious and cultural heritage. After some dispute, a union ballot proved that members were content to allow Sandhu (who was by now sacked for failing to comply with company regulations) to wear both a beard and a turban. They were more worried about the state of the bus service itself and whether the buses ran on time. Out of 900 members, 336 voted for, 204 against, with 38 spoiled papers.

It was only when the decision passed over to the local council's Transport Committee that the dispute escalated into a nationwide issue. Pannchi became known as the national leader of the Sikhs in Britain which elevated him to a position that he perhaps did not fully deserve. The fact that he had to communicate through an interpreter, despite living in England for ten years, did not further his cause or improve his image with the public at large. His position was eclipsed, however, by Mr Jolly's brinkmanship at a critical point in the campaign.

Jolly was also a member of Akali Dal, and was based in Hounslow in west London. In his public statements he declared that he was prepared to sacrifice his life on behalf of the ninety per cent of Sikhs in Britain who did not wear turbans. Privately he was also concerned at the prospect of a significant number of young men who were attracted to the secular politics of the Black Power movement, taking their cue from the civil rights struggles across the water.

In 1967, the year that Sandhu took the life-changing decision to let his hair grow, India was celebrating the end of its second decade of independence. The fact that Sikhs were well represented (wearing turbans) fighting alongside British soldiers in the Indian Army, was meaningful to those who had themselves fought in the 1939–45 war, and for this they were likely to sympathise with their cause. But this proof of loyalty to the Crown did not hold much water with those mourning the loss of empire.

Manifestations of British and English nationalism often expressed a sense of humiliation that this once great imperial power was being overrun by former colonial subjects. When these intruders appeared to show little respect for the British way of life, however that was defined, this added insult to injury. When they seemed hell-bent on bringing the country to its knees – a strange expression one heard a lot growing up in the 1970s – and demanding that native Britons adopt their alien customs, this was altogether too much.

The sight of dark-skinned immigrants and their supporters marching through Wolverhampton streets demanding special privileges fed a very specific form of fear that the country was being ruined from within. In April 1968, only months after the Indian Workers Association had come to him for support on the turban issue, Enoch Powell, MP for Wolverhampton, stood up in Birmingham and prophesied that the British experiment with immigration would lead inexorably to bloodshed. The chapter of British history that ensued has been written and rewritten many times from different angles. However, as further examination of the local context suggests, this small but persistent campaign to win the right of recognition for minority practice on religious grounds had more significant consequences than anyone thought, either at the time or later.

David Beetham, a philosophy lecturer, wrote an invaluable account of these campaigns in a slim book simply entitled *Transport and Turbans*, published soon after Jolly's brinkmanship in 1970. This is a comparative study that recounts and analyses the events in Manchester and Wolverhampton with reference to local and national press coverage. Not only does it provide documented evidence of each campaign and the background events that help to explain their different trajectories, the book also draws conclusions in the light of national debates about the rights of new minorities, especially those concerning religion.

One of the strands of Beetham's account is the way that the question of religious freedom for incoming groups such as the Sikhs challenged the concept of 'integration'. This was a relatively new concept in British political life, having been defined most succinctly by Roy Jenkins in 1966 when he famously spoke of it as 'equality of opportunity with cultural diversity in an atmosphere of mutual tolerance'. The Conservative politician's formulation was to prove the meridian of the theory of multiculturalism over the intervening decades. In the late 1960s it sounded admirably fair as an abstract premise for accommodating cultural differences, although the real test was yet to come.

For those who were broadly accepting of immigration from former colonies, as opposed to the nationalists who were busy working themselves into a lather, it was the prospect of making unfair exceptions for newcomers that was problematic rather than the ideal of social integration itself. Many commentators, from humble letter writers to national politicians, preferred their own version of 'racial harmony', an alternative term for not making a fuss about immigration. This demanded that minorities blend in to the extent that they were invisible, rather than claim special privileges for their peculiar customs which were often regarded as being very un-British indeed.

To recount the tale of the Sikh transport workers' struggles simply as a triumph against pathological British racism would diminish the possibility of understanding how this country has changed in the intervening years. Making the history of that national campaign invisible, and failing to appreciate the details of local variations, also obscures the fits and starts of Britain's evolution as a self-consciously pluralist nation. Perhaps it might be more productive to accept that we are merely condemned to a muddy, untidy, complicated, contested and unfinished business of negotiating how to live with the convergences and consequences of history.

Chapter Three: Memory Loss

People who use digital cameras have no idea how hard it used to be to take good pictures in bad light. Having only recently acquired some basic photographic skills in a Workers Educational Association evening class for beginners, I wasn't exactly equipped with a long telephoto lens and nerves of steel. This was the first assignment that I failed because I was trembling so much I couldn't hold the camera steady. As a result I turned a perfect photo opportunity into a grey blur.

Searchlight, the magazine for which I worked, had received a tip-off about a gathering of National Front members to celebrate Hitler's birthday. Maurice Ludmer, the editor, drove us out to the bleak housing estate in south-west Birmingham and parked strategically in the street near the designated block of flats. It was 21 April 1980, barely a year after the general election that saw Margaret Thatcher elevated to prime minister, and the start of the eighteen-year Tory rule.

In that election, the National Front, the precursor of the present-day British National Party, had fielded an unprecedented number of candidates, masterminded by a man called Martin Webster who had famously boasted that the organisation would 'kick their way into the headlines'. Having achieved some worryingly high polls in certain areas, their strategy in 1979 had been to raise their profile across the country in an attempt to look like a real political option for disgruntled voters. Media attention was good, as long as it made them look as though they represented public opinions that were being suppressed or bottled up. Being exposed as thugs or hypocrites was still publicity, but they were aware that the country was not quite ready for neo-Nazi solutions. They did their best to conceal the admiration for Hitler that they celebrated in private. A snapshot of paid-up NF members strutting around in Nazi uniform would have provided valuable evidence that the image of a respectable democratic party was a sham.

In the front seat of the car, however, on that grey spring day in Birmingham, we were not sure what to expect. Suddenly Maurice hissed, 'They're coming out, get ready.' Two figures appeared on the balcony, three floors up. I prepared to take a photograph, crouching behind the dashboard of the Ford Escort trying to focus my modest zoom lens on the group.

We could see quite clearly in the gathering twilight that they were wearing uniforms, and one of the men sported a swastika armband. Just as I was about to press the shutter, Maurice, who was eager to record this puerile event, suddenly exclaimed, 'They've got a gun, he's holding a gun. Quick, get a picture of that!' Any composure I had managed to muster collapsed as I struggled to hold the camera steady. I felt as though they were looking straight at us, and had worked out who we were. Bob who worked with me in the *Searchlight* office was in the back of the car laughing and swearing at the same time. Even the fact that he was a karate black belt was little consolation as we sat in the line of fire.

As soon as I had taken a couple of pictures the men went back inside and we sped off, looking anxiously behind to make sure we were not being followed. Maurice was jubilant that we had caught them in an act, and rang the police to report seeing firearms as soon as we reached home. I rushed into the darkroom to develop the film, only to find that even the best picture was so indistinct it was almost unusable. The armband on its own wasn't much good since its owner's face was unrecognisable. The gun turned out to be a replica, according to the cops, and it wasn't clearly visible either, so the local paper was not interested. Maurice wrote about it in *Searchlight* and we used the picture in all its blurriness as proof. Consequently the story had the effect of making the local NF branch aware that they were being watched.

There were several reasons why it was important to reveal the true agenda of these individuals and the networks to which they belonged. It wasn't just the NF, either. There was an array of groups ranging from the out and out Hitler-worshipping British Movement to the Monday Club, a select organisation composed mainly of Conservative Party members. One of *Searchlight*'s tactics was to show the links between the various factions in order to demolish the idea that their brand of racism was a patriotic response to immigration.

Maurice was from a Jewish family, born and bred in Salford near Manchester. He traced his decision to devote his life to fighting racism and fascism to his experiences in the army. In 1945 he was part of the force that liberated the Nazi camp at Belsen. At the time he was a young man barely twenty years old. The British nationalist movement was a legacy of Oswald Mosley's British Union of Fascists which had openly emulated the German Nazi Party in the 1930s. After the war it was composed of people who wished that Hitler had successfully invaded Britain, and who refused to believe that the holocaust of Jews and others in Germany had taken place. Their propaganda was full of advertisements for revisionist material including the infamous pamphlet, 'Did Six Million Really Die?'

Branding the fascists as Nazis proved to be one very effective strategy in the 1970s. At that time, many political activists, trade union members and ordinary anti-racist women and men had lived through the war and their early lives had been shaped by the disruption and destruction it had wrought. The enduring power of those memories – particularly the bombing of the docklands by German planes – could still be felt when Derek Beackon was elected as the first BNP councillor in 1993. The fact that the tabloid newspapers identified the party as 'Nazi bootboys' was a sign that the memory of the war as a victory against fascism was still intact in the popular imagination. However, that so many were prepared to vote for the BNP regardless of its connections showed that people were more concerned with their immediate worries. Oral memory of solidarity and hardship has been replaced by a chronic form of nostalgia for a time when Great Britain was victorious, regardless of against whom or in what cause. By 2007, a poll commissioned by the *The Jewish Chronicle* to mark Holocaust Memorial Day showed that over a quarter of eighteen to twenty-nine-year-olds in Britain are not sure if the Holocaust actually happened.

↫

Knowing about history is an important means of avoiding the conflicts experienced in the past, according to a poll carried out by History Matters, a new consortium of British heritage organisations. Just a small percentage of those who responded to the online questionnaire thought it had any relevance to identity. Martin wasn't sure of the details but being a history teacher he had found the results encouraging. He mentioned the website early in our conversation when I went to visit him one day at the George Mitchell secondary school where he worked.

I was back in the north-east again, as usual with no map and a hazy memory of the directions I had been sent by email. I had alighted from the overground train at Leyton, just one stop before Leytonstone, as the school lay somewhere between there and the cafe La Rosh. Setting off along the main road I looked about to get my bearings. It was a sunny afternoon in early autumn, and there were plenty of people on the streets.

I came first to the Good News Shop, a cornucopia for any-one who likes party games with a religious theme. The window display offered sets of Bible Charades, Bibleopoly, and Bible Brainstorm, along with specialist books, frames and cards. Above the shop there was a Healing Room. Next door but one was the Authentic Caribbean Takeaway which looked from the outside like a regular fish and chip shop. A smallish supermar-ket was next, and on its windows I noticed a sign advertising six cans of Polish beer for six pounds. A chicken and pizza bar called Drum and Bass came after that. Apart from the Bible shop the street fare was routine fast-food multiculture. But there were a few twists, I was happy to see, as I came to an old pub that had once been called The Three Blackbirds according to the old sign that swung above the front door. It was now an African and Caribbean restaurant on one side and a nightclub called Club Desire with Polish strippers on the other.

By the time I got to my destination I was feeling quite nervous, the way you do when you are going back to school no matter how long ago you left. I was going to meet Martin Spafford, a history teacher to whom I had been introduced through Leyla a few weeks earlier. As I waited for him in the foyer I read the notices. A chart showed the forty nations, from Albania to Zambia, that made up the school's intake. When Martin appeared I had already decided that this was a special school, and by the time I left I was sorry that I had no more children of my own to send there.

We sat in the staffroom and talked first about the school's catchment area. Martin had over twenty years of experience working with children from many different communities. At one point he had worked closely with Bangladeshi families, and as the generation of new settlers decreased over time, he had remained friends with many former students who were now of Suja's age. Since the 1990s he had developed close links with Pakistani, Turkish Kurds and Afro-Caribbean families, as well as Somali students, like Leyla's cohort, whose families had been forced to flee Somalia when civil war broke out in 1991. Having close contact with so many different groups had taught him the importance of shared social class as a factor affecting how families coped with the transition.

'This community for the last ten to fifteen years has remained incredibly mixed and harmonious,' he said. 'Although our students are ethnically diverse they are socially homogenous. In general they are almost all from the families of lower-paid skilled or unskilled workers and this unites their experience.

'Of course there are problems,' he added, 'but gangs and conflict are more likely to be about postcode than ethnicity. It is territorial rather than being about race or culture which I see as a positive thing. But it is fragile and at risk of being changed.'

I asked Martin which communities were not doing so well, and remembering my conversations with Peray, I wondered if the Turkish-speaking kids were faring better in educational terms than they were in neighbouring boroughs. He confirmed that they represented the second-lowest achieving group but they were not at the bottom. Now that we were talking about the performance of particular minorities his voice acquired a more urgent tone.

'The lowest achieving group in the school is white. They make up less than ten per cent of the intake. This is not counting Eastern Europeans who have different and distinct experiences. This is the only group where girls do consistently worse than boys. Talk about an invisible community.'

Martin explained that those who resented the new immigrants had gradually moved further east. Those who stayed were on the whole more comfortable with the diversity or they just got stuck there. Many families were connected through intermarriage between blacks and whites.

'In 1997 children in school were solidly New Labour. Now they mainly express support for the Liberal Democrats, and

Respect, the anti-war party, is popular too. You have to ask what the community has received from the Labour government in the last few years. Sure there's no denying there has been a welcome attention to child poverty, access to health care, and government programmes like Sure Start, but from the perception of where they stand, they have had nothing.'

The school recognised the potential dangers of this situation a long time before the rather belated acknowledgement by government think tanks and reports that emerged in 2007. When Derek Beackon was elected as BNP councillor in Tower Hamlets in 1993 and the young teenager Stephen Lawrence murdered in South London the same year, Martin took the lead in devising an anti-racist project that reached out to the entire catchment area of the school. He was proud of the results.

'We wanted it to be something the white community would be enthusiastically involved in. So we looked at the contributions of all the communities in the Second World War.

'We had people who lived through the Blitz in the East End, and old guys who had been firemen coming in with Somali seamen who'd been in the merchant navy, Pakistanis, and a Sikh who was a Battle of Britain pilot. We were looking at shared experience through a piece of history, history that white people could feel good about, could identify with. It is so rare that it's no surprise that there is sometimes anger. There has been a continual history of exclusion.'

The cultural historian Patrick Wright suggests that we might think of history as a 'submerged, unmanageable charge'. A year after London won the bid for the 2012 Olympics he gave a lecture in the Docklands on John Burns' theme, 'The Thames is liquid history'. But he was not just using poetic language to evoke the way that our past lies beneath the surface as unfinished business 'ready to blow up in our faces'. He was using the example of a potentially explosive shipwreck lying in the mud at the mouth of the Thames.

'Thanks to the scale and extent of its industrial and maritime past,' he explained, 'the estuary is full of articulate ruins. Take the USS Richard Montgomery, a sunken American munitions ship packed with bombs and drums of phosphorus which, since the Second World War, has lain just south of Nore Sand where the river Medway runs into the Thames. Ordered to anchor in shallow waters as the result of an error in Southend harbour – where it is said to have arrived just as a Luftwaffe bombing raid was expected – this Liberty ship got worked into the sandbank in a spring tide, and its hull broke before retrieval was possible. Judged too dangerous to move even half a century later, the Richard Montgomery remains a well-known local feature, its masts still sticking out of the sea in its buoyed-off 'Danger Area', and reputedly still capable of obliterating the nearby town of Sheerness on the Isle of Sheppey.'

The force of his argument, sharpened by this extraordinary image, was directed against those who characterise history as a resource to make us feel more comfortable about who we are. Over twenty years ago his book, *On Living in an Old Country*, warned that Britain's heritage industry was in danger of turning the country into a theme park. History, he argued, ought not be reduced to a costume drama in which we recognise earlier versions of ourselves in fancy dress. It is a powerful tool that must be put to work in the present, which as we all know, is rarely comfortable and not always predictable.

Although broadly supportive of any initiative to bring the topic of history into public view, Patrick has grave doubts about the most recent campaign launched by the group that Martin had mentioned to me earlier. History Matters was created in order 'to draw attention to the contribution of history to all our lives and to encourage more people to get involved'. Its website is full of quotes from notable celebrities exhorting individuals to declare their support for the campaign, to 'get involved' and generally join in the celebration of just how important history is for the health of the nation.

Patrick was particularly vexed by something that Stephen Fry, one of the founding members, had said when he launched the campaign in the summer of 2006: 'History is not the story of strangers, aliens from another realm; it is the story of us had we been born a little earlier.' This call to enter imaginatively into the worlds of our ancestors is not misguided, but it brings us into dangerous territory where we do not confront those things that we cannot imagine, either because they are too ghastly or just too complicated. 'History is full of strangeness,' said Patrick, 'full of fractured and often polarised conflicts between different communities and factions.'

∽

In the affray of the picket, among the jostling crowds and the slogans hurled at the neo-Nazi mob just a few yards ahead, Tapan chewed on the paan. He felt the caustic juice sipping down his gullet, but didn't think much of it until he began to spin and levitate higher and higher… Suddenly he leapt through the barricade and flew up, spreading his wings in the sky. He swooped down on the racist mob and began to cause panic, blitzing them with his beak and talons.

In his novel *Burrow*, Manzu Islam creates a fictional story about a Bangladeshi philosophy graduate called Tapan who drifts into illegal status when his student visa expires. The plot and the context draw largely on his experience of working as a racial harassment officer in the Brick Lane area of London in the late 1970s, a time when young Bangladeshis were getting organised to defend themselves against consistent racist attacks. Because it is based on a real place and evokes the memory of things that really happened, like the murder of Altab Ali, the novel helps to remind readers of the history of Bangladeshi life in London. But it does more than this. Tapan, the novel's main character, was born in Bangladesh and lived there until he was sent to college. The dreams, flashbacks and reminiscences that haunt him throughout the novel tell us something about the country he left, bringing the history of Bangladesh into London's literary world.

Manzu was, like his main character, born in Bangladesh, although his own life story was very different to Tapan's. When I spoke to him before my trip he was just finishing a new novel, *War in the Delta*, a love story set against the backdrop of Bangladesh's war of liberation from Pakistan. He mentioned that this was a difficult subject for him. I was aware that his father had been a leading politician who was assassinated in the mid 1970s but I had little idea of how this had happened and certainly, how this was connected to the constitutional crisis that was unfolding when I arrived. When we spoke, he urged me to contact his family in Dhaka and told me that they would take care of me.

Manzu's younger brother Shafayatul, a retired briga-
dier who was now a businessman, offered to take me to the
national monument which was located in Sarvar, a few miles
to the north of the city, and I got the impression that this was
something they thought I should see. As we walked through
the gates into the park where the monument was located, I
realised that this visit would provide a key not just to the constitutional crisis, but actually to an ongoing, deeply contested
process of forging national memory in Bangladesh. Straight
ahead of us, at the centre of this eighty-four-acre park, rose
a giant concrete edifice formed out of seven narrow triangles
that rose from a joint base to a single pinnacle. Each triangle,
Shafayatul explained, represented the seven stages of the struggle for independence from Pakistan.

The sun was hot on that day, but free from the oppressive
humidity that can linger on at the end of October. Two small
children sold us small garlands of flowers for our wrists, and
then trailed after us shyly as they had nothing else to do. As we
walked towards the monument across the red brick paths and
almost artificially green lawns, we passed a sign explaining its
history.

'The war of liberation began on 26 March 1971, and ended in
victory on 16 December 1971. Three million undaunted patriots
laid down their lives in this struggle for freedom. The memorial is dedicated to the memory of the heroic struggle of the
people and as a mark of respect from an indebted nation to the
martyrs...'

This was not simply an example of a public monument and
a place for reverence. The park and surrounding gardens also
included a stage, a mosque, a cafeteria and other facilities for
public gatherings and state functions.

A group of young men were leaning against the grey cement
structure taking advantage of the shade it offered. My hosts
and I took pictures of each other, and then began to stroll back
to the car. On the way, Shafayatul told me that when the war
broke out his whole family had moved across the border to
India where they first stayed in a refugee camp. Their father,
Syed Nazrul Islam, had been a close ally of Sheikh Mujibur
Rahman, the leader of the Awami League, who was imprisoned in Pakistan throughout the conflict. The day that war

broke out he left Dhaka wearing a veil and took up the role of acting president, helping to coordinate the armed resistance in hiding. Manzu and his brothers received military training but as Manzu told me later, he was only fifteen at the time and worked in the camp rather than fighting alongside the older men.

Later, as we waited for Nazma to put the finishing touches to a sumptuous lunch, Shafayatul patiently explained the tortuous history of the newly liberated country that had led to his father's murder just a few years after independence. In 1975 there was a coup. Sheikh Mujib was assassinated and their father was one of four politicians imprisoned. Seeing that they were outnumbered and likely to be defeated, those responsible for the failed coup had the four prisoners murdered before they fled. Although the murder suspects were identified they were never brought to justice, something that had been enormously painful for all the families concerned. As it happened the following day was a national memorial day for the four, known as Jail Killing Day.

After lunch we turned to discuss the roots of the current political crisis that had erupted just days before I arrived. The shocking part was not so much the details of the conflict between the two main parties, but the underlying and unresolved struggle over what kind of nation Bangladesh was to be. I simply had not grasped that the Bangladeshi National Party, which had just ruled the country for five years in coalition with the conservative Jammat Islami, had not been in favour of splitting from West Pakistan, as it was called before 1971. I had not realised that the Awami League, the party that led the opposition and the prime mover responsible for bringing the country to a halt, had been the vehicle of the independence movement. The conversation brought home to me that the two political blocs challenging each other over electoral procedures represented the different positions taken in the struggle to secede from Pakistan. Many representatives on both sides had actually fought in that war, as well as losing members of their immediate families to violent deaths. In my ignorance I had not realised that this was a struggle to keep the country not just a democratic republic, but a secular one, too.

But more than that, I was struck by the repugnance which

the young people I had met up to that point had expressed towards the entire political establishment. Politics, they said, was a game, a business, a way of life for a corrupt elite. For the previous three days I had talked and argued with students, activists, writers and artists who had uniformly stressed their alienation from a political process that denied them any sense of democracy and prevented freedom of expression. Sickened by the street protests that had raged the previous weekend, and by the sectarianism that led to individuals being clubbed to death by mobs, they felt disappointed, anxious and often in despair at the direction their country was headed.

How was I to interpret that overwhelming disillusionment with politics as I listened to someone whose entire family had risked their lives in a bitter war for the ideal of a secular democratic republic? How to process this overriding impression of a young generation that had benefited from their parents' struggle, but who now felt excluded from building on their achievements? I knew that young people in the UK felt quite cynical about the political process in Britain, but I had not necessarily expected this to be the case in a young country like Bangladesh. Was this to be a pattern of educated, metropolitan young people across the globe, I wondered.

The day before, in another traffic jam, this time in Chittagong, I listened to Nazzina talking about the legacy of that war within her immediate family. In 1971 her mother had witnessed a beloved uncle being shot by Pakistani soldiers. Another relative now living in Toronto had turned away from religion having seen members of his family killed in front of his eyes by Pakistani soldiers wearing Islamic attire. He had only survived because he fainted and was presumed dead. From other conversations I had learned how the memories of massacres and mass rape haunted the older generation, how some enemies could not be forgiven.

That legacy of profound resentment was often exposed in everyday life. It could be a simple avoidance of talking face to face, or it could be a more subtle way of refusing to forget what had happened, reflected, for example, in how one dressed. One Bangladeshi woman I met who lives in Britain admitted that she wore a sari rather than the fashionable Bangladeshi shalwar kameez. Wearing the former might identify her as Indian, but that was preferable to being mistaken for a Pakistani, who would in turn try to avoid dressing like an Indian. As much as she was committed to dialogue and reconciliation she confessed it had become an ingrained habit that was difficult to change.

Nazzina, now in her twenties, had grown up hearing these stories from her parents and grandparents, but she felt determined not to take these patterns of aversion into her own life. As we sat inhaling traffic fumes from Chittagong's rush-hour traffic, I turned to my other travelling companion, Mohammed Jahangir. He was slightly distracted. A journalist and broadcaster, he was fielding phone calls on behalf of his brother Mohammed Yunus who had just been awarded the Nobel Prize for his lifetime's work on reducing poverty in Bangladesh through the Grameen Bank. I was asking him whether he thought that the younger generation had views on British colonialism, or whether it was too far back in the past, especially given that their parents had to live through the partition of Bengal and the war against Pakistan before they were born.

'There's a big problem with this generation. The young don't care for history. Our generation knows about the British period, the Mughal period and so on. We were part of the Pakistan movement. Young people today, they might visit England, and go to Piccadilly Circus maybe. They are not interested in historical things. They just know what they have read in textbooks. That's all.'

Part of the problem, he thought, was that their lives had been easy, so far. 'The Pakistani government was suppressing us, we had to fight. We had a fighting spirit.'

This sounded dangerously familiar, a senior citizen chiding the younger generation for their apparent apathy and frivolous interests. Yet MJ was not as despairing as he made out. He had founded an NGO called Centre for Development and Communication whose main objective was to increase an awareness of democracy through the media. He acknowledged the bankruptcy of the main political parties but his response was that they should start a new one. 'Get together,' he urged, 'form your own groups and talk about things.'

∽

'Identity sometimes comes from the gut,' said Swati. She was talking about the way that what we eat reflects who we are more often than we think. She had grown up in a family that had been torn apart by the division of India into two nations in 1947. Although many Hindus and Sikhs remained in what is now Pakistan, thousands decided to flee to India where they thought they would be safe from persecution.

Swati's reaction to hearing her family's accounts of the bitter conflict propelled her to be a vegetarian. It was partly a form of protest, partly because she could not bear to be responsible for violence towards any living creature. Her desire to escape the stories she had imbibed from childhood did not equip her to understand the roots of the conflict, but she was determined not to let the past affect her own political outlook. She decided to go to Pakistan herself and visit some friends she had met through college. She broke at least one other taboo by travelling alone with a male friend, but in the course of her journey she gained some valuable insights.

Now Swati had already made it clear when she was telling this story that she was not interested in cooking elaborate meals just for the sake of tradition, mainly because this demanded too much time from women. Diwali had just ended and she had been climbing the walls of her family home as a result of claustrophobia and over-eating what she called 'heavy festival food'. For her, identity was also about what you didn't eat. She was perfectly happy with pasta and salad and getting on with more important things, which didn't include preparing herself for marriage. When her mother had asked her to bring some masala spices back from Pakistan she had been puzzled but put it on her list.

The first morning she woke up in Pakistan at her friend's home she had a shock. The smell of cooking coming from the kitchen was just like home. 'Suddenly,' she said, 'the whole thing about India and Pakistan being two entirely separate countries strikes you. I had always accepted that as a fact, but from that point the masalas forced me to question the whole version of history I had been fed.'

Like Nazzina in Bangladesh, Swati had grown up with an ominous sense of the crimes committed against her family by another national group. As a result they felt impatient with their parents' preoccupation with the past, whether it was Partition in 1947 or the more recent war in 1971. According to historian Urvashi Butalia this was a pattern that was replicated across their generation. When I met her in Delhi she was in the process of editing a new collection that explored these reactions among younger women writers across all three countries. Entitled *A Sense of the Past: women's writings on Partition*, it would be a mixture of fiction and non-fiction she told me, a sort of extended dialogue between the generation of women who lived through Partition and those in their granddaughters' age group for whom it had very different meanings.

Urvashi had taken me to her favourite cafe for tea and apple pie. We sat outside so we could enjoy the afternoon light and listen to the birds singing in the beautiful Lodhi Gardens just next door. New Delhi was plastered with notices that read 'Green Delhi' and I had just seen a sign in the park declaring it a 'plastic bag free zone'. I was enjoying the feeling of being back in a city that had changed as much as I had over the intervening decades.

Zubaan, the independent publishing house founded by Urvashi a few years earlier, is an offshoot from India's first feminist publisher, Kali for Women. The word 'Zubaan' comes from Hindustani and has many meanings. Its literal translation is 'tongue' but it can also mean voice, language, speech and dialect. Urvashi is also a well-known writer herself. Her first book, *The Other Side of Silence*, published in 2000, explored oral histories of the traumatic displacements caused by the partition of India.

In the new collection, *A Sense of the Past*, the writings would not only span three countries, a rare undertaking in itself, but they would also approach it through a wide range of styles including oral history and first-person writing. Urvashi mentioned two small anecdotes that were remarkably similar to the one that Swati told. In the first, a young Pakistani woman travelled to India and reacted viscerally, like Swati, when she saw the similarities in lifestyle, language and culture. Another, from India, went across the border in order to trace her family roots and to see the things her parents had talked so nostalgically about throughout her childhood. She had been upset by what she saw as indifference to the fate that had befallen her family, but then she went to a cricket match between India and Pakistan. Suddenly there it was, staring her in the face. She felt a real sense of the deep historical chasm that seemed to have survived across the two generations.

Urvashi felt that the collection would reflect a new era of investigation that she had detected elsewhere on her travels. 'There is a lot of interest in regional and minority experiences of Partition,' she said. 'How the Sindhis experienced it, for example. They did not face a lot of violence but they did lose their homes and their country, too.'

She had recently been to speak at a Sindhi college in Mumbai. This was one of several institutions that had been founded in an attempt to give the displaced community a focus and to keep the history alive. The college was now attended by Christians, Parsees and Punjabis, and Urvashi detected a new confidence in returning to the human aspects of this history, through writing, talking, filmmaking and art.

But the real story that Urvashi was interested in exploring was the long legacy of Partition, not in terms of what actually happened in 1947 but as a longer, ongoing process that connected majorities and minorities across these imposed national borders. 'It is interesting to see new areas opening up in Partition research, new awareness. There is lots of work on the Dalit experience. Also Muslims who went to Pakistan and came back, as well as those whose stayed.'

She had recently begun to work with a new group of displaced people whose stories were even less well known. 'A number of Hindus had stayed in Pakistan and then over the years gradually started to move to India. The most recent mass movement was in 1971. A hundred thousand came over and settled in Rajasthan. It is peculiar – they are mostly Hindus with Pakistani passports waiting to become Indian citizens. Many continued to cross-marry, Indians with Pakistanis. The negotiations across the border foul up notions of citizenship.'

As the afternoon light began to fade and we drank the last cups of warm tea from the pot, we talked about the way that the experience of earlier generations was beginning to be addressed through art and fiction that crossed national borders, as well as academic research and oral history. Perhaps this imaginative interpretation of what happened would encourage paths of reconciliation rather than avoid suppressed histories and taboo subjects that might erupt in other ways. Urvashi remembered another important book on Zubaan's list of forthcoming books. 'It's a novel by a writer called Shaheen Akhtar about the 1971 war in Bangladesh. We've had it translated into English, and it's now called *The Search* (*Talaash* in Bengali). It is structured round the life of a woman who was raped – she was one of the Birongana, one of the thousands raped by Pakistani soldiers at that time. The novel examines the legacy of pain and anguish that scarred the bodies of so many women. It makes you question the whole notion of independence.'

∽

I have never read a book by John Grisham but after a few weeks in the major cities of Bangladesh, India and Pakistan I began to feel like I was missing something. In every traffic-filled street, wherever I went, boys would walk up and down the trapped lines of cars and rickshaws offering a variety of books for sale, always including *The Innocent Man*, Grisham's latest novel.

When I turned away, or showed my disinterest by shaking my head, they would hold up another title. Sometimes this would be Amartya Sen's *The Argumentative Indian* and at this I would try to gesture that I already had it. Also popular were *Freakonomics*, *The Monk Who Sold His Ferrari*, and *How to Talk to Anyone*. On several occasions I noticed they had Kiran Desai's prize-winning novel *The Inheritance of Loss*.

But the number one favourite, the one that they tried to sell the hardest was *In the Line of Fire* by Pakistan's President, Pervez Musharraf, which looked to the naked eye an exact copy of the edition published by Simon and Schuster a few weeks earlier. The fact that it was being sold on every street corner was either a sign of its popularity or alarmingly skilful marketing.

It's surprising what you can learn if you go to a good bookshop, though. Browsing in the Oxford University Press store just next to my hotel in Islamabad I observed to the assistant that there were a lot of new books about Partition. 'They are all from India,' he explained. 'India experienced Partition as a loss; for Pakistan it was a victory.'

I heard a scratchy noise overhead which sounded suspiciously four-legged. I looked inquiringly at the assistant to see if he was concerned. They sounded awfully near and dreadfully numerous. 'Actually,' he said, 'they are rats. They came in the container and started breeding. We are going to kill them all this weekend. We also get them after floods – people say they come from India.'

We began to discuss rats as a problem in cities generally. In London, I told him, they say you are never more than six feet away from one. 'I have never seen a rat in London although I was there for a year,' he said. 'It was very clean, not like America, or so I have heard.' I told him about the graffiti artist Banksy and his interest in rats, and the responses that they evoked. He said he had noticed that Europeans feel very bad about rats and spiders too. 'In Pakistan we don't have a problem with rats and spiders, but we hate lizards. Cockroaches too are difficult to deal with, but we have noticed that the bigger ones which used to be common are mainly found in sewers now. We have a small variety that has come from Germany, probably in a container, and they are very hard to get rid of.'

This conversation reminded me of the fuss that was made at the opening of the Channel Tunnel that links England to northern France, which heralded the end of Britain's history as an island – or a group of islands – that could only be invaded by air or by sea. For decades the very concept had produced nightmare visions of rabid foxes, dirty foreigners and strange diseases slinking into the country unannounced, polluting it with harmful outside influences that could no longer be held at bay. Now the UK is invaded by all kinds of creatures that threaten its biodiversity, like the devastating Harlequin ladybird or the Californian pathogen that causes Sudden Oak Death. In this era of avian flu and the threat of global pandemics no one is sure how these enemies arrive but as the sinister effects of their free-floating presence become evident, the Channel Tunnel has been let off the hook as a symbolic conduit for bringing in contamination from mainland Europe.

⤳

Michal sends me a picture from the Polish Tourist Board. A cheery pilot beams from a Spitfire cockpit. 'Londoners We Are With You Again!' it reads, in direct reference to the Battle of Britain in 1940. The poster was issued shortly after the 7 July attacks in London, implying that the spirit of World War Two flows seamlessly into the War on Terror.

Then he bombards me with another email. 'I am sorry for distracting you but this something you *must* read.'

I open the link and find I am reading from Hansard, the official record of parliamentary debate. The discussion is all about leaky church roofs and the heritage protection reforms planned by government. I scroll down to see something more controversial, although I do think that architectural heritage is related to national identity somewhere along the line. But Michal had warned me to expect a torrent of nationalist, stereotyping rubbish so I kept going. What he was directing me to was the transcript of a debate about Anglo-Polish relations led by the Conservative MP Daniel Kawczynski. I recognised it when I found it.

The exchange had taken place in May 2006, shortly after one of Britain's celebrity chefs had made a disparaging remark about Polish waiters. This was not the cause of the debate, though it was mentioned in the opening stages. The reason that Kawczynski had tabled the subject was because he wanted to enlist Poland's aid in bringing about a major European coup. In short, he wanted to argue, he said, for a strategic UK-Polish partnership that would challenge the Franco-German axis 'which has run the EU for far too long'.

He put all his cards on the table at once. 'I passionately believe that the United Kingdom – the fourth largest economy in the world and a major military power – has the opportunity, within my generation, to become the leading partner in the EU and to take control of the future strategy and vision of the EU. However, it needs strategic, key allies – junior partners – in order to be able to play that leading role. Poland is one of the key allies that I believe we need.'

Over the next hour and a half there ensued a stream of effervescent eulogy for Poland. Kawczynski launched into it with a hymn of praise for the new economic migrants, revealing the interesting fact that most of the NHS dentists in the town he represented were Poles of recent origin. This was followed by admiration for the country's economic health, greatly boosted by British investment and partnerships. But the real meat of his speech was reserved for the shared military connections between the two countries, beginning with the observation that they were fighting the same war in Iraq. 'There is a long tradition of Polish soldiers fighting alongside British soldiers,' he said. 'That was certainly the case in the Battle of Britain and at Monte Cassino and Arnhem.'

The MP was alluding to the fact that one in five of the pilots in the Battle of Britain was a Polish national. Then he added, 'Speaking as somebody of Polish origin, I find it difficult to think of a time in the past 100 years when Britain has not come to Poland's aid. I sometimes think that we in this country do not blow our own trumpet enough, because Britain has done more for Poland than any European country has.'

The debate continued with fulsome support from MPs from all parties who seemed to be competing with each other to praise Poland to the skies. I could see why Michal was so upset. Although he does not live in Poland he is deeply tied to it through family and friends as well as through his work. When he read the Hansard report of the debate he felt let down by those in the Labour Party whom he expected to take a different stand. For one thing, he would have hoped for a different language of connection: a tone that was not infused with a self-righteously patriotic fervour; a perspective that looked to the shared values of contemporary, democratic citizenship instead of revelling in the glories of long-gone military victories; an awareness that what is driving many young Poles to leave their country is a sense of alienation from a regressive, nationalist and socially conservative government.

Daniel Kawczynski represented himself as a child of an earlier generation of Polish migrants to Britain. During the period 1939–45 there were an estimated 250,000 Poles seeking refuge in the UK. Roughly 150,000 of these stayed behind, forming communities that played a vital role in linking networks of refugees from the Communist era across Europe and North America. Small numbers came to London from the 1950s to the 1970s, and the 1980s saw an increasing number of asylum seekers, like Michal's step-father, sympathetic to the banned organisation, Solidarity. After the fall of the Berlin Wall in 1989 a new generation of economic migrants began to move west, and since 2004 the trend continues to rise.

These successive layers of migration do not automatically

sit well on each other. For many reasons, the Polish diaspora in the UK has had to work hard to overcome mutual suspicion and incomprehension between the generations. Michal had sent me another picture, this time a photo of young men and women cleaning Polish war graves in a cemetery in west London. The image is intended to appease the incongruity between an older generation that settled in Britain after the end of the war with Germany, and those who arrived recently as economic migrants with a different sense of Polish national identity. Like the poster of the Spitfire pilot, it suggests that the historical links between Poland and the UK can still be asked to supply a simple narrative of patriotic solidarity against a common enemy.

But Polishness has plenty of other narratives to contend with that go far beyond its 'special' relationship with the UK. Situated on the perimeter of Europe, the nation has long seen itself as a bastion of defence against non-Christian invaders from the east, whether Turkish or communist. For some nationalists, their adherence to Catholicism, long defined against the Russian Orthodox Church as the true version of Christianity, qualifies the country as the guardian of an important element of European identity under new threat from multiculturalism and migration. There are less heroic strands too that make it harder to maintain the country's image as a staunch survivor of invasion and occupation. In common with other European countries occupied by the Nazis, Poland has been required to face unpalatable truths about its role in the war. This has proved especially difficult since current nationalist sensibility draws on a sense of victimhood.

In 2001, one of the most respected historians of twentieth century Europe, Jan T. Gross, published a book called *Neighbours*, based on the events that took place in July 1941 in the small Polish town of Jedwabne. It was a little known but recorded fact that virtually every one of the town's 1,600 Jewish residents was killed in a single day. Using eyewitness testimony Gross demonstrated that they were not murdered by Germans occupying the country, but by their Polish neighbours. When the book was published it caused an unprecedented re-evaluation of Jewish-Polish relations during the war, bringing about a public debate that reached into the heart of Polish identity. For many Poles it was unacceptable that an outsider had drawn attention to the massacre.

More recently, in 2006, Gross, a professor at Princeton University, published a new book called *Fear: Anti-Semitism in Poland After Auschwitz*. The book recounts how 200,000 surviving Polish Jews returned to their country after the war which saw ninety per cent of their community – 3,000,000 people – slaughtered by the Nazis. They came back to find levels of anti-Semitism that were, if anything, higher than they had been before or during the German occupation. Jews were stigmatised, terrorised and, in some 1,500 instances, murdered, sometimes in ways that deliberately recalled the Nazi pogroms.

The publication of these historical accounts, based on careful readings of the recent past and first-hand testimonies of perpetrators as well as victims, has had a profound impact on debates about Polishness and national identity in the twenty-first century. But the experience – and extent – of migration to countries that are engrossed in their own struggles with racism, exclusion and diversity opens up new opportunities to rethink European identities, too.

In Lisahally near Derry in Northern Ireland, another wartime vessel lying underwater has been identified as an articulate ruin, but unlike the *USS Montgomery* in the Thames estuary, one that offers possibilities for peace education rather than symbolising the 'submerged, unmanageable charge' of history. The proposal to lift a surrendered German U-boat which had been guided into the harbour by the Polish navy in 1945 has been enthusiastically supported by the British, Irish, Polish and German navies. The plan provides welcome opportunities for the 2,000 Poles living in Derry to contribute to a new history of multiculturalism in a city eager to leave the past behind.

⁓

Checking Zubaan's website a few weeks after my conversation with Urvashi, I made another discovery. In 1932 a woman called Bina Das was sent to prison after shooting (and missing) Stanley Jackson, the British Governor of Bengal, at Calcutta University. A new translation of her memoir was about to be published, giving an account of her growing political awareness that led to her espousal of violence against the British rulers. As I read the brief paragraph describing the new book, it crossed my mind that this event must have terrified members of the Bengal Club, the heart of Raj society in Calcutta. I wondered about this as I had stayed there myself and could picture the building both inside and out.

I can safely say that I did not know the full meaning of the term 'starch' until I had breakfasted at the Bengal Club and I wasn't thinking of carbohydrates. My napkin seemed to be made of cardboard. But that was the least of my troubles. At first I thought it amusing, walking into the building knowing that I had a room booked in my name. Founded in 1827, everything about it was infused with a sense of the colonial past. The lift was one of those that rose up a wire cage shaft inside the staircase, with wooden doors and brass fittings. Later, when I decided to walk downstairs I saw that the walls were graced with fine old prints of Calcutta's historic buildings.

The most wonderful thing about this institution is the library. It has a huge collection of leather-bound books on and from the colonial era, as well as a fascinating cross section of contemporary fiction in English. As soon as I discovered it I snatched six books off the shelves and rushed to the air-conditioned reading room, knowing I had little time to read them. When I came back later all of my stash had been returned to slightly different places on the shelves, but in looking for them I found others equally interesting.

Crammed alongside each other was title after title bearing witness to the long relationship between Britain and the Indian subcontinent. I picked out a leather-bound volume at random entitled *India: Its Life and Thought* by John P. Jones, author of *India's Problems: Krishna or Christ?*

'It is amusing,' it began, 'when not discouraging, to witness travellers, who have rushed through India on a winter tour, publish volumes of their misconceptions and ill-digested theories about the people with an oracular emphasis which is equalled only by their ignorance.'

Somewhat taken aback, I read on, only to find that his admonition was qualified by a brief preface: 'To the people of the West, the inhabitants of India are the least understood and most easily misunderstood of all men.'

As scholars like Edward Said have elaborated, creating a body of knowledge about the people that you conquer and control amounts to a form of domination in itself, even if you modify your claim to know about them by saying that they are easily misunderstood. Thus inscrutability becomes one of their key characteristics. It is important to remember, however, that the traffic in travel writing flowed in more than one direction, and that there is a sizeable body of literature explaining what Indian writers thought about Britain. *London and Paris through Indian Spectacles* by Paramesvara G. Pillai caught my eye and I made a note to check it out in the British Library in London when I got home.

Kolkata is full of archives. One day I braved the humidity to run to the South Park Street cemetery to see for myself the burial ground of European settlers which had recently been restored. Once a habitation for homeless people, stray dogs and snakes, it has been cleaned up and preserved in recognition of its value as a historical record. The restoration, which began in 1978, is still in progress, but the main section of the cemetery has been landscaped and the tombs repaired and scrubbed. As I read the inscriptions on the graves, wandering through the tropical plants in astonishment at the architecture of the obelisks, domes and mausolea, I recalled the dedication in Mr Jones's book. '*Dedicated to my dear children who have bravely and cheerfully endured the separation and loss of home for the sake of India.*' There were many who didn't make it, such as David Smith who died at seven months and his sister Amelia who was three years and four months. Their mother Dorothy who died at the age of twenty-eight shared their tombstone which gave no clue as to why they perished together.

The booklet published by the Association for the Preservation of Historical Cemeteries in India explains how the cemetery was rescued and why it is such a valuable record of the city's social history. Reading it now gives a sense that the European presence in Calcutta, first as traders for the East India Company, and then as representatives of colonial government, or simply travellers, writers, and relatives, was an important part of the city's heritage.

'These sentinels of the past speak silently of the way of life, the habits, hopes and fears of a generation that walked and talked in the once fevered expanse of this city a century or two ago. For posterity to permit a total eclipse of the testimony of their existence would be to lose surely the sense of history without which the story of mankind would be poor indeed.'

The graveyard was used from 1767 until the 1830s, and the stories about some of the characters buried there paint an extraordinary picture. This was an era of expatriate society grafted on to the city in the days before the Raj was established as a form of colonial government. The tedium of tropical weather clearly made a lot of time for gambling, adultery, and other pastimes that often arise from boredom. But there were also printmakers, writers, schoolteachers, historians, entrepreneurs, and other professions that make up civil society. This was the period that saw the founding of the Bengal Club and the construction of many of the buildings and spaces that I had glimpsed in the prints on the wall. A historian I met later that day told me that the city had once been divided into 'white town' and 'black town', describing parts of the city that still bore the imprint of colonial planning. And then when I returned to London my mother reminded me that her grandfather, who had died long before she was born, had been a doctor in Bengal. There is no one left to ask about what he was doing there or if he left any record of his life. Although he would have lived in the city long after the cemetery was closed, I wished I had had longer to consult the cemetery records to see if his forbears had been buried there.

‿

'How do we want to be remembered after we die?' Wahida wanted us to imagine her as an angel, addressing a new batch of customers who had passed away and were waiting for news of their final destination. 'What did you do in all the different stages of life,' she asked, 'and what would you do differently if you had another chance?'

The group consisted of a Christian, a Muslim, a politician, a married woman, a businessman, a trader and an old man who had been a member of a local mafia. Some of them answered in character and others spoke more from their own experience. From time to time Wahida turned to include the unsuspecting audience, asking one new mother, for example, what advice she would give to prospective parents. 'That we do our best, but we all make mistakes?' she suggested with astonishing prescience.

Waina complained about his education as a young boy. 'We were made to work from seven to seven and on Sundays, too. We were told over and over again, we must be number one, this is the best school. I failed. We became number two, but this sense of coming second best stuck to me all through my life.'

The businessman boasted of his success. 'I spent most of my life working. I wanted to go out with my concubines but I had a big family and didn't have much time.'

The exercise was designed to show how people's life experiences were shaped by many different factors, apart from the obvious ones of money and social class. It questioned how much individual choice there was in a country dominated by a political elite that manipulated ethnic and regional differences. By asking us to look back over a variety of fictional lives led by penitent, disappointed or complacent characters, the group was exploring the idea that it is possible to learn from what has already happened if we are to do things differently in the future. For them, the topic of identity was not simply who are we, but how did we become what we are?

It took only six people and five scenes to tell the story of Kenya. It began with a vision of pastoral bliss and ended in a British Council office. And it wasn't strictly confined to Kenya either, since half of the actors had grown up in the French colonial system. But the audience got the message.

The first scene made much of the harmonious and sustainable origins enjoyed by Africans before the Europeans arrived. By the end of the second scene the French had invaded, full of promises to show the natives how to use the land more productively, what it meant to buy and sell title deeds, and how to communicate in their language. The colonists were noisily dispatched in the same scene, but not before they had lined up their successors. They were shown quite deliberately educating and grooming a number of individuals who gladly took over the reins of the newly independent country.

In the following scene the country had entered its post-colonial phase. Aid was pouring in from the United States, the government ministers all spoke French and the new citizens were treated much as they had been in the colonial era. By the fourth scene we had reached the twenty-first century. This is where the actors departed from a simple script and spoke their lines with conviction.

'We are all educated now, our eyes are open.'

'We have seen how our people became colonials themselves.'

'What we need now is food.'

'Crime comes from hunger.'

'Aids comes from poverty and desperation.'

'Why do we let our brothers and sisters die from hunger?'

'Why is it that we cannot allocate our resources equitably?'

And as they posed these questions, one replied, 'I am going to the London School of Economics to learn how to help run my country.'

But the play was not over yet. The final scene was set in the present, in the meeting room loaned by the British Council in which we were sitting. A young English woman called Catherine had come to Kenya to write a book about 'social issues'.

'Hello everyone,' she said, in a warm and jolly manner, addressing the row of African students sitting in front of her. 'Welcome to the British Council. I would like to talk to you about ways in which we can help you. We feel so terribly sorry for what happened in the days of the British Empire. We want to be your partners in this new era instead of dominating you.'

The five remaining actors laid out their requests. Some were keen to study and work in the UK. One, a Nigerian, wanted to be granted UK citizenship. The last one asked for a grant to start her own NGO to work against HIV and Aids.

Up to this point the play had been verging on comedy, despite making some devastating critiques of the country's political system. The fact that Catherine's part was being played by David, a young Rwandan man speaking his fifth language, was both hilarious and unbearable at the same time. In the fifteen minutes it took to stage this impromptu drama, we had been presented with a story that poignantly showed how a rising generation understood the historical relation between Africa and the West. Their perspective was not developed from an 'us and them' mentality. In a sense, they were saying: 'This is how the past has shaped our countries in this part of the world. We understand that it is up to us to determine how we tackle the enormous problems of inequality and poverty that we face. We neither look up to our possible allies in the West, nor do we look down on you – although we are entitled to make fun of you. If you want to do something, give us the resources we ask for and let's keep talking.'

In the discussion that followed, another group was equally insistent. Organise, don't agonise, they declared. What is important is that we transcend national identities and find commonalities. We need global ideas about how to end poverty, crime, racism and violence.

↬

Dithering between avocado, mango and tree tomato, I asked for a mixture of all three. I wasn't unhappy when I was handed my glass of vermillion tree tomato juice, but I would have liked to try the mango and avocado that my companions had chosen.

I was sitting with Zarina Patel and Zahid Rajan, editors of the Nairobi based journal, *Awaaz*. Zarina is a writer, artist, environmentalist and historian, while Zahid has been a journalist for decades. They had kindly agreed to meet me although they were in the middle of holding their Samosa festival of Kenyan South Asian music and arts. Zarina was telling me how her curiosity about her grandfather's mysterious life had turned her into a writer as well as a political activist.

A. M. Jivanjee died when she was six months old, and as far as the family was concerned he had been a philanderer who ended his life bankrupt. His brother had been given an OBE by the British, and this had further divided the family. Zarina was born in Mombasa and trained as a physical therapist. She was also an artist and did voluntary work among craft workers in the city. When she moved to Nairobi to set up a community and race relations project in the National Christian Council of Kenya she was warned not to mention her grandfather who was known as a hustler. It was years later, in 1991, when President Daniel Moi tried to develop a small park that Jivanjee had donated to Nairobi at the turn of the century that she decided to find out who he was. During the course of the campaign to block the proposed destruction, she began to research his life and this ultimately led to a biography.

'I was amazed at what I found. I was writing about a whole period of Kenyan history. My grandfather was in fact the founder of the nationalist political movement in this country. He founded the the *African Standard* newspaper in 1902 (now the *East African Standard*) and the East African National Congress in 1914. Then other compatriots, South Asians, carried on the anti-colonial struggle in league with African leaders.

'The Indian community in East Africa can be traced back to several sources. In the late nineteenth century the British imported labourers to build the Uganda Railway and to grow sugarcane. But, for generations, traders had settled along the Indian Ocean coast, forming communities in port towns like Mombasa and Dar es Salaam. Those who were prosperous started their own businesses, employing Africans to do the work. Because of their financial success, South Asians were often accused of segregating themselves from Africans at the same time as exploiting their labour. But it was not always like that. Jivanjee himself was a trader who ran a chain of shops and bazaars in colonial towns. The garden he donated to the public was on the site of a small bazaar that had burned down. His involvement in nationalist and cultural politics had not been unusual in his own time.

'It was that cooperation that the British colonialists tried very hard to break up, and to block. It's because the South Asian role in the freedom struggle has always been very progressive, coming out of the Indian subcontinent. They came here with Gandhian ideas, basically pro-people ideas. After independence, of course, the Kenyatta regime became inwards looking and started to promote its own vested interest. All the people who had these socialist ideas were left by the wayside, African and South Asian. The South Asians became politically inactive after independence.'

Zarina's book *Challenge to Colonialism* portrayed early Nairobi as well as telling her grandfather's story in the process of rewriting a chapter of Kenyan history. Following this she wrote two versions for school children: *Rebel of the Empire* for younger children and *The Makers of History* which was part of a series for high school students.

'Today,' she added, 'nobody talks about nationalist politics in this country without mentioning my grandfather. And his was an unknown name before I wrote the book. The tendency has been that communities write about their own history, from their point of view. So Europeans wrote their history as settlers. As a result the African was just a servant and the South Asians were just ignored. Africans then began to write their own history and South Asians were left out. It is only of late that people have begun to write the South Asian history back in.'

Zarina was doing most of the talking because writing history was her specialism. Her second book had just been published, part of the same project to incorporate South Asian political activists into a historical narrative from which they had been excluded.

'It started in a similar way,' she said, 'I was curious about a man called Makhan Singh but it turned out to be a history of the trade union movement in this country. It is a part of Kenyan history which had been totally unknown, because the Central Organisation of Trade Unions (COFU) burned all his early records in 1984. The only record that we have is Makhan Singh's own work *The History of Kenya's Trade Union Movement*. Pulling out those papers and writing about that history has really helped to make people appreciate what he did.'

Little is known of Makhan Singh's private life. He was born in India, and was largely self-educated. He spent eleven and a half years in prison because of his attempts not just to found a trade union movement in colonial Kenya but to make it part of the struggle for liberation. While he was in detention he translated Karl Marx's *Das Kapital* into Punjabi, but he was released into a newly independent Kenya that had little time for his brand of politics. He died in 1973, destitute but with his principles intact. Zarina's book, *Unquiet: the life and times of Makhan Singh*, was also used as the basis for a documentary.

Zahid had also been a writer for many years, actively involved in the movement for democratisation in Kenya. He and Zarina founded *Awaaz* as a regular journal in 2002, but it had emerged out of earlier attempts to create debates about identity and history in terms of Kenyanness and the South Asian community in East Africa. Frustrated that there was virtually no voluntary participation in public life, and that people were living behind secured fences, too afraid to mix with the rest of Kenyan society, the group turned to art, film, music and other cultural projects as a way to break down barriers. The Samosa project which was being held in Nairobi's biggest art centre was advertised all over town.

'Our board is completely multicultural,' stressed Zahid. 'We are journalists, playwrights, we have an environmentalist based in Mombasa. *Awaaz* is also distributed to South Asians living in the diaspora – in the UK, the US and Europe, and of course Tanzania and Uganda in East Africa.

'We do a lot of human-rights work, too,' he added. 'We've explored the question of race relations and inter-marriages and had lots of interesting responses from people asking us not to publish things like that – telling us that we are making things worse by talking about them.'

↩

The India Museum in Kolkata was the first institution of its kind in British India, and the ninth oldest regular museum in the world. In 1814 it was established in the Asiatic Society headquarters, founded earlier by a Danish botanist called Nathaniel Wallich. The current museum to which we were now headed was built in 1878.

We got there out of breath having spent too long enjoying a Bengali-style Chinese lunch with endless cups of jasmine tea. We managed to buy tickets before the office closed and rushed straight into the hall displaying exquisite examples of Kalighat Patas, the brightly-coloured folk art of Bengal. Pratap ushered us further into the building, hoping aloud that the particular room that he wanted to show us had not been closed to the public. I still did not know exactly what we were looking for but followed expectantly in the full knowledge that he had been here before. We finally found the right room and were able to take as much time as we needed to explore its contents.

The gallery contained a replica of the Bharut railing, part of a Buddhist stupa discovered in Madhya Pradesh in 1873. Carved in red sandstone, it depicts scenes from Buddha's pre-birth stories, providing a visual storehouse for the reconstruction of political, social, economic and cultural history of India in the second to first centuries BCE.

'In the seventeenth and eighteenth centuries a lot of this kind of stuff was being destroyed, neglected, forgotten,' Pratap explained. 'Some of the early orientalists arrived from Britain, and in addition to all the exploitation which we know about, there was a genuinely open attempt to understand this great civilisation which appeared to British eyes to be decaying and nearly lost.

'One of my teachers put it very succinctly: Before the orientalists and other British scholars came we had a past but did not have a history. So the story of Buddhism was all wrapped up in myth, and Buddha thought of as a mythological, Vedic figure, a god. But the recovery of the historical Buddha and his teachings is significantly connected with the arrival of Western scholarship.'

'How did you know about this?' I asked Pratap. I was moved by his passionate interest as he explained the relevance of the scenes carved on the structure.

'I was making a series about the relationship between Britain and India pre-Raj. What fascinated me was that we had a much more open relationship that was so nearly something much richer than what came to pass. Before the militarisation of British settlement and the increasing growth of racist, colonial thinking there was a period when that wasn't the case. We don't know enough about that – we being most Indian and British people – because we have been sold a different version of history, whether it's the imperialist story or the Indian nationalist one.'

⌒

'Make sure you go to the National Archives,' I was told when I arrived. But I was only in Nairobi for a few days and I knew from my experiences in Kolkata that you can't do a library in a rush. My guidebook assured readers that the institution was more interesting than it might sound to the non-historian, despite or possibly because of the fact that the building contained hundreds of thousands of documents. However, it had also told me that the Jivanjee Gardens were named after one of Nairobi's first Indian businessmen, adding that he was also a philanthropist. I made sure I visited the little park on the way to the Archives and stopped to appreciate the beautiful modern sculpture of Zarina's grandfather that she and others had commissioned to commemorate his revised history.

The building that houses the Kenyan national archive collection is itself a monument to the success of Indian business in East Africa. Originally designed in 1931 as the headquarters for the Bank of India, it was acquired by the government in the late 1970s as a repository of national and regional documentation. It is a grand white hunk in the middle of the city's downtown area, directly opposite the Hilton hotel and easily accessible to the curious passer-by.

The interior consists of a single massive exhibition space divided into compartments. This houses numerous examples of art, craft, photographs and other records of East African life and culture, and the visitor might easily assume that this was the sum of its public exhibits. It is easy to be detained by the exquisite pieces of sculpture and fabric, and by the stories of the women and men who collected much of the material. In one section, for instance, there is an array of paintings belonging to the John Boyes Collection, purchased in an auction after his death. Described in a caption as one of the more 'colourful' figures of Kenya's colonial past, Boyes was the first English trader to establish himself in the area that became known as Nairobi in the late nineteenth century. He was apparently known as the 'king of the Wakikuyu' and a famous game hunter. His exploits and the art that he amassed have now become part of Kenyan heritage.

Upstairs, a gallery running round the outside of the main hall displays an extraordinary photographic record of the country's political landscape during the era of colonial rule which began in 1895 and ended in 1963. The photos show the first years of independence taking the viewer almost up to the present day. It begins with a portrait of Dedan Kimathi who was hanged by the British in 1956 in an attempt to suppress the Mau Mau insurgency. By that time Kimathi was a legendary leader within the nationalist movement, but the previous decade he had fought for the British colonial army in Burma.

Another print shows Pio Gama Pinto, a journalist active in the struggle for independence who founded the *KANU* newspaper in 1960, and later the *Pan African Press*. Born in Nairobi and educated in India, Pinto was assassinated in 1965 by a fellow Kenyan national.

The photographs are supplemented by glass cases containing

sample historic documents that provide a flavour of what lies out of sight, filed away in boxes, on shelves and in microfiche form in the bowels of the building. I noticed a bundle of papers on display with the telling words: Land for Detribalized Natives 1933–48 (Open for Public Inspection).

On entering the archives I had been given a brochure that outlined the purpose of the institution in modern-day Kenya. Its vision, it stated, was 'to excel as an archives service in view of all Kenyans and to serve as the Memory of the Nation'. Its mission was to preserve all valuable public records and to make them accessible to present and future generations.

The documents referred to in the guidebook are not on view to the public but available for inspection through catalogues in the adjacent library. They cover the colonial period from 1895 to 1963 and consist of provincial and district annual reports, record books, and handing-over reports, correspondence, intelligence reports, debates and other documentation of governance. The resource allows scholars of national and regional history to pour over this material in order to challenge accepted accounts of the past and to develop new insights into what happened. But the implications of this research go much further than East Africa. They reach right into the heart of current debates about Britishness.

Just a few weeks before this trip, I had made a detour to call on writer and scholar, Caroline Elkins, who is based at Harvard University in the United States. Her prize-winning book, *Imperial Reckoning: The Untold Story of Britain's Gulag in Kenya*, was published in 2005 to great acclaim among historians and analysts of colonial wars. As I was passing through Boston I contacted her to ask her about her work, not just as an academic specialising in this area, but as an expert involved in a court case that had just been launched by the Kenya Human Rights Commission. This concerned a carefully prepared case by ten survivors of British incarceration during the Kenya Emergency which ran from 1952 to 1957. The claimants have begun the long process of suing the British government for what they claim was officially sanctioned torture and other human-rights abuses.

Fortunately Caroline was in town, between trips to Kenya to make a new documentary based on her research. In 2002 she was the subject of a BBC film called *Kenya: White Terror* which had caused a certain amount of controversy when it came out. When I met her we began by talking about what led her towards this particular field of study.

'You can't understand Africa without knowing global history, and it makes you think about the relationship between empire and indigenous peoples. There are large areas of African history that have been studied but there is a lot that we still don't know.'

Her interest in the Mau Mau period was fuelled partly by the discovery that the British administration had repeatedly tried to cover up their attempts to suppress the rebellion. Many of the reports detailing the mass detentions, torture, sexual abuse, flogging and even murder of 150,000 Kikuyu men and women were destroyed before the country became independent. Her book is based largely on eyewitness accounts by survivors of camps set up to hold the thousands of prisoners after they declared a state of emergency in 1952. But as well as exposing the extent of the atrocities that took place, the book also contains a detailed account of campaigns in Britain formed in protest at what was happening. In 1955, when news of torture and execution was contradicting the official reports from colonial administrators, the Labour politician Barbara Castle, in opposition at the time, declared:

'In the heart of the British Empire there is a police state where the rule of law has broken down, where the murder and torture of Africans by Europeans goes unpunished and where the authorities pledged to enforce justice regularly connive at its violation.'

A mere decade after celebrating the Allies' victory against fascism, the British government was accused of permitting some of the same tactics used by the Nazis against their opponents. But this is not a chapter of history that has remained in public consciousness, nor has it achieved the mythic status of battles fought to retain the honour of the British Empire. The young US historian's academic commitment to exposing the horrors of colonial warfare waged by the British is an example of a new generation of scholars and researchers writing about empire as a politically-charged field of study. As Caroline Elkins said when we met, 'Historical questioning changes a lot based on contemporary political circumstances. My generation of historians who are in their thirties are thinking about the world, raised in a different context. Clearly the post-9/11 world certainly influences how people are asking questions and how they are thinking about things.'

She was confident about the responsibilities facing her as an author of books that exposed crimes previously overlooked or buried in official denials.

'There is an intimate relationship between writing the "new" histories and political claim-making. New histories give coherence and force to claim-making in the same way that contemporary political circumstances drive the kinds of questions that we are asking. We can't step away from that. In this case I think, unfortunately, this claim will get held up in the courts for years. But ultimately the question becomes what happens in the courts *and* what happens in the court of public opinion. This is the first time that a former colonised population has sued the British government for injustices during the colonial period. Obviously it will have an enormous impact on other populations thinking along the same lines.'

↜

English people can scarcely believe in the wickedness of actual war. Its civilised and legal operations are terrible enough, but without an iron hand to repress, there is no cruelty, no crime, however dreadful, that will not be enacted under its shade.

Mrs Muter, the woman writing these words, was looking back over her life half a century earlier as the wife of a colonial official in India. I read her book in the Bengal Club library, expecting it to be sensationalist about Indian war crimes, not ones committed by her own countrymen. The war to which she was referring was the Indian Mutiny, or the Sepoy Revolt, as it was then known, that lasted from 1857 until the following year. For generations, British children learned that the dreadful episode was the result of a clumsy approach to cultural sensibilities. School textbooks related how the Hindu and Muslim soldiers who were serving in the British Indian Army were expected to grease their guns with cow and pig fat. It made a vivid picture in the classroom but it did not explain the context for the widespread insurgency that it sparked across the country.

Subsequently renamed the First Indian War of Independence, the uprising has been revisited by many generations of historians whose disparate and widely varying accounts agree that 1857 was a turning point in the history of British rule in India. The East India Company, forerunner of the modern-day global corporation, had developed from an outfit primarily motivated by trade to a colonial power in its own right, complete with its own army, a burgeoning civil service and a selective programme of 'Westernisation'. By 1857 all the remaining independent states had been conquered and were subject to new laws banning social practices such as suttee and child marriage.

Many other colonial wars had taken place by the time Mrs Muter published her recollections in 1911, and the British Empire was in its heyday. Three years later the 'war to end all wars' would break out in Europe. Perhaps it was the awful sense of looming catastrophe, as well as her experience of unrestrained carnage, that gave her book its moral tone. Not knowing anything else about her, I appreciated her readiness to bear witness to some of the crimes committed in the name of preserving civilisation. Writing a scene that she must have composed countless times, she revisited the aftermath of the first outbreak in May 1857 which happened when the Europeans were in church:

> The sun rose on a scene changed in a manner words cannot describe. It was not only that it had sunk on a peaceful charade for church and rose on blackened ruins and murdered Christians; it had also sunk on good and kindly feelings, and now rose on the wildest storm of men's passions.

Looking back with hindsight, she writes as though this was the revolt against colonial occupation that they all dreaded as their worst nightmare:

> We felt intuitively that it was a great revolution, a cyclone that had merely its centre at Meerut, destined to sweep with a violence that would startle the world, over the

length and breadth of the land. Perhaps the framework of English rule would go down before the tempest, and if so, what was reserved for us?

Much of the book is taken up with finding her husband who was away from Meerut at the time, and escaping with him on foot until they were able to leave the country. This was not before he had come across many instances where the British troops had taken their revenge for the rebels' rumoured targeting of civilian wives and children. She writes that her husband saw the bodies of several young girls lying dead by a well into which five young women had leapt to escape the troops advancing to capture the city. It was this that caused her to talk of the wickedness of actual war as opposed to the 'legal and civilised' version.

'Were the number of blameless persons who were sacrificed truly estimated,' she continued, 'the British public would be horrified at the result.'

᷍

The day I met Caroline Elkins was one of those glorious New England fall treats of bright-blue sky and freakishly warm sunshine that tempts you back into your shorts for one last time. The leaves had barely started to turn, but there were signs that the trees would soon produce the fireworks that were expected in this part of the world. On my way to our meeting I passed one of the city's many graveyards that act as a constant reminder of how relatively young this country is. The rugged tombstones clustered together in this open space between the buildings and the street caught my attention as the shafts of sunlight pierced through the old trees growing in their midst. American flags were dotted around the cemetery, the red, white and blue contrasting sharply with the greys and greens. I noticed a blue oval plaque attached to the railings as I walked past. It read: 'Old Burying Ground: Burial Place of early settlers, Tory landowners and slaves, soldiers, presidents of Harvard and prominent men of Cambridge, 1635.'

New England is full of visible evidence of its colonial past, and the cemeteries dotted throughout towns and villages date back to the early seventeenth century and no further. The Boston area is saturated with reminders of the American

Revolution since it was there that the first shots were fired. There is a 'freedom trail' running throughout the city, the stirring narrative linked by a red stripe running along the pavement. For those interested in African-American history and the story of the anti-slavery movement there is a Black Heritage Trail that celebrates the courage of the many abolitionists who were based in the city. There are statues of revolutionary heroes at every turn, and placards and monuments along main roads and crossroads.

The notion of history as costume drama is compounded when you read brochures for nearby Plimoth Rock. There, people dressed as settlers take you round a settlement based on earliest accounts of the Pilgrim Fathers, showing how they found food and survived the hot summers and freezing winters in those early years. This public heritage helps to turn Boston and its surrounding towns into a tourist haven. It offers visitors and residents a constant reminder, not just of the early days of the city itself, but of the country's founding moments first as a colony and then as an independent republic.

Since Britain is not a settler country that developed as a result of being colonised, its historical landmarks do not provide much evidence of founding moments. Instead we have medieval castles, churches, prehistoric burial mounds and mysterious old ruins like Stonehenge to remind us how far back we go, and to link 'us' to a past shrouded in mist. Never mind that when those responsible were moving their mammoth boulders 4,600 years ago, the area now known as the Middle East was enjoying art, sculpture, music and law.

Others would argue however that Britain was really born 300 years ago, when the Treaty of Union in 1707 officially brought England and Scotland together to form one country called Great Britain. By dissolving the parliaments in both countries and forming the Parliament of Great Britain in Westminster, the Act cemented a more formal relationship that had begun a century earlier when Scotland and England agreed to share the same king.

On my last night in Nairobi the TV was on while I packed. A local channel was showing a programme called *Face the Nation* and the topic of the studio discussion was leadership and ethnicity. The majority of participants were arguing that ethnicity was unimportant, especially for young people. They were highly critical of the way that those in power made it a significant factor which had the effect of prolonging conflict and rivalry. Justice and equality came from the careful distribution of resources and should not be linked to ethnicity. But one gentleman disagreed with the consensus. Look at what Tony Blair has done by setting up the Scottish Assembly, he said. The British are not shy about the ethnic differences between the English and the Scots. Let us look at what they are doing, how they manage their different ethnicities.

↜

'If you go back a thousand years, there was a market in Leyton shopping centre and people were speaking Danish, Norman, Saxon, French and other languages. We know from excavations that there has always been that diversity round here. This was always a society of flux and migrant communities.'

Martin had been involved in drawing up proposals for the new history curriculum for eleven- to fourteen-year-olds. He was happy that the government had been receptive to the ideas put forward so far.

'We want to get away from just teaching British and world history chronologically for the sake of it without any clear reason or context: what we teach has to be relevant to children's needs. The plan is to design a course where kids know why they are learning history. Individual schools will have the autonomy to teach about their own location and the makeup of the communities in which they are based.'

'How would that work in practice?' I asked him.

'Well, here we are doing it in three stages. With the youngest ones, we start by asking how the local area comes to look like it does. The next stage is to find out how we came to be governed like this, and then thirdly we ask how the world came to be so unequal. All three questions run from the ancient world to the present, but by using different examples we help them understand how to use history to make sense of the world around them. One important strand, for example, would be the continuing diversity of Britain and the impact of migration into and out of the country.'

'What about the history of the British Empire?' I asked, 'How would you approach that using this model?'

'I'd start, myself, with our own stories,' replied Martin. 'I'd ask where we've all come from and start to unravel why we are all here.' Then he added, 'It's interesting that the only bit of content that everybody insists on, across the political spectrum, is the British Empire. I agree with this, I think it is so important.'

I wasn't sure about asking kids to talk about where they had come from. It worried me that the ones who didn't think of themselves as immigrants anywhere along the line might feel left out. To me it had echoes of a tokenist approach that valued *other* cultures, implying that there was something homogenous, white and rather dull at the heart of majority Britishness.

'What happens to those who don't know where their parents came from, or who think of their ancestors as, well, just Londoners?'

'It's the same for them,' said Martin, agreeing heartily when I put this to him. 'Nearly every Londoner is descended from a migrant of some kind or another – whether from Scotland, Wales, Ireland or different parts of England, perhaps as a result of the Industrial Revolution. Round here their families may have come from rural Kent to factories in the East End, or to the docks – they came for the same basic reasons as all migrants. Their families moved to where they could survive.'

'Well, OK,' I said, 'but how would you teach the Empire without some kids turning round to others in the class and saying, "Look what you did to us"?'

'I understand your point. I don't personally think it's helpful to teach it as "what Britain did to the rest of the world." You've got a problem as soon as you approach it like that. It's important to make it clear that it's what people in powerful positions did in order to further their own wealth or political power. A Lancashire mill worker might have seen her or himself as connected to that British identity forging the Empire, but they were also fighting their own case in their own corner. I think it's crucial to present it through the lives of real people.'

Earlier we had talked about the new literature on the repression of the Mau Mau in Kenya and the question of the government atoning, or not, for acts that were increasingly being viewed as war crimes. The question I really wanted to ask Martin was how to teach the history of empire without either offering a facile supremacist account, that everything was for the best, or making students feel alienated because it was basically a string of invasions, occupations, repression and exploitation, all carried out in the name of British superiority.

'Well,' he pointed out, 'this is true almost anywhere in the world. Certainly in the European empires of the eighteenth, nineteenth, and twentieth centuries.'

He reminded me that the French and Japanese governments had intervened in debates about what could or couldn't be taught about their colonial pasts in school history lessons.

'It throws up huge questions, and mustn't be ignored. As you say, what's been coming out of Kenya in the 1950s, and I suspect will emerge from the 1960s in Malaysia, is painful, but on the other hand this new interest in the British Empire is causing people to do that work and uncover realities.'

↬

You don't need directions to find your way back to the history of colonialism when you alight from the train at Bristol's railway station. The signs for the British Empire and Commonwealth Museum are right in front of you as you exit the ticket barrier, and the museum itself is about a two-minute walk. Opened in 2002 in an old railway building, the museum has been carefully designed as an educational resource for the national project of remembering, revisiting and re-evaluating Britain's colonial past. Its location in Bristol, one of the country's most active slave ports until the trade was banned in 1807, is no coincidence. It represents the importance of acknowledging the city's collusion in the slave trade and therefore facing a particular responsibility for exploring its legacy.

The day I chose to visit was the day the government announced the new history curriculum for eleven- to fourteen-year-olds which included slavery as an important new component. The museum was already gearing up for a major exhibition called 'Breaking the Chains' to mark the bicentenary of abolition. One of its regular contributions to the teaching of this history is the availability of artefacts deriving from the abolitionist movement. Teachers are invited to borrow these Slavery Handling boxes for use in lessons so that children can examine coins, badges and plates and other items used in the public campaigns against slavery.

Gareth Griffiths, Director of the Museum, explains that the aim was to give teachers the right information and skills to take back to their schools to teach children about the abolitionist movement. He said, 'Because slavery can be a controversial subject, particularly when discussing whether people today should apologise, it is often avoided in the curriculum. I think the government is right to make it compulsory in history lessons. Pupils find it fascinating once they realise that the abolitionist movement was the forerunner to mass campaigning activities today such as Live Aid. The abolitionists were the first people to campaign for something on purely humanitarian grounds, where they had nothing to gain personally, and those values have been carried forward to many charity campaigns today.'

Making the past accessible to the present in tangible form is an admirable way of asking questions about these kinds of continuities. The idea that today's wristbands are the direct descendants of 200-year-old anti-slavery buttons can be used to provoke curiosity about whether other campaigns against global injustice took place in between. But asking school students to imagine a connection between today's current events and more recent periods of Britain's shameful history is another matter, and a burning question that looks to government heads rather than schoolteachers for resolution.

I didn't visit the museum solely to investigate its verdict on what happened in Kenya, but it was high on my list. Starting at the beginning with the exploits of the East India Company in the seventeenth century there was much to detain us. But as we progressed in time it seemed to me that the organisational themes became more fragmented. By the time we reached the twentieth century and the independence struggles had begun to stretch the resources and patience of the British government, the notion of any chronological narrative was dispersed. I searched for the Mau Mau story and found it on a board entitled 'Land and Freedom in Kenya'.

Three documentary pictures accompany a short text describing the bare bones of the period 1952–57. One shows Dedan Kimathi being arrested, and the caption explains that he was executed in February 1957. Unlike the portrait in the Kenya National Archives it omits to mention that he fought in the

British Colonial Army in Burma in the 1940s. But the picture does show him in the captivity of another African, described as a Kenyan policeman. This visually-striking evidence further indicates another complicating reason why the story of the Kenya Land and Freedom Army cannot be collapsed into a simple story of black Africans against white settlers.

As my friend pointed out, the panel gave a very careful 'transitional' account of what happened in Kenya from 1952 until independence in 1963. It acknowledged that thousands of mostly Kikuyu were killed and detained by the British, recognising that their attempts to suppress the insurgency left deep scars which continued to divide the new nation. The brief version presented in the panel was neither the imperialist account of history nor an official nationalist view. Rather, it was a careful, self-conscious tiptoe through a territory where the landmines had been identified, but not removed. Within the context of the museum itself, the unmanageable charge of colonial history is being slowly and cautiously handled in the hope that it does not blow up in our faces at a later date.

⌇

Over dinner in Dublin someone called Ian (his mother, though Catholic, had given him this normally Protestant name as she was a huge fan of Ian Fleming, creator of James Bond) revealed to me a way to keep swimming lengths of the pool without either dying of boredom or losing track of how many you had done. I do them in eights, he explained, eight of each stroke, and I go at a leisurely pace. It only took a couple of months to get up to 80. Eighty, I pondered, remembering that the day before I had managed to get 20 under my belt before retiring to the steam room. I don't think I'm going to be doing that in a hurry.

On my return I thought I would give it a try. It worked a treat and soon I was able to crack the half an hour barrier for the first time in my life. There was something so beautifully simple and shapely in the four pairs of there and back, repeated four times.

But today something strange happens. I start off all right and begin to relax into the rhythm. About halfway through I begin to get confused. Is this the second length of breaststroke for the second time? I keep swimming, my mind full of shallow thoughts, mostly about what I have been writing. I plough up and down the pool at a very leisurely pace, but by now, not only have I lost count, I feel as though I am always in the same place. A problem has been bothering me all this time, holding me back as though it was trying to reach the water's surface for air.

I am remembering a conversation with a young academic I met who teaches at Queen's University in Belfast. 'Irish history is not a popular subject,' she said, 'unless you go back to the seventeenth or eighteenth century, to the Flight of the Earls in 1798, for example. But even that can be divisive.'

She had mentioned the example of two students in a colleague's class who were studying the Reformation. They had each traced the source of their religious convictions to this period and a fierce argument developed. 'In Northern Ireland,' she said, 'society doesn't want us to discuss religion or politics.'

The interpretation of history is so tied up with people's individual and collective identities that few people are prepared to discuss it with strangers. It is simpler not to talk about it.

This conversation had reminded me of the Irish students I met who were studying journalism. They made it clear that they did not want to look back at the Troubles. When I asked if they felt sympathetic towards Muslims who were being constantly profiled as security threats, just as anyone who looked or sounded Irish used to be until very recently, one said that he felt detached from the past and tried not to think about it.

This much I could understand, although my own experience was utterly different. Having grown up myself in the shadow of the 1939–45 war in a part of the country that had not suffered visibly from being bombed, I was not interested in hearing about it and I didn't think my parents particularly wanted to remember it. Partly it seemed too awful and terrifying to imagine what it must have been like, as though an abyss had opened up in your parents' lives and then closed over just before you were born. And this was in a country that never stopped reminding itself that it had won.

The polarisation around history in Northern Ireland resonated with what I had learned through talking to young people in Bangladesh as well. As Sabrina explained, each political administration rewrites the textbooks to reflect what happened in 1971. 'We just don't care any more,' she said forcefully.

But the sensitivities involved in writing, discussing or teaching history is not the problem I am grappling with. I understand that societies trying to build a more cohesive sense of national identity face a particularly difficult task in coming to terms with the difficult and divisive periods of their history. What is bothering me now is not how the past relates to the future, but what to do about the present.

The fact that I was able to talk about history in that way with Irish academics and students was a result of the ongoing negotiations between the British and Irish governments and representatives of the two communities in Northern Ireland, inaugurated by the Good Friday Agreement in 1998. These negotiations, often referred to as the peace process, have produced an extraordinary unfolding of events over the past decade. Each week, it seems, there are developments and setbacks, revelations and confessions, which often barely register among those who are not paying attention. But they hold enormous significance for debates about Britishness.

Onlookers can be forgiven for not being able to keep track of who has agreed to what or how the political framework of the new Assembly is shaping up. More disturbing are the revelations of collaboration by British security forces that led to sectarian murders and sustained the momentum of the war. A police ombudsman for Northern Ireland had just published a report providing clear evidence of collusion between members of the banned Ulster Volunteer Force (UVF) and some police officers in north Belfast over a period of twelve years. The report showed that Special Branch officers had failed to prevent up to fifteen murders in the interests of protecting loyalist paramilitary informants.

Writer Bea Campbell, who once updated George Orwell's famous *Road to Wigan Pier* and who is now compiling a book on the Good Friday Agreement, had waited some time for these revelations to be made public. I had just read her powerful comment in *The Guardian* insisting that this recent episode be factored into British historical memory.

'All these pressures are bearing down on Britain. It has been exposed not as peacemaker but as perpetrator, spreading terror and spilling blood; as the most powerful presence among the warlords. That is the national narrative we need to contemplate before we can consign collusion to the past.'

As I force myself to think this through, I abandon all hope of enjoying my swim. What is really weighing me down is not the revelation of crimes committed in secret. It is the burden of what we do know about what is happening in the present, in our names, which some day children will study as history. And perhaps they will wonder, as we do now, what British people thought about those daily crimes being committed among ordinary people in other parts of the world, and what they did to try to stop them or to salve their consciences. Perhaps Wahida's question is the one we should be asking: How do we want to be remembered when we are dead?

I head for the steam room where I find a strange assembly of people. A man suddenly starts to speak and I realise he is a leader of some kind. Well, he says, are we all relaxing? Try to find your third eye, your inner eye, which looks on to your spirit. Make contact with your spirit, the real you. That will lead you to your true identity and you will be strong.

Chapter Four: Multiplicity

'How would people react if you said, "I'm proud to be a white British man"?' asked Yvonne.

The question was a little incongruous as we were passing over a moat at the time. As our vehicle squeezed through the gatehouse that was built for four-legged transport some 600 years earlier, our fellow travellers gasped with delight at what lay in front of us. We had arrived at Broughton Castle, an English manor house owned by one family from 1377 to the present day. And there were the current occupants, the gracious Lord and Lady Saye and Sel, waiting in the snow to greet us and give us a guided tour.

Our party of assorted visitors was possibly a novelty for them as well but there were no indications of surprise on their part. Their ancestor who had bought the house in the fourteenth century was none other than William of Wykheme who came up with the motto: Manners Makyth Man. Within minutes of entering the house, and at their instigation, Altaf and Atif were staggering under the weight of heavy metal helmets and chest plates, and Mariam was attacking them with a sword. Madhu was reeling from the news that a scene from her favourite film *Shakespeare in Love* had been shot in that very room, starring her favourite actor Joseph Fiennes, who to cap it all was a distant cousin of our hosts. Here was a comfortable past, even if it was extremely cold and draughty, and it invited us all to imagine ourselves as we might have been, had we been born here centuries earlier. There was Chinese wallpaper, Turkish and Persian rugs, ceramics and furniture from the far corners of Europe, and a hall carpet donated by Walt Disney. It was the perfect setting for a heated debate about who we really are.

But as usual, Yvonne's question hung in the air and we returned to it later over scones and tea. It was the kind of question that didn't really need answering as much as taking apart. In fact it was designed to show up some of the problems involved in talking about Britishness in the present day. 'What would happen if you left out the "white"?' I suggested.

'How would people react if you said that you were proud to be a British man?'

The candidates to whom this was addressed wriggled appropriately. 'Under no circumstances would I say either,' said one, 'although, I am aware that this is an important aspect of Britishness, to be embarrassed to say you are proud of being British. Other nations, like Canada and the US don't have this attitude and it really shows.'

'But doesn't it depend where you are? We are in Britain at the moment so it would mean something different if you said it here,' objected Sabrina. We had since moved to Jane Austen territory, staying at the eighteenth century Ditchley Park for a residential weekend talking about Britishness. 'I don't think of myself as being Bangladeshi when I am there. In fact I didn't think about it at all until yesterday when I got stuck in Dubai changing planes. The people I was travelling with from Dhaka were all speaking Sylheti and I couldn't join in, but they invited me to sit with them and looked after me as a fellow Bangladeshi. But back home I am too busy defending other aspects of myself to worry about my national identity.'

'But wait,' said Madhu, who had travelled from Kolkata to join us. 'If someone says I'm a proud Indian man, that's very different from saying I'm a proud Indian woman. Or a proud Brahmin, or a proud Dalit. I think it's all to do with economics and your status in society, where you are in the hierarchy.

'Like Sabrina, I have so many things to deal with in my home territory, like gender, earning a living, and they are really more important. National identity is redundant in our own country, it's a given.'

Later I heard Madhu describe herself as a 'rather atheist Hindu' as she talked about the problems of fundamentalism in any religion. On that occasion she was gently chiding a group of mainly white British men for their carelessness in talking about Islam and terrorism interchangeably. 'I'm Indian,' she said, 'and you don't fixate on us because you're scared. We are too rich for a start.'

Atif was a seasoned traveller as he was used to attending international conferences on disability. When I first met him in Islamabad I heard him speak about his experiences in Mecca performing the Hajj. Listening to people describe what it is like to be caught up in a swirl of peace-loving humans from all over the world offers a glimpse of global unity that is diametrically opposed to the violence of sectarianism. But Atif's observations about conference behaviour were altogether different, and for him more of a puzzle.

'I was at an event in Cairo recently,' he said, 'and there were delegates from thirty-five different countries in the opening session. After lunch on the first day I noticed that everyone went back to different tables depending on where they were from: Britain, the US or Asia.'

Altaf was still recovering from the trip to the castle. He had trained as a journalist in India but had come to live in Sheffield for a year to 'dabble in a multi-faith programme,' as he put it. I was hoping that he would use my photo of him wearing the suit of armour for the article he was writing. His glasses had looked a bit incongruous under the helmet but his normally serene demeanour had been transformed into a snarling warrior, in my picture, at least.

'At home I am aware of being Indian on some level, but I really think of myself as a Mumbaiker,' he offered as we sat balancing our cups and saucers and cream teas on our knees. I had made sure they did it my way – cream on the scone first and then jam and it had gone down well.

'But I've learned all sorts of things by coming here, and not just about myself, either. My family belongs to a very conservative Muslim sect, but being a Muslim is only a small part of my own identity. I would never have gone to the mosque if my mother hadn't made me. But it's different now I am here as a visitor. I am living in a white working-class area of Sheffield, and it feels quite unsafe. People warn me to be careful about coming home late and that sort of thing. I am sharing a house with a British person whose family is also Indian and from Gujarat too, like mine. At first I was quite happy about this, but actually now it makes me feel more different. For a start he doesn't like Hindi movies! When he criticises them I suddenly feel my Indianness is being attacked. Then I literally heard him say, "I am a Brahmin Hindu." I have never heard that in my social circle at home, I was shocked. Basically, though he dissociates himself from India as a country, he is mad keen to invest there. It is convenient for him that he has contacts there.'

Altaf's curiosity at his housemate's behaviour was compounded by the loneliness entailed in living in a new place that seemed unwelcoming, if not hostile. 'I felt a need for connection,' he explained, 'and thought it would help to go to a mosque. But I was worried about what I would find in a British mosque after all we had heard about them in India. Eventually I found the Muslim Welfare House of Sheffield which was just what I needed, and now I volunteer for them a few hours a week.'

Nazmun's sense of her own national identity was changing before our eyes. Although she spent the first thirteen years of her life in Sussex, she felt sure that she could never feel anything other than Bangladeshi. A year back in the UK to study at university level had only confirmed how much more at home and comfortable she felt building her life as a lawyer in Bangladesh. Over the course of a three-day conference on Britishness, however, she was discovering the value of reasserting her right to be both, as opposed to one or the other. Impatient with the way that fellow Muslims were being tarnished with the sweeping brush of terrorism, fundamentalism and cultural practices that contravened human-rights laws, she decided to reposition herself not as an outsider but as someone entitled to speak from within.

Nazmun's sense of 'bothness' was partly a convenient way of making her voice heard but it was deeply felt and came from the heart. It also rested on the strategic importance of the little word 'born'. Her bilingual approach to national identity allowed her to switch what some commentators might call 'allegiances', making her one of the feared constituency of British citizens whose primary loyalties lie in more than one country. But, like everyone else, Nazmun had plenty of other options up her sleeve. Her nickname was Jenny, which her grandmother had given her as a child, and she was the proud member of the 'hijabis' as they called themselves on this occasion. She was also the chief exponent of the 'Deshi' sensibility that began to emerge during our time together.

The word 'Deshi' or 'Desi' means literally indigenous, or native, in Hindi, Urdu and Bangla, but its implications depend a great deal on context. It is widely used among the English-speaking South Asian diaspora to connect people with origins in the subcontinent, but in India, for example, it can also be used to describe goods that are made locally rather than imported from abroad. When members of our party who had travelled from India, Pakistan and Bangladesh started using it to describe themselves, I remembered Farhana acting out the role of the British Born Confused Deshi in the sketch in Islamabad. Seen from the standpoint of an originating country, the tenuous links that emigrants make to their 'homelands' can look very peculiar indeed. I wondered if Altaf had ever called his housemate a BBCD either to his face or behind his back. I decided it was doubtful, though he sounded like a prime candidate from what Altaf had said, especially the part about Brahmins.

I was sitting in the front of the bus when we set out for the castle, so I couldn't tell whose idea it was to start singing. It was clearly a Deshi moment, though. At first my heart sank. Oh God, I thought, they are going to ask us to sing an English song. It was always a crisis about what to choose. I could hum 'Greensleeves' and bits of 'John Barleycorn', but I was no Billy Bragg. I could never remember the words to any other folk songs much as I loved the music. Nor could I hold a tune, especially unaccompanied. But I needn't have worried as they were engrossed in finding something that they all wanted to sing. Two Pakistanis, two Bangladeshis and two Indians were all talking at once. Some singing broke out and everyone joined in for a verse or two.

'Wait a minute,' I said, 'how come you all know the same songs?'

Pakistani pop music is really good, they explained. Indian pop is rubbish but Bollywood songs are great.

'So let me get this right,' I said. 'Indians and Bangladeshis listen to Pakistani pop, everyone listens to Bollywood. What about Bangladeshis?'

'They have beautiful folk music which everyone else listens to.'

Sujata from Kolkata leaned over and said quietly, 'Actually the folk music is from the whole area of Bengal.'

I made the mistake of telling them that English people can never agree what to sing in these situations. It makes them feel awkward because the Scots, Welsh and Irish have lots to choose from and singing is part of their identity.

'Are you kidding?' they cried. The whole bus burst out at once in a hearty rendition of 'For he's a jolly good fellow' and I was firmly put in my place.

 ⌒

'Which part of you is British?' Although Yvonne's question was more light-hearted this time, everyone thought carefully before answering. Yvonne was named after Charles de Gaulle's wife and lived in Nairobi. She described herself as terrestrian, with her umbilical cord deeply buried in Kenya and hence in Africa. This time the participants were composed of a select group of students, activists, artists and writers in Nairobi. The exercise was designed to kick off a two-day seminar on questions of identity in the context of East Africa.

'Afternoon tea, catholic religion, complaining,' said one.

'My name, language, clothes, eating habits, accent.'

'Timekeeping, strong routines,' said a third.

'There are some things you do without realising. For example, if someone drops round to see you and you say, "Oh, I didn't know you were coming, so I didn't prepare anything," people say that you're so cold, so British.'

'My love of English literature,' said Yvonne. 'I grew up reading Enid Blyton,' she added, and later we exchanged fond memories of the *Famous Five* and their siblings *The Secret Seven*.

Some protested. 'I was brought up in the British system so it's hard to define. Most of what is me is British.'

'Kenya itself is a British construct – we can't escape that aspect. Why are there so many expats here and a whole generation of my family over there?'

'Britishness is the idea that the world is shaped with you at the centre. The feeling that you are better than anyone else. Even their version of colonialism is supposed to be better than others. I would hate to be from Mozambique and to have been colonised by the Portuguese!'

'The mentality of colonialism has affected us like second-hand cigarette smoke,' observed Binyavanga. 'I think we give too much credit to the imperialists though. It's difficult to pinpoint what's British and what's Western. The way we dress, for instance, or having an individualistic approach. The love of money, the fact that a lot of us even think in English. Is this British or American?'

'I think we should be asking what part of us is not British,' said Wahida, the angel, when it was her turn to speak. 'Can we say what it means to be Kenyan?'

'Knowing which aspect of our identity to put forward at any time,' was one response.

Later I picked up a book called *How to be a Kenyan* in a shop in the city centre. First published in 1996 and reprinted several times, my copy is a revised version issued in 2002. A quote from *The Guardian* adorns the back cover: 'The volume allows Kenyans to laugh at all things that set the international finger wagging – corruption, opportunism, racial self-depreciation (sic), AIDS, lies, and incompetence.'

I note that the revised version has an extra chapter entitled 'Of beepers, flashers and vibrators'. Since 1996, the mobile phone has made as dramatic and transformative an appearance in Kenyan social and commercial life as it has done in many other parts of the world including the UK. Reading the contents of this chapter I laughed out loud at several of the observations, not because they were making fun of Kenyan social etiquette, but because they reminded me of exchanges I had had with others on my travels. The ingenuity of people everywhere to avoid paying through the nose for services that could be obtained at minimal cost is a wonderful human characteristic. Two rings for 'call me back'. Three for 'I'm on my way home'.

The book had obviously been flying off the shelves for a decade and I wondered if the joke was getting stale. Perhaps the author made fun of certain patterns of behaviour that locals could read as nationally-based characteristics, offering them a humorous way to recognise things that actually drove them mad half of the time. National stereotypes usually contain a grain of truth when held up to the light.

Soon after I was back from Nairobi I was riding the escalator somewhere in the London underground system, minding my own business. Suddenly a menacing voice barked out of nowhere: *If you don't touch in and touch out with your Oyster card you will be charged the maximum fare.* My response was to stick my chin out, as if I had been threatened with punishment for breaking a school rule that I didn't even know about. Why do we have to be spoken to like that? I asked myself, since

there wasn't a human being in uniform to whom I could protest. For the amount that we have to pay to use public transport
you would think they might treat us with a bit more respect.

Nor is it just spoken orders that we are being subjected to.
Travelling across the city we are likely to be photographed more
than 300 times by ubiquitous security cameras. Everywhere we
look there are public notices informing us of the rules that we
must obey and the dangers that we face. The over-use of the
imperative was getting on my nerves before I went away, but
it was really in Nairobi that I started to think about it from a
visitor's point of view.

'It is 1963, one month into independence in Kenya, you
are eighteen years old, and you have a peek into the future.
You look at the *Standard Newspaper* and it says all citizens of
the British colony have one month to choose British citizenship. Knowing what you know now in 2006, what would you
choose?'

'The worst place in the world to be young is an old country where there is no place for the young,' said Binyavanga, in
answer to his own question. This statement struck me as profound in its simplicity as I wrestled with the fact that in many
Western European countries the proportion of young to old
people was the inverse of that in most developing nations.
Demographic data from 2005 showed that eighteen per cent
of the UK population were less than fifteen years old, compared to forty-three per cent in Kenya. Put it another way: the
median age in Britain in 2006 was forty, while in Kenya and its
neighbouring countries it was just eighteen years old.

The average age of those in the room was likely to have been
mid-twenties, although one or two members, like Charity,
were grandmothers with long experience of living in different
places. The session began with her harrowing account of living
and working in the UK and the United States for a number of
years as she struggled to support her sons through their education, working as a nurse. Charity had chosen British citizenship believing that she could provide a better start for her
family by living abroad. She had talked movingly about her
homesickness and her sense that no one outside Kenya ever let
her forget that she was a foreigner. Returning to live in Nairobi
had restored some of her faith in mankind and released a lot

of the tension that had been stored up inside. She told us how relieved her son had been when he too came back to live in the country where his mother had been born.

'He felt so happy to be home,' she said, 'and to be able to fit in without being made to feel like an outsider.'

The question of choice proved to be a good way to get everyone to put some cards on the table. Murad, who had earlier read the disturbing extract from the novel *Londonstani*, was concerned about levels of fear and loneliness in Europe, and in particular the fate of old people living in institutions. He had studied at Nottingham in the 1990s and even though he had enjoyed his time there, he said there was no question that he would choose Kenyan citizenship, given this hypothetical choice.

A filmmaker now in his early thirties, Murad made another unsettling point. He remembered some advice an uncle in London had passed on to him in the 1990s, when he had turned up wearing a rather unusual Tibetan hat. 'Try not to stand out,' he said. 'This is a multicultural society but everyone can get on with their lives provided they don't draw too much attention to themselves.'

Visiting him again recently Murad had found that his uncle's attitude had shifted markedly. He was making plans to leave the country, complaining that it had become a far less tolerant place, particularly for Muslims. When he told this story there was a demurring in the room. Several spoke of Asian friends and relatives who were leaving the UK and returning to East Africa, worried about their future prospects in Britain. The Deshi grapevine had taken root in countless gardens around the world.

The question of the British fondness for rules and the consequent lack of freedom came up several times during the course of that particular discussion about choosing citizenship. Those who chose Kenya said that they felt altogether more free and comfortable there, and that the proliferation of signs irritated them. George said he would never want to feel like a second-class citizen, and he didn't like the weather or the food.

However, not all the participants took the patriotic path out of this dilemma. Jane, who remembers her parents' difficult discussions on this issue when she was a child, pointed out that the vast majority of Kenyans did not have access to free health care and education. It was important to identify the real issues that made everyday life hard, whether it was living in exile or having fewer resources in a country where skin colour was not an issue. Two said they would definitely choose British citizenship for economic reasons, certain that this would give them a better standard of living and better educational opportunities.

The question annoyed Myriam as it touched a raw nerve. Her mother was German and her father Kenyan, but neither country permits dual citizenship. This meant that her choice, such as it was, has had real ramifications that affected her relationship with her family and her ability to travel freely back and forth.

Although she had studied in the United States and lived abroad for several years, she had made her home in Nairobi, establishing herself as an artist. Keeping her Kenyan citizenship meant that she stayed close to her father's family and there were no complications involved in living in the country. Travelling to Europe, including Germany, or to the United States, was a real pain, however, as it entailed applying for visas each time and being treated with suspicion at airport immigration checkpoints.

Her sisters had chosen German citizenship, which had broken their father's heart. It was hard for him to see it as a purely logistical decision that enabled them to travel more freely and obtain the benefits of being EU citizens. Myriam remained close to her sisters but felt very frustrated at the injustice which could so easily be avoided. Being forced to choose entailed a rejection of half of one's family heritage, and it inevitably went deeper than the convenience of travel.

Britain is one of a minority of countries that recognises dual citizenship, allowing individuals to retain two passports and hence claim the right to belong to more than one country. It was clear that history had taught several people in that room to raise both hands when asked to make a hypothetical choice between staying British or becoming Kenyan.

‿

When Farhana acted out the role of British Born Confused Deshi in Islamabad it was hard to see whether she was playing it for laughs or following a script. Her character didn't seem very confused to me. She behaved more like the classic visitor from England who didn't have a clue about Pakistani politics but thought they knew everything. But it was from her that I learned a good deal more about what it meant to be British and Muslim without there being any contradiction, conflict or confusion, for that matter.

Despite her resistance to her parents' pressure to accept a marriage partner from Pakistan, Farhana was open about the fact that she would have found it hard to marry someone who didn't fit into her family. By this she did not just mean a Muslim but one who was from a Sunni background, as well. I learned a lot from listening to the complex negotiations involved in walking her own path. The care she took to consider her parents' feelings, particularly regarding their status in the extended network of family and friends, seemed connected to a deep understanding of where they had come from and how far they had travelled in their own lifetimes. Her commitment to their happiness had an edge of protectiveness too, as though her ability to feel comfortable in the country of her birth could shield her parents from hostility towards Muslims in general, especially ones from Pakistan.

I had heard Farhana describe herself as an 'inbetweeny', someone who was happy to have grown up in Banbury within a liberal Asian community. It was more of a blend rather than a choice between two different options. Today she was wearing a combination of jeans with a dark olive-coloured long shirt with embroidered sleeves. I had noticed when we travelled in Pakistan that her suitcase was at least as heavy as mine although she was barely away for a week. She had told me that she had lots of relatives to see and she was looking forward to shedding much of her load. Today, however, we were going shopping for her nieces back home so there didn't seem much chance of that. Our destination was the bazaar in Lahore, the corner that specialised in jewellery and women's shoes.

This was not just a chance to do some early Christmas shopping. I was getting used to making a break from the hotel whenever an opportunity arose and I felt I owed it to Tariq, the Pakistani student I had met on the train to Leeds, to have a look round Lahore. In 1975 I had passed through the city having just crossed over the border by bus. This time I had flown from India in the company of men and women wearing business suits. When I settled into my seat to read my copy of Amartya Sen's *The Argumentative Indian* which I had bought in Kolkata, the kindly air steward for Pakistan Airlines observed with a twinkle in his eye: 'You'll need more than an hour and twenty-five minutes to read that.'

Now in the bazaar I chose a necklace for my daughter in about five minutes flat and waited for Farhana to decide which of about fifty different bangles her nieces would be happy with. It gave me time to wander further into the narrow passages of the bazaar, stocking up on embroidered tea cosies and picking through Kashmiri shawls, bedspreads and blankets. I found many people to talk to about the state of the world and almost forgot how long I had strayed away. But I needn't have worried, as Farhana was still negotiating her way through her seventh jewellery set and contemplating buying some beaded sandals for herself after that.

The vast array of glittering footwear filled case after case, stall after stall, calling women of all ages and across social distinctions, as well. It reminded me of an experience in a Clarks factory shop in north London. Clarks is the ultimate English shoe company, founded by a Quaker family in the mid nineteenth century and providing sensible well-made footwear for adults and children ever since.

A few years ago I went to the local branch looking for bargains. It was a hot summer Saturday and the streets were busy. I poured into the shop in the company of the world's wives, women from several different continents and generations. Competition looked tough, but I needn't have worried. There were more than enough shoe types to satisfy all the different tastes, and plenty of perfectly feminine styles to match the different dress codes. It seemed a wonderful illustration of what unites women across cultural differences as well as what divides them sharply. It also underlined the connection between what you wear and who you think you are.

I was pondering this experience in the Lahore shoe shop as I waited for Farhana to choose between turquoise and pink. The room was full of females, all local as far as I could see, but varying widely in degrees of modesty as well as age. I had registered that there were signs of thriving fashion industries operating in each country I visited. As in the Clarks shoe shop, there was something significant being explored in the relationship between clothing, individual taste and cultural identity.

I remembered Roxana telling me before she left London that she had become fascinated by the ways in which Colombian women made a home away from home there. She had started to investigate the role of beauty parlours, asking questions about the function they served helping women feel good about their bodies, their appearance, their identity as Colombians. It made her want to return to her country to explore this phenomenon on a regional scale, and to explore the notion of cultural distinctiveness through looking at comparative notions of beauty.

A special pre-Eid feature on fashion in one of Bangladesh's main newspapers shortly before I arrived demonstrated perfectly the link between dress sense and a nationalist sensibility. *The Independent*'s weekend supplement began with a review of local designers' seasonal offerings. Amid the descriptions of new collections, fashionable styles and colours, Jatra is described as a 'fusion between the traditional Bengali taste and contemporary design'. In an article on fashion and the Bengali male by Arshad Sawar, an Indian designer is quoted as saying:

'I pity men with dull wardrobes. The West has enslaved us to notions of masculine dress codes, forcing Indian men to turn away from their rich heritage. Both men and women in our country were fond of dressing up – from Mohenjodaro to the Mughals.'

This sentiment celebrates Bangladesh's burgeoning consumer culture, and in particular the arrival of elegant men's fashion in Dhaka. 'Making a fashion statement,' writes the author, 'is no longer a female domain. What is more, men are also beginning to frequent beauty parlours "in droves".'

A third feature outlines the history of fashion culture in Bengal from the distant past to the present. Regional dress habits were constantly changing as a result of influence from successive invasions by Turks, Pathans, Afghans, Mughals and the British. Throughout most of these sartorial assaults, however, Bengal stood firm. The region was renowned for its cotton and silk textiles, and Bengali women famous for their defiance in the face of outside influence. Their rich traditions of designing fabrics and styles of dress, as well as their aesthetic sense, became famous throughout the world. Unfortunately, he points out, it was this success that drew the East India Company like a magnet and ultimately led to the British dominating India.

'With their artistry the Bengalis overwhelmed the world community. Dhakai muslin overawed the whole world and the success of this textile brought about the downfall of India as the British interest in merchandise gradually shifted to creating a dominion.'

As more and more raw material from India was shipped back to the looms and mills of northern England in the nineteenth century, the infrastructure of locally-made Indian fabrics was destroyed. Parts of Britain, like Lancashire in the north-west, were transformed as a result, with thousands of poor women forced to work long hours in the new factories in conditions that had not even been imagined before.

Now Bangladesh is one of the main production centres of garments for Western outlets, often in comparable conditions. Shops that sell cheap garments on British high streets, like the branches of Primark and Matalan that I spotted in Leytonstone, are under increasing pressure to pay a living wage to factory workers in countries where the clothes are made. A recent report by War on Want, however, indicates that their fine words are not matched by deeds in the supplying factories. The majority of garment workers in Bangladesh are women who work for longer than sixty hours a week with no protection whatsoever and on minimal wages.

It was Mahmud who had pointed out the garment workers walking to and from work in Dhaka. He had published a book of his photos of women in Bangladesh and had followed their path as they trudged through the city's traffic each day. Many of them lived in the corrugated iron and cardboard huts near to where he lives.

But as an artist himself he was also interested in the burgeoning design scene in Dhaka, and took me to several shops selling handwoven fabrics and artefacts made locally. One was run by Roxana, a friend of his from Sylhet who had trained in fashion design in London. She had recently returned to Dhaka, married, and become more committed to her Muslim faith. She specialised in turning out Islamic abayas for a Malaysian market, but her outlet in Dhaka sold sophisticated evening-wear that was popular with the expatriates in the city.

When I finally got home after all my travels my friend brought me the student newspaper from the London School of Economics. He knew that I was interested in the way the institution functioned as a beacon for students seeking scholarships from all over the world. The headlines were all about the *Celebrity Big Brother* row over Jade Goody's behaviour towards Shilpa Shetty, but inside there were many different features, columns and news articles reflecting the diversity of the student body. The Islamic Society had organised a 'Discover Islam' week and there were several pieces dedicated to making a few things clear. I found an article on fashion entitled 'Muslim Dress SOS'. A colour photo of three models wearing head-to-toe designer outfits was captioned: 'And you thought it was just about wearing a headscarf.'

The article was intentionally humorous, and there were two underlying jokes. The first was that wearing items of Muslim dress such as the hijab and the loose-fitting jilbab allowed women to cover up so they didn't have to agonise about feeling fat or having a bad hair day. The second was that they let you go about your business while wearing whatever you liked underneath. The only problem was one of perception.

'What I so enthusiastically perceive as slightly Bedouin, cultured, and modest,' wrote the author, Ruhana Ali, 'others think of as "confused", "extremist" and "oppressed". I guess it is a case of miscommunication.' She concluded: 'But, whatever anyone thinks about the way that we Muslims choose to dress, the main thing is that I enjoy it and it makes me feel good. Ironically, even if I don't want to stand out in a crowd, if my clothing does make a statement, I hope it would scream alternative fashion, Muslim, and extremely proud.'

～

'Why don't you tell me something about yourself that's important to who you are,' I said to the students. 'I know you all know each other, but just tell me your name and say a little bit about yourself.' I had interrupted a class of South Asian Studies at a Further Education Institute in east London. Out of the eight present all but one were from Bangladeshi backgrounds and only one was female. The first to speak was Ashraf.

'I was born in Bangladesh and came to the UK when I was six or seven. I live in the East End, and I have a two-year-old son...'

The class registered their surprise. You have a child? We never knew? The next to introduce himself was Saddique. He too was born in Sylhet and came to London when he was five. He told the class he was married with two kids, a fact they already knew. The thing he identified with most symbolically was his USB stick which he carried with him out of fear of losing his files.

As we went round the room the students followed the pattern set by Ashraf: where they were born, when they moved to the UK, if that was relevant, and whether they had kids. Gerald was from Uganda and came when he was seven. His child was just two months old, and he was the only one to declare his intention to return to his land of birth. Then we came to Zahra who had been quiet until then.

'I was born here and grew up here, and I work around here as well. I would say I am a Muslim first, then Bangladeshi, and then British, in that order.'

The atmosphere changed immediately. 'That would apply to all of us,' said one of the guys. 'Of course if you follow Islam then the most important part of your identity is being Muslim.'

This reminded me of a conversation with Farhana as we travelled through Pakistan. We were meeting many young people who were quick to identify themselves as Muslim before everything else. This was in striking contrast to Bangladesh and India where faith-based identity appeared to be more of a private issue among the young people I met. So I was surprised when I asked Farhana how she would identify what was most important to her, and her reply was 'being a Muslim'.

'It shapes my world view,' she explained. 'It guides my everyday behaviour, makes me who I am. And it doesn't have anything to do with whether I am British or not. I don't see why everyone makes such a fuss.'

Gosia, who had dedicated herself to helping young Polish migrants to acclimatise in London, had said something similar when I asked her about the importance of being Catholic. 'For Poles it's a primary part of our identity,' she explained patiently. 'It's our culture.'

Now in the group discussion in London, I definitely picked up a sense of annoyance that Zahra had shown the men up because none of them had mentioned their faith. Fatherhood had emerged as an important reference point because it was an experience that most of them shared. However, as we went on to talk about Britishness Tanvir recovered some ground.

'Obviously there are some good things about adapting to the way of life here. But if Britishness means going out drinking and mingling with the opposite sex then I don't see myself as British. I am a Muslim first and foremost.'

I wondered if that comment was pointed at Zahra who clearly was there as an unaccompanied woman. But as they opened up to each other about where they felt at home, the discussion ranged over familiar ground. Britishness was a confusing concept as it could mean so many different things. The consensus was that it was easy to identify with east London and speak in a cockney accent. Citizenship was about paying taxes and possessing a passport, so there was definitely no contradiction between being British and Muslim on that score. The problems arose when you felt that you were not accepted, especially if you had a beard or were easily identifiable as Muslim in other ways. The current levels of hostility and non-acceptance were making people feel defensive and insecure.

A few weeks later I heard it from Altaf's perspective. His experience of living in Sheffield for a few weeks had opened his eyes to the way that Islam was perceived by mainstream society. For a start, he said, people are amazed that a Muslim from India speaks so well. They have such a narrow view of the world. But their ignorance about his religion was beginning to make him feel his identity was being invaded.

'I definitely sense a reaction that you're either with us or against us. It's like you are presumed guilty unless you can prove yourself innocent. I've noticed that in the headlines, Islam is always attached to criminal activity. They always make it look as though what those criminals do is connected to their religion.'

The day that I met Altaf in Mumbai I had steam coming

out of my ears, and so did my compatriot Pratap. We had just read the same headline in the newspaper that the hotel staff had slid under our doors: 'Beckett asks UK Muslims to "stand up and be counted".' Britain's Foreign Secretary was on an official visit to India ahead of us, just as Prince Charles was waiting for me in Pakistan and Tony Blair would follow me to Islamabad. Beckett was using her platform in India to speak to British Muslims (especially those who reject violence) about their special responsibilities. It fell to them, she urged, to serve as ambassadors in South Asia as a way of bridging the East-West divide being fomented by Islamist extremists. The article noted that this challenge represented 'the government's desire to take the war on terror to the heart of Britain's settled Muslim communities'.

This headline came hard on the heels of Home Secretary John Reid's demand that Muslim parents watch their children for telltale signs of being brainwashed. He made this speech a stone's throw from the school where Martin teaches history. When I met him the following month, just before I left for South Asia, the effects were continuing to unsettle his students.

'Speeches by politicians can be very divisive but the John Reid meeting was just round the corner and there was so much publicity. Afterwards the kids were saying, "Every headline appears to be attacking us as Muslims". Being so close they took it really personally. What's being presented is a sense of a separate community that doesn't want to be part of Britain. I find it heartbreaking. I have spent twenty years with mainly Muslim communities in London, watching them embrace London life in its complexities. They are proud of being part of London which for them is what Britain is like. Like this diverse community that we have here. They feel part of it.'

'Now,' he continued, 'things are different. There is enormous disillusionment because of how they are feeling about their identity as British Muslims at a time of war. International politics has squandered the potential for young people's sense of optimism and involvement. They say we feel blamed for something that is nothing to do with us. Feeling under attack themselves makes them feel more identified with people under attack in Iraq. There was an element of this in 1991, but it was

massively greater in 2003. We had many conversations in
school. The demonstrations before the war were attended by
many British Asians. The fact that there was strong support
across communities made a huge difference. This summer
they were watching the bombing in Beirut and thinking: "This
is happening in my name." That throws them into confusion,
and they feel forced into feelings of pain and guilt. Their relatives in Holland and France see the same footage but it is not
happening in their name. They are not alienated from being
British, not feeling forced into a cultural ghetto. It's not a case
of not wanting to be British, but it's what's happening out there
that makes them feel separate.'

↬

'Handbags are my weakness,' said Leyla as we strolled through
the market. She had been magnetically drawn to a stall selling
little else, and as we looked through them I dwelt on the irony
that feminists had fought long and hard for their daughters'
entitlement to own multiple handbags. I had learned about
this syndrome from having a daughter myself, but I also knew
it was a global phenomenon that touched women across generations as well as continents. Somewhere in my cupboard I
too had a very snappy Made-in-China Prada bag that I bought
from African street vendors in Italy.

Leyla had offered to show me Europe's longest street market which was one of her favourite parts of London. We were
in Walthamstow, just a couple of miles from Leytonstone, and
it was a Wednesday afternoon. As there were not many stalls
open, we could see the shops on either side and get a real taste
of what the area was like beyond the market itself. Leyla knew
the lie of the land and was pointing out some of the more popular establishments. She had just mentioned something that
happened a few weeks ago. She was shopping in the market
one day when her mother was away on a trip to Somalia. A vegetable stallholder had asked with some concern. 'How is your
mother, I haven't seen her in a long time,' he said, 'I hope she
is all right.' Leyla had been coming to his stall with her mother
on and off for fourteen years and as far as she knew they had
never really spoken to each other before. I asked where he was
from. 'He's English, white,' she replied.

We passed a shop selling jellied eels and pie and mash, one

of those relics that looks as if it belongs in a book of black-and-white photos. A few doors along there was a bagel shop, a House of Shawls, and opposite that a busy Arab cafe serving shisha. The fish shop looked good and there seemed to be hundreds of cheap shoe shops. I decided I would come back on a Saturday and see the market in its full glory. We walked over to the new shopping centre adjoining the market street where Leyla wanted to show me an exhibition of photographs showing the historic background of the area. She was very struck by the extent of the bombing in the Blitz and what was still recognisable today.

As we sat in the mall cafe drinking tea and eating flapjacks we looked out over a brand new playground. 'Look at the way those little girls are dressed,' Leyla pointed out, 'they are completely British and Asian. It's fascinating how the area can influence the way you dress. It's quite different if you go over to the other side of London.' I knew from our previous conversations that she often felt angry that she had to justify the fact that she thought of herself as British. 'I refuse to choose,' she said. 'It's perfectly OK to be both. But I really don't want my daughter to have to think about it.'

Becoming a mother four years ago had changed Leyla's life in ways she could not possibly have foreseen. Her pregnancy was extremely difficult and her doctor not very understanding. She found her way to the African Well Woman's clinic which provided her with support until her daughter was born, although giving birth was a traumatic experience. As soon as she was able Leyla went back to their clinic as a volunteer interpreter. It was there that she realised the terrible toll that Female Genital Mutilation (FGM) was taking on girls and women.

'The clinic had some money to treat Somali women homeopathically because they were presenting symptoms of infection that did not show up in tests. This meant that I had to translate their stories. It was amazing, they talked about all these traumatic things that had happened to them, and just sat there smiling. It really made me question the environment that allowed this to happen. I decided that I was going to work with young women who had undergone this practice, and that I was going to do everything I could to stop it. But first I had to face my own demons before I could start doing this work. I had to go back to my own trauma which I had blocked out. But I knew I couldn't live with myself if there was one girl out there who I might have saved from having it done to her.'

When Leyla talked about herself with such openness and conviction she remained calm and composed. But when I asked her what she thought about Ayaan Hirsi Ali she developed a fierce bout of hiccups. 'Yeah,' she said, 'people often ask me about her because of the work I do. I think she's a cowardly woman. She had to use the Islam thing to promote herself, and I wouldn't do that. I wouldn't talk about someone else's religion for a start. She's obviously very intelligent, but I wished she'd used her brain to do other things for women. She's working for Bush now.'

Leyla had just come back from Brussels where she attended a conference organised by Euronet, a network of organisations working for children's rights in the EU. She had been invited to be one of the main speakers on FGM along with women from Nigeria and Sierre Leone, but was surprised to find that she was the only youth worker on the platform actually doing preventative work. Through being a volunteer at the Africa Well Woman clinic she had since been appointed as youth outreach worker by the local National Health Service. She was very clear about what this meant.

'Educating men is a big part of my work. I discovered that so many of them have no idea what the procedure involves. We have a youth group that tries to target boys as they are going to be future fathers. But we have to use different tools to educate them about other aspects of life. It's hard to talk about this when they are dropping out of school or have bad home lives. We have to get them to see that they have the power to change things. It's dangerous though, being a black Muslim woman, trying to fight a culture that has been suppressing women for centuries. Especially when it's done by women to their daughters. It's a battlefield and there's always someone in authority trying to control you. FGM may be a traditional practice but it damages you for the rest of your life. Now that I have a daughter I see her in every little girl out there. I wasn't ready for her when I got pregnant, but I know she came into my life for a reason.'

'On the other hand,' she says laughing, 'I found my Regular Achievement Folder from school the other day, and it said that Leyla is never happy unless she is helping someone.'

∽

What is British? Is it a red Burberry stiletto lying beside a pool of yellow vomit? Is it the Queen? Is it a young girl giving two fingers to the camera? Or is it a zebra standing in front of a half-timbered house? The exhibition of the work of seven photographers on this theme made it very clear that one picture wasn't going to answer the question. Nor was I very impressed with what my friend called the montage approach, the collection of different headshots intended to show what British people look like today. That seemed a little obvious given that the gallery was located in Spitalfields, at the intersection of the old City of London, the East End and the heart of the fashion district. You could see faces from all over the world in the street outside.

More pointed was the row of family portraits demonstrating new ways of living together. This time it was not just physical appearance but also dress styles and the gender of the parents that was designed to say something new about Britain. There were two mums with a son, two guys with a dog, a white mother and black daughter, and so on. The British family may still be nuclear, but according to these images it is an important mechanism for nurturing a more modern sense of who we are as a nation. It is in our homes that we are freest to challenge deeply-held beliefs about who is allowed to love whom openly, legally and privately.

I remembered Roxana telling me just before she went back to Colombia that when she saw the film *The Queen*, she suddenly understood the way that the class system worked in Britain. The portrait of Her Majesty in the gallery had been altered digitally and placed against a rather sinister backdrop. I came back to the picture of the red shoe. The image alongside showed the owner's bare legs lying in the street, and the caption for both was 'hen-do'.

The alcoholic reference in this frame came closest to providing a knee-jerk response to the question: What is British? Not so long ago the victim would have been male. Making an icon out of a drunken female dressed up for a night out bordered on a cliché these days. The image expresses how far gender roles have changed as well as patterns of drinking. But what it says about the country is more complicated. Has it gone to the dogs because women are free to act like men, or is it the other way round? Perhaps it's the case that no one really cares what you do as long as you are spending money. The alcohol companies don't seem that bothered where their products end up.

The US civil rights leader, Malcolm X, was very clear about why it mattered when women behaved badly and what this said about national values. Visiting Beirut after performing the Hajj at Mecca he professed shock at the extent of European influence on Lebanese women based on what they were wearing. 'It showed me how any country's moral strength, or its moral weakness, is quickly measurable by the street attire and attitude of its women – especially its young women.' He gave no indication of how they behaved, but Arab women in the Middle East were not really on his mind.

'Wherever the spiritual values have been submerged, if not destroyed, by an emphasis upon the material things,' he wrote in his autobiography, 'invariably the women reflect it. Witness the women, both young and old, in America – where scarcely any moral values are left.'

The combination of spiky scarlet shoe, vomit and prostrate female legs would have been familiar to Malcolm X from his earlier life as a coked-out hustler which he also wrote about in his book. That was possibly why he felt so strongly about moral values. The book was published in 1964, long before British hen parties were spilling out on to Europe's streets, decades before the term *binge-drinking* was invented – although not the practice itself. His disapproval of women's freedom to dress provocatively is in direct contrast to Jack Straw's finger-pointing at the niqab worn by some of his constituents. In both cases there's an underlying political agenda. It's as though what the women are wearing tells us not just where society has gone wrong, but also that it's their fault.

Altaf was finding the alcohol question difficult in his sojourn in Sheffield, but it wasn't necessarily due to the way women behaved in Yorkshire. Among the young people he met, alcohol was the main mechanism for social exclusion as well as cohesion. There didn't seem much point in going to the pub if you didn't drink, and this drastically reduced the number of places to be sociable. Previously he had lived for a short time in Glasgow and it was no different there. Since he was staying near the big football ground at Ibrox Park he could see that it was the male drinkers who caused the most problems, but it wasn't vomit that provided the evidence.

Thinking about Altaf's feelings of being left out because he didn't drink alcohol, I remembered other teetotallers I had met who had grown up in Britain, and who felt similarly excluded, especially on university campuses. Asmat, for example, from Lancashire, said, 'British culture can be exclusive as it involves drinking in pubs and clubs. It's the most British thing to say you are going for a pint. People like me can't experience that because we don't drink. If I could say anything to the government I would tell them, if you agree that Britishness revolves around drinking, then you have a responsibility to make it more inclusive for Muslims who don't drink.'

But as Nazmun pointed out when we talked about this a few days later, being a Muslim was a personal thing for her. 'It's not really about practical issues,' she said. 'I have a real problem with imposing rules on people. Being strict about your religion is sometimes associated with being middle class in Bangladesh. Most of civil society is not practising religion in the strict sense.

'My sister is in the corporate world,' she added, 'and they are always having cocktails parties at their meetings and conferences. A lot of my friends drink in Dhaka, and some get drunk, too.'

It's not about whether you drink as a nation or even what, it's more a question of how. Alcohol was invisible on the surface in Pakistan – they didn't offer it on the plane I noticed, and the perfume was alcohol-free, but there were plenty of stories about fast cars and high living in Karachi, Lahore and Islamabad. That didn't mean that it wasn't available if you knew where to find it or that it wasn't consumed in large quantities in safe company. But it was still associated with men misbehaving in private rather than women.

In Dublin I was woken at three in the morning by a random fire alarm going off in the hotel, and as I lay awake I heard a horse clip-clopping past my window. In the morning I discovered that a horse and carriage was a popular way to get home after a night out. Ireland is the land of Guinness, and a pilgrimage to the former brewery in the heart of Dublin is essential to any visit there. For those who miss it there's always the virtual tour available free of charge although without the opportunity for tasting. This also includes a visit to the 'Choice Zone' on the third floor where you can take part in an interactive exhibit to learn about safe drinking habits. As Ireland's economic growth has soared, the corporate face of this iconic brew has responded to meet new demands. The original brewery has been converted into a state-of-the-art museum which makes the affinity between nation and alcohol look like a manageable feature of modern Irish heritage.

↬

'I might call myself British,' said Maggie, who was born in Bangor in Northern Ireland, 'but it would depend on the situation. Sometimes I say Irish if we are talking about cultural identity. To say you're British in Northern Ireland is to make a definite political statement. It's much more complicated than national identity.'

Maggie clearly remembered the first ceasefire, and described herself as being in the last generation of people who had direct experience of the Troubles.

'Being Northern Irish is increasingly seen as a blend that allows you to be neither completely British nor completely Irish. It's proving a popular way of describing yourself as it gives people a way of being able to take control. They are testing it in integrated schools at the moment.'

We were talking about whether young people in Northern Ireland were drawn towards a broader European identity.

'Thinking of ourselves as EU citizens offers us a way to lift ourselves out of the old national identity issues,' she said, 'and I think that people like it for that reason.'

The presence of EU migrants in Northern Ireland was having an impact on identity there too, particularly in Protestant areas where more housing was available. For the ever-expanding Polish communities, their identity as Catholics had led them into situations where they were unwittingly caught up on both sides of old sectarian battles. In 2005 over thirty Polish employees had walked out of a meat-processing factory in Lisahally, claiming that fellow workers had subjected them to racist and sectarian abuse during a two-minute silence held in honour of Pope John Paul's funeral.

More recently the Republican Sinn Féin party accused them of being mercenaries and collaborators when it was revealed that Poles were being successfully recruited to join the Police Service (PSNI) to make up the Catholic quotas. The PSNI was formerly called the Royal Ulster Constabulary and viewed by nationalists as an arm of the British state.

I asked Maggie about attitudes to migrant workers in Northern Ireland. She had mentioned that the economy was growing at a staggering rate and that property prices were the fastest rising in Europe.

'There is increased migration,' she said, 'but it is still mainly white European – apart from significant numbers of Filipino nurses. But yes, the figure for hate crimes is high which is not surprising given the history of sectarianism. But you have to remember that the PSNI records racism and hate crimes differently from the rest of the UK. It's not just if a person perceives an incident to be racist, but also if a passer-by or witness perceives it to be – that counts too. That's partly why it's so much higher.'

Poles make up a high proportion of newcomers settling in the Republic of Ireland too, finding work across a range of sectors. Dublin's local evening newspaper has a Polish language supplement and a Polish school is due to be opened where children will be able to follow a Polish national curriculum. President Mary McAleese urges Irish citizens to show that their own experience of migration can be put to good use making others feel welcome in their country.

But throughout Ireland as in Britain, the term *Eastern European* has become a dubious code for the new immigrants from anywhere east of Germany. It signifies 'white' without anyone having to spell it out. This has different implications depending partly on the new migrants' expectations of their right to belong – and their attitudes towards those who are not designated as white. But remembering what Michal had told me about Poland's history as a buffer between east and west, I asked Gosia if Poles actually thought of themselves as being from Eastern Europe. I was also wondering how membership of the EU had changed their relationship to their neighbours in the former Soviet Union.

'Yes, of course we identify as Eastern European,' she replied. 'We feel a connection to all the countries that were part of the Communist bloc. We have a similar way of understanding things, of speaking, of everyday life. It's easy to relate. I have some Russian neighbours two doors away, and we are always going to each other's houses for tea without making an appointment.'

But, as she explained at greater length, the shared political histories had deeper implications. 'In the Communist bloc you couldn't ask too many questions, you learned not to take risks. You couldn't be an individual. That's why we love coming to Britain. It's OK to take risks, and people respect you for it. We love the values of Western Europe and the freedom that comes from being able to speak your mind.'

While Maggie was optimistic about her generation's ability to negotiate the tangle of Irish, British and European paths out of narrow identity politics, she was seething with anger about the way that Northern Ireland was being left out of the debates about Britishness, especially in relation to security.

'In Northern Ireland there's enormous frustration that we've been through what we've been through and it's not being taken into account now. Three and a half thousand people were murdered, and many of them in England, too. To think that within a generation they can ignore that experience and repeat the same mistakes makes us feel as though all those deaths were in vain. We all laughed at the uproar about security searches after the bombs went off in London on 7 July. The fuss they all made in London about having their bags searched. It took us years to realise that you didn't need a day to go from Bangor to Belfast. It used to take hours because you got searched going into every single shop. Now the government is making a huge mistake by targeting Muslims. Look at the way they treated those suspects in Birmingham, the ones who are calling Britain a police state. When the RUC used to take people's husbands and brothers in the night, the IRA would come round the next day and tell their families: "That's British justice for you. We will protect you." They don't seem to have learned anything.'

꙳

I was always learning new words from Yvonne, or rather new ways of understanding old words. The latest one was 'narratologist', which I took to mean 'one who studies the art of telling a story'. Yvonne was an artist at telling stories herself, and had been awarded the Caine Prize for African writing in 2003. I heard her use this word in a discussion about the value of constructing new narratives of British national identity, particularly in the field of education. My whirlwind trip had convinced me that Britishness was rather like cloud cover. How you viewed it depended on whether you could discern it at any given time, and what it looked like from a distance. It certainly wasn't confined to the borders of the UK, and those who thought in planetary terms tended to prefer the view from above. Having seen it through the eyes of those whose countries had been shaped, or even created, by the diktat of British colonial rule, I appreciated that Yvonne was not talking about narratology as a particularly British problem. She took it for granted that every nation is formed out of stories told by the powerful about the weak. The art arises from listening to the voices of those who have been silenced.

In that Nairobi workshop it was Yvonne who had insisted that we watch a clip from the successful British film, *The Constant Gardener*, which was both made and set in Kenya. The perils faced by the largely voiceless Africans in the film correspond to those that many Kenyans face in the very real world. Poor health, poverty, inter-ethnic conflict, exploitation by multinational pharmaceutical companies, corruption, and so on. But these terrible forces are reduced to incidental details that drive the main plot forward. Africans are victims; they do not play an active role in defending themselves or taking power into their own hands. There is only one significant black speaking part, taken by a Belgian doctor who is in league with the central character, the English activist, Tessa. He comes to a gory end hanging from a tree. The audience, and some of the white characters in the film, are made to wonder if there is something more between them, as they are so clearly in cahoots, only to find out after their double deaths that he was gay, so conveniently out of the picture.

The whites, however, are seen undergoing a range of emotions that give clues as to their motives, desires and fears. Tessa is driven by a righteous fury that many people feel at the duplicity of Western governments conniving with multinational corporations at the expense of the global south. The film was very popular, partly because it worked as a love story regardless of the veracity of the plot. The political and ethical issues raised by the thriller provided welcome opportunities to reveal the injustice involved in holding trials for new drugs that are not intended to benefit the people undergoing the experiment.

So what is the issue with Western audiences being coaxed into learning unpalatable truths in the name of entertainment? It's a long and honourable tradition after all, especially in the cinema. But the success of *The Constant Gardener* and the more recent *Blood Diamond* marks the beginning of a new trend in blockbuster movies. The target audience is the Live Aid generation, eager to address global injustice by making changes in their own lives. The problem was that the Kenya I saw through the eyes of the characters and cinematographer was flattened, humiliated and gagged, a chimera of the country I had just visited. The film made me remember an essay by Binyavanga called 'How to Write About Africa.' There was one paragraph that had stuck in my mind.

> Broad brushstrokes throughout are good. Avoid having the African characters laugh, or struggle to educate their kids, or just make do in mundane circumstances. Have them illuminate something about Europe or America in Africa. African characters should be colourful, exotic, larger than life – but empty inside with no dialogue, no conflicts or resolutions in their stories, no depths or quirks to confuse the cause.

I hear his voice in the writing now we've met and remember saying to him that I had liked that piece. He had replied wearily: 'People always remark on that rather than any of my other work.' Even then I wished I hadn't said it. Now that I have read through copies of *Kwani?*, the annual journal that he edits from Nairobi, I can see why it's irksome that he is known for the Granta piece – a short, satirical, diatribe – rather than his own fiction, or for that matter, for his capacity to bring other Kenyan and East African writers together.

Although Binyavanga, recipient of the Caine Prize the year

before Yvonne, is also an artist at telling stories, I am not sure if he would consider himself a narratologist. His interest lies in bringing disparate voices together, voices that do damage to old ways of thinking as well as bringing forth new stories. He is definitely not one for a chronological account of what it means to be Kenyan today, nor is he searching for a continuous thread back through the past. He has made this abundantly clear in his own work, but he spells it out in capital letters in a *Kwani?* editorial, writing back to critics who accuse the journal of not being sufficiently serious.

> Kenya's literary community sometimes behaves as if literature is a lineage: that some chosen somebody passes on the light to another chosen somebody, and so on. I prefer to see Kenya as a diverse place which needs diverse conversations…What I hope for as a reader is as many literary engagements as possible, in all languages possible, from all schools of thought possible.

The pages of the editorial are splattered with ink blotches that signify the fury of creating with words and a two-finger gesture to elitist expectations. The Kenya of this writer's imagination is emerging as an unbounded space in a new political era that corresponds to the end of ex-President Moi's grip on the country after the elections in 2002.

'There is a new Kenya growing out of these ashes. It has learned to need nobody; to be competitive and creative. It speaks Sheng, it is the Kenya we are waiting for.'

᷍

One sentence from Binyavanga's essay reminded me of conversations in Bangladesh: 'Among your characters you must always include The Starving African, who wanders the refugee camp nearly naked, and waits for the benevolence of the West.'

This image took me back to a discussion in Dhaka in which a group of students were asked how they thought Bangladesh was represented in the global media. What would they expect to find if they looked for information about Bangladesh on the Internet?

There was a brief silence from everyone in the room at these questions. 'Bad news,' ventured one, 'pictures of floods. A small boy up to his waist in water with a goat under his arm.'

'Or mobs rioting,' said another, mindful of the events of the previous weekend when rival political demonstrations had clashed in the streets. This latest phase of political unrest had led to over forty deaths in different parts of the country. Everyone was feeling anxious and upset, ashamed at how the near-collapse of democracy must look from the outside.

'It's also about geography,' someone added thoughtfully. 'India comes across so easily because of its vast geographical position. We have no Bangladeshi music on television, it's all Indian, mostly sung in Punjabi which we don't understand. There are very few Bangladeshi films, just Bollywood which dominates our cinemas. It is no wonder that the country is perceived as a disaster zone. People only see what is visible, and all that there is out there is bad news. Apart from Mohamed Yunus and the Grameen Bank, of course.'

The person who had asked about the image of Bangladesh had his own agenda. Sazidul Islam was a manager of DJuice, a youth-oriented mobile phone service promoted in a number of countries – including Pakistan and Ukraine – by a multinational communication corporation called Telenor Mobile. DJuice is also connected to a Bangladeshi company called Grameen Phone, owned jointly by Telenor and the Grameen Bank. Sazidul's purpose was to instil a sense of agency among young people so that they felt motivated to change this situation, to put a different Bangladesh on the map. He was full of corporate enthusiasm and modish catch phrases but you had to admire his act. His dynamic presentation was designed to inspire and cajole a new generation to use new technologies to break this cycle of negative imagery. Make better-quality music videos, he urged, and create your own websites that celebrate the positive aspects of life in this country.

He gave examples of how technology could change the way that people expressed themselves. 'We need to produce Bangla songs that guys can play in their cars, you know, the kind that vibe their woofer.'

Music was a key component of the corporate strategy to make young people feel good about being Bangladeshi. He made comparisons with rap and hip hop which, he emphasised, provided a model. It came from black youths representing their thoughts, and it had its own originality. *We need to find our own voice and medium. We can do better if we make our own songs that were like what we had before.*

One practical step the company had taken was to ensure that artists were paid royalties if their songs were used for ringtones. Another was the promotion of youthful renditions of Bangla and Baul music by running talent competitions.

Young people were offered free use of their phones after midnight, but this was judged to encourage promiscuity as well as lack of sleep. Parents complained and the company withdrew the offer. But this corporate sensitivity gives a misleading impression that youth culture in Bangladesh is uniformly subject to the controlling hand of the grown-ups. No one familiar with Bangla heavy metal would agree with that for a start.

It was Sabrina who told me about Warfaze, and I found 10,000 links to them on Google after that. She mentioned their impact as the best known of the bands that became popular in the early 1990s, part of a new wave of music expressing a unique mix of Bangla with rock. 'We need to talk about the role of arts and culture,' she insisted, holding up a supplement from a Bangladeshi newspaper called *The Daily Star*. It was a special issue on 'Deshi pride' exploring the link between patriotism, youth culture and national identity. The central spread was called 'youth vibes' and described the work of a new generation of organisations committed to addressing poverty, deprivation and inequality. One of these I noticed was ProjectDYouth, a collaboration between Project Bangladesh Foundation and DJuice. 'The target,' it read, 'is to create or mould a generation who will be self-confident and smart and also care for their community.'

Elsewhere the supplement explored the new wave of youth culture struggling to articulate a sense of belonging in a global sphere as well as a distinctive national space. Several writers reflected on the way their lives had been marked by the 1971 war and its legacy. There was a widespread acknowledgement that the children of the generation that fought for the country's independence had imbibed enough optimism about its future to be utterly disillusioned with the reality as it unfolded in the 1980s and early '90s. 'Feeling Bangladeshi fell out of vogue and patriotism dissolved into a sketchy ideal,' wrote Quazi Zulquarnain Islam, whose father had fought in the war as a nineteen-year-old. His own conclusion was that J. F. Kennedy was right when he said that true patriotism lay in asking what you could do for your country rather than how it could serve you.

The most interesting article as far as I was concerned was about typing messages in Bangla. It is easy to be glib about the phenomenal spread of mobile phones and Internet cafes throughout the developing world. It is not often that people stop to ask how these new forms of communication affect local languages. In their enthusiasm to reach out to the country's youth – thirty-three per cent of the population is under fifteen and the median age is currently twenty-two – the DJuice flag-fliers recently ran a nationwide advertising campaign that spoke to young people in their own language. Banners and billboards urged them to communicate by phone, using slang words and phrases considered to be a travesty of Bangla heritage. Once again the older generation was not happy, and there was pressure from on high to remove the ads.

The reaction to the DJuice campaign in Bangladesh suggested that new shorthand codes of talking, mailing and texting were being formed below the radar of official speech. But according to writer Asifur Rahman Khan there was little cause for alarm.

'The important thing to notice is that writing an SMS in Bangla is far more strenuous than just writing in English, because almost all the mobile phones do not have incorporated Bangla dictionaries. Hence, in these cases, the user has to spell out each Bangla word to be stored for later use, and although many would proclaim the Bangla nation as being lazy, it is surprising that teenagers and their older counterparts actually go through all the trouble.'

The reason why they are prepared to show their appreciation of Bangla, he argued, is that there are some things that can't be translated into English and retain the same meaning. I remembered the seven grey triangles making up the national monument that I visited with my friends in Dhaka. One of them represented the language movement that began in 1952, shortly after the partition from India when the Karachi-based government insisted on making Urdu the official language. This helps to unpack the patriotic orientation towards the mother tongue. 'Writing SMS and emails in Bangla is not a big deal, but it does show a part of you, a part that is proud to be Bangladeshi.'

I turn back to the new Nairobi-based literary journal, *Kwani?*, a Kiswahili word meaning 'So?' Some of the stories and poems are written in Sheng, a hybrid language mixing English with Kiswahili. It is not normally found in literary circles, and is considered more of a street dialect. I don't understand Kiswahili, but I find a rap poem I recognise as Sheng. It is called 'Prophecies to the Dry Bones' by Kama, one of the pioneers of Kenyan Swahili rap and a member of a threesome called Kalamashaka. It begins:

> *Ka unaweza fikiria haziwezi live, uliza the big n the strong/*
> *Unambiwe na biggie smalls you dead wrong*
> *Oh ye dry bone skieni Jah na mlive on/*
> *hii song ina prophesy to the 4 winds, dj, grafiti, breakin na emcees*

I wonder if Sheng would qualify as 'slanguistics', a term I first encountered when London rapper Skinny Man used it in a discussion about the historical influence of black music on British street culture. When I heard it in the TV documentary *Soul Britannia*, it reminded me of a scene in Pratap's film, *Found in Translation*, where Jackie Bygrave was teaching a class of fifteen- and sixteen-year-olds in south London how to analyse a poem by John Agard. 'You have to understand youth culture,' she said, between explaining to the class how to differentiate between words like 'infer' and 'imply'. 'These kids speak a fusion of dialect and slang that largely comes from Jamaican ways of speaking. We encourage them to express themselves in the ways that make sense to them, but in order to pass the exams they have to know the right terms to use, and understand what they mean.'

Later I read a feature about London's gang culture written in response to a spate of teenage shootings in the capital. The spread included a special section on the language used to speak about drugs and guns. I note that according to this, Urdu and Arabic are now beginning to find their way into the common tongue of British gang warfare.

⌐つ

'The worst place in the world to be young is an old country where there is no place for the young.' Binyavanga's poetic observation rang true at the time but none of us had any idea that it was about to be backed up by a global survey. When UNICEF published their international league tables on the physical and emotional well-being of children in the world's wealthiest nations, British children ranked at the very bottom. The day the report was published, the media echoed the findings in ways that made everyone feel miserable: Britain's children: unhappy, neglected and poorly educated, ran the *Independent*'s front page. 'UK is the worst place to grow up, say UN.'

Some of the data supporting this conclusion came from official statistics measuring child poverty, educational achievement, health and safety, and measurable indices of deviancy like the rates of teenage pregnancies. Some of it came from interviewing children themselves. The Harry Potter generation of eleven- to fifteen-year-olds admitted to being more likely to have been drunk or to have had sex than their peers in any of the other twenty countries that took part. They were more likely to have been involved in a fight over the previous twelve months, and more likely to have been bullied. Less than half had found their peers to be 'kind and helpful'. In terms of rating their own unhappiness, British children were the most likely to feel left out, awkward and lonely.

Looking at the rankings according to each category of well-being, the UK consistently comes near the bottom. The only dimension where the country scored slightly better was in health and safety. British children were found to be least likely to die as a result of an accident, although this figure was affected by relatively high infant mortality rates and low levels of immunisation. Having raised two teenagers in the United States, I thought it was interesting that American children fared hardly any better than British ones. They scored slightly higher in educational terms but there was no recorded result for their levels of happiness.

A few weeks before I left I had kept the text of an open letter to the government composed by over seventy experts in child psychology and development, writers, teachers, child advocates and social workers, setting out their analysis of the problem afflicting British kids.

Society has lost sight of children's social and emotional needs they argued, and this is compromising the mental health of a significant proportion of young people. Their brains are still developing and they cannot cope with such a rapid pace of technological and cultural change. They are not learning to interact with adults since they are left for far too long on their own in the company of electronic stimuli, and their diets of junk food are harmful to their physical development. Education has become another area of pressure instead of providing a refuge from the adult world.

'They also need time,' they wrote. 'In a fast-moving hyper-competitive culture, today's children are expected to cope with an ever-earlier start to formal schoolwork and an overly academic test-driven primary curriculum. They are pushed by market forces to act and dress like mini-adults and exposed via the electronic media to material which would have been considered unsuitable for children even in the very recent past.'

The letter ended with a plea to bring debates about the well-being of children into the very centre of public policy. I had kept a copy because I was working on the hypothesis that the debates about Britishness would, sooner or later, be forced to confront this mounting crisis and set it alongside the fixation on multiculturalism as the source of its ills. I had lost count of polls, surveys and reports showing that rates of depression, self-harm, low self-esteem, bullying and anti-social behaviour were rising among children at an increasingly young age. Yet it was very rare to see these topics discussed under the heading of national identity and British values, let alone teaching Britishness in schools.

∽

'You remember that song that was a hit last year, I can't remember who sang it,' said Leyla. She was referring to 'I wish I was a punk rocker' by Scottish singer Sandi Thom. I was out of the demographic loop and hadn't heard it, but it was easy to find on YouTube. There was a lot of forum discussion about it partly because the record company alleged that it had become famous since being 'webcast' from the singer's basement. But the sentiment was controversial too and a lot of people were bothered by the way it collapsed punks and hippies. The thirteen-year olds that I canvassed hated it because once they heard it they couldn't get the tune out of their heads.

The song begins: 'Oh I wish I was a punk rocker with flowers in my hair/In '77 and '69 revolution was in the air/I was born too late into a world that doesn't care'. It comes across as a lyrical lament for the innocence of a pre-digital world that existed before Thatcher's era, long before New Labour was invented. Leyla noticed it because she was envious of the revolutionary spirit that energised youth culture before she was born. She was also fed up with running into authority and disapproval at every turn. Even among her own generation it was hard. 'People are so materialistic and selfish now,' she sighed. 'They just think about themselves. I think I was just born at the wrong time.'

I wondered what Leyla would think of Radio Bagdad's version of 'London Calling' that came out at the same time as this. Unlike Thom's solo vocals sung against a drum beat, the Polish 'London Calling' retained the actual sound of punk in imitation of The Clash's version released in 1979. But the sentiment behind the two contemporary songs was entirely different, too. Where Thom longs prettily for a world where ignorance could still be bliss, Radio Bagdad claims more tunelessly: 'I never felt so much alive'.

This catches more of the animus that rocked the foundations of Great Britishness in the 1970s. In the daytime I was writing about fascist propaganda and racist violence in *Searchlight*. At the weekends I was going on counter demonstrations organised by the Anti-Nazi League with thousands of others determined to defend their towns and communities against the National Front. The militancy of a new generation of black and South Asian Brits, born in the UK and schooled there, was now converging with more traditional political activism, from trade unions to Troops Out and numerous international solidarity groups. It also drew in people who had never picked up a banner before, let alone stood up to a line of police in riot shields. The resulting movement against racism and fascism was galvanised by slogans like 'Never Again, Nazis = No Future and certainly No Fun'.

The first time I was aware that it wasn't so bad to be born in the UK was in a darkened room in Birmingham's Digbeth Civic

Hall with the vibrations from a giant bass speaker rearranging my internal organs and rewriting my DNA. 'Kingdom rise and kingdom fall, Babylon back against the wall.' The revolutionary lyrics throbbed through a sound system that came from an English market town called Leicester. There was nothing in that space to remind me of my past, just an overpowering sense of excitement about what we were all doing in the present.

Black music helped create a youth culture that expressed how people felt about the world they had inherited. It also helped articulate a demand for human rights and justice. When politicians still talked about the possibility of sending immigrants back 'home', music provided a defiant way to prove them wrong. This was formalised in 1976 when Rock Against Racism was founded, an event that had much more profound consequences than the ANL. It helped to create a critical mass of dissidents who understood the ability of youth culture, especially music, to make a political stand against injustice. Punk was a hugely significant part of that too, partly because it could have so easily gone the other way. There were plenty of admirers on the far right who tried to claim it as a distinctively 'white' sound, and who were drawn to the more shocking paraphernalia of punk such as wearing Nazi regalia.

The Clash played a particularly important role in bringing hordes of disgruntled girls and boys into contact with anti-racism. Their 1976 hit 'White Riot' was written in response to the riots at the Notting Hill Carnival. Both this and their earlier reggae hit 'Police and Thieves' called on white youth to rise up alongside their black counterparts to vent their anger against oppressive policing. In his recently published memoir, *The Progressive Patriot: A Search For Belonging*, Billy Bragg recalled that The Clash showed him the way to ditch his day job and become a full-time punk rocker.

> Conformity won't get you noticed, punk – confrontation is the quickest way to get people's attention. You're not pretty? So what? Show the world you don't care by putting a safety pin through your cheek to make yourself even more unsightly. Can't sing? Who cares? It's what you are singing about that matters. Don't understand the workings of the music industry? Well don't worry, we're

going to turn that world upside down. And, hey, don't wait for someone to come along and do it all for you. Do it yourself.'

Billy Bragg was a budding songwriter and performer whose life was certainly never the same again after he heard The Clash in 1977. The following year he took part in the first ANL/RAR Carnival Against the Nazis along with thousands and thousands of others from all over the country. I was there when the front of the march arrived at Victoria Park in Hackney and we were told that there were still people waiting to leave Trafalgar Square six miles away. That day must have transformed so many people's lives. Unlike the big anti-war march in February 2003, it actually made us feel that we could change this country regardless of what the government decided to do.

But as Billy sagely writes almost three decades down the line, groups like The Clash turned out to be better at posing than politics. The real work needed to come not from the performers so much as the audiences. 'What a performer *can* do, however, is to bring people together for a specific cause, to raise money or consciousness, to focus support and facilitate an expression of solidarity.'

While this observation underlines the achievements of that generation of political protest which brought human rights into popular culture, the value of music as a galvanising force is a mainstream view these days. This has had unfortunate consequences. It has also meant that, with the best will in the world, music may also have lost some of its extraordinary power to change it.

～

Leyla's lament reminded me that I had encountered the spirit of the young Billy Bragg in a pizza restaurant in Dhaka. As we sat chewing the fat after our meal, my companion, Mahmud, leaned over and drew my attention to a family on the other side of the room. 'That couple is very proud because their son is singing a song in English,' he observed. I watched the little boy who was shyly enjoying being the centre of attention. He couldn't have been more than six. Knowing what Mahmud thought about English-medium education in Bangladesh I expected him to be more scornful, but he was more amused than irritated.

Just then I heard the strains of Simon and Garfunkel's 'Scarborough Fair' wafting out from the kitchens. Having just left London two days earlier I was in a mood to forget England entirely but I had always loved that melody. Here was a very English folk song, sung by two Americans in 1968 when I was still at school. I had been thinking about it only recently as I had read about it in Billy Bragg's book.

Billy cites that particular song as the spur for a moment of clarity when he first glimpsed a connection between his own identity and the country in which he was growing up. Something about the words, the tune and the counter melody threading through the voices combined to draw him back in his imagination to a place and time that he recognised as England:

> My mind starts racing back to a time before I was born, long before my century, to a time far yet near, to a place I can see but cannot find, that I know but cannot name…
> For the first time, I feel a connection that goes beyond nationality. This is who I am. This is where I come from.

It's not that he was unaware of his family origins before this moment. Of course he knew he was English, that this was his nationality and his language. He grew up in Barking near the River Thames estuary, and had learned at school about the country's history as a former empire. The English football team had won the World Cup two years earlier and he had been old enough to share in that moment of triumph. But hearing an old English folk song offered him a recognition of another kind of Englishness that was almost shocking in its reverberations. The words 'parsley, sage, rosemary and thyme' evoked an ancient knowledge; the mournful tune, which he later identified as a kind of plainsong, summoned up images of medieval monks inhabiting the now ruined abbey along the river.

The experience came at a time when he was emerging into adolescence, a time when many children begin to struggle with the demands of a more complex social universe outside the orbit of family and school. Following the source of 'Scarborough Fair' he found his way to the album by Simon and Garfunkel, and opened himself to the energy of popular music as it forged the political consciousness of a new generation.

The act of writing his book, many years later, required him

to listen closely to a version of 'Scarborough Fair/Canticle' that was recorded on *The Graduate* soundtrack album, a track that he had lovingly taped on to the end of a compilation years earlier. Determined to understand why this song in particular had haunted him when he first heard it – indirectly starting him on his own musical journey as a performer and songwriter – he approached it through the political context in which it was recorded.

Straining to hear the counter melody weaving through the words and tune of the old folk classic he suddenly became aware of the alternative lyrics written by Paul Simon:

> The lyrics are hard to make out at first, something about a clarion call. In the verse, the phrase 'polishes a gun' leaps out from behind the main vocal. In the penultimate verse, as the song reaches its climax, the lyrics of 'Scarborough Fair' finally succumb to the weight of the counter melody, which comes to the fore to deliver the lines:

> *Generals order their soldiers to kill*
> *And to fight for a cause they've long ago forgotten.*

As he listened to this old song in the early years of the already blighted twenty-first century, Billy realised that almost forty years ago Paul Simon had used 'the beautiful melody of an English folk song' to smuggle an anti-war message into the homes of Middle America. This discovery strengthened his conviction to reclaim an alternative sense of national identity. He wanted to offer a counterpart to the way that groups like the British National Party – which had temporarily taken over his home town of Barking – had commandeered the idea of patriotism and turned it into a nasty, narrow doctrine that dictated who did or didn't belong.

The reason my own heart stirred at the sound of 'Scarborough Fair' was not that I was homesick. It was in solidarity with Billy's desire to explore the roots of his dissenting faith: 'internationalist in spirit, collective in principle, committed to social justice and determined to hold those in power to account.'

Chapter Five: Organise, Don't Agonise

One day I was returning from Leytonstone when it struck me that I had been to the area before in an earlier life. I was standing on the platform waiting for a train, buffeted by strong winds and dampened by the incessant drizzle of a Monday afternoon in January and it suddenly came back to me that I had used this route in 1994 when I went to visit the famous Claremont Road occupation, a site of direct action against the extension of the M11 motorway. The tactics of the new DIY protest movement, as it subsequently became known, put this area of east London on the national media map for almost a whole year.

The proposed link road entailed driving a six-lane highway through a number of residential areas in north-east London. For over thirty years the communities tried to block the development through all the conventional means: planning inquiries, petitions, lobbying. But the Tories decided that the link road was crucial to their plans to rationalise the motorway system. The bulldozers arrived in the autumn of 1993 condemning 350 houses to demolition, thousands of residents to displacement and acres of parkland to destruction. All at enormous cost to save six minutes' journey by car.

The most celebrated acts of resistance took place in neighbouring Wanstead. The new road was due to cut through one of London's last ancient woodlands, which by then consisted of an area of common with a number of elderly trees. A huge oak, famous for its girth and age, was scheduled to be felled. Activists climbed up into its branches, registered it as a postal address and asked supporters to write letters to them there. Since it is illegal to knock down a dwelling without due process, this tactic delayed the inevitable and drew national attention to the cause.

The actions of the protesters were not designed to reverse the government's decision since the battle had clearly been lost. What emerged during those months was a social movement that placed great emphasis on creativity and imagination, intentionally bringing art back into politics in an effort to give both new meaning. Often the tactics worked as a brilliant strategy to get sympathetic media attention. When squatters closed a whole street off and declared it the Independent Free Area of Wanstonia, journalists were offered passports and invited to become citizens for the day. The green, yellow and red Union Jill was flown from the rooftop, and utopia was glimpsed on the upper reaches of the Thames Valley.

As I climbed into the train bearing me away from the windy platform, I was grateful at least that the service was more reliable than it used to be. A cancellation meant waiting at least half an hour on a lonely platform – there were no computer screens and no announcements in those days – and I dimly recalled trying an alternative bus route home which took forever. In 1994 Leyla was well settled in her secondary school, Shamser was probably a student in Manchester, and neither would have paid much attention to these wild creatures converging on Leytonstone from all four corners of the country. Since then, the M11 link road has probably been resurfaced more than once as well.

But there was a burning question that I had been asking myself for some time and I was glad to be reminded of this distant era of pre-9/11 political activism. In April 1997, just before the general election that saw the Tories booted out and New Labour surging into power, I took part in a large and boisterous demonstration in central London. It was historic in its way partly because it was organised jointly by the Reclaim the Streets movement and the trade unions that had come together in solidarity. What brought them together was a bitter and long-running strike by dockers in Liverpool.

In 1995, six years after the Tories abolished the National Dock Labour Scheme, Mersey Docks sacked 500 men who had refused to cross the picket lines outside one of their subcontractors' gates. The dockers soon realised that this had been a trap to give their employer an excuse to fire them, but by then their jobs had been advertised. Represented by the media as relics of an earlier age, and receiving half-hearted support from other trade union leaders, the dockers were forced to look beyond conventional labour-movement politics for support.

Some of this came from abroad in an unprecedented show of support from as far afield as South Africa. Within Britain the defiance of the dockers touched raw nerves among many who had had more than enough of Tory rule. A new T-shirt appeared that symbolised the convergence of old and new ways of doing politics. It simply read: 'Support the Liverpool Dockers' but the letters 'c' and 'k' were printed exactly like the Calvin Klein logo which was emblematic of the escalating fashion for wearing designer brands.

I remember the demonstration for three reasons. First, it was truly extraordinary to see the mingling of more conventional militants with elements of the road-protest activism that forswore the conventional tactics of law-abiding struggle. Banners calling for the public to vote for trees were waved alongside those calling for an end to Thatcherism. The demonstration was more like a strange carnival procession with drums and painted banners, and as it crawled over Westminster Bridge it created an explosive sense of disillusionment and optimism in great proximity to the seat of power. That was the second thing I remember, which I have had many occasions to recall in recent months. I am not sure that any demonstration of this size would be allowed to pass so near the Houses of Parliament these days. But that is another matter.

A third reason for remembering this day is that I spotted an aunt on the underground on my way home. She had scolded me over the years for not behaving like a dutiful daughter to my beloved parents. On this occasion I had a bright pink sticker stuck to my chest bearing the legend 'Fuck Middle England'. It was one of a series that appeared all over the underground as a riposte to the main political parties' attempts to compete for the electorate outside the metropolitan centres. I was glad she didn't see me as I felt she only would have considered it further proof of my juvenile tendencies. In any event I sheepishly zipped up my jacket, turned the other way, and felt guilty for not going over to say hello.

The anger, cynicism and even despair of the demonstrators were utterly familiar from years of taking part in such events, inspired by a host of targets. But I will never forget that impression of sheer disdain for everything that parliamentary democracy stood for. So many placards called on people to boycott the voting process altogether, which was strange for a pre-election rally. This was not a rejection of participatory politics though, nor can it be read as disinterest. Looking back, it was a manifestation of what so many young people feel when faced with the choices open to them as new voters. When I ask myself where all of those particular people went, I also know that little has changed.

In 2005, just over half of the eligible voters bothered to vote in the general election that saw New Labour returned with a reduced majority. Of the four Western European nations that held general elections that year, just sixty-one per cent of the electorate turned out, compared with sixty-five per cent in Portugal, seventy-seven per cent in Norway and eighty-five per cent in Denmark.

✎

On 24 February 2007 a row of well-dressed men stood with their backs against the wall watching the crowds filter past with their banners held high. Speaking in an American accent one remarked, 'Gee, there are about ten different causes wrapped up in the same demonstration.' I was hovering nearby taking photos, scanning the protestors in search of a familiar face. I turned to the expensive cashmere overcoat and remarked as acidly as I could manage: 'I think you'll find it's one cause. They are all against war.'

Later I had plenty of time to watch the march through his eyes. I joined in the stream in Piccadilly and walked down to Trafalgar Square to listen to the start of the rally. After hearing one speaker declaim that this event showed the true values of the British people for peace and justice, I decided to wander back to check that this was a representative sample of good citizens. The demonstration had been called by the coalition group Stop the War and CND under the joint banner 'No Trident, Troops Out of Iraq'. There were indeed many printed placards eliciting other causes, such as 'Free Palestine', 'Don't Attack Iran' and 'Blair Must Go'. I stood for well over an hour near the statue of Eros as what I thought was the tail end of the march turned out to be larger than what had gone before. Banners from groups all over the country passed by, proving that the sum of local outrage added up, geographically at least, to a nation of angry people. But ten different causes? More like two: end war and make peace.

Demonstrations can occasionally make history even though

they don't often manage to change its course. Four years ear-lier, on 15 February 2003, the world witnessed its first col-lective, coordinated protest. This in itself was a momentous happening, encapsulated for posterity in photographs of peo-ple in all climates making a stand against the imminent inva-sion of Iraq. In London the march itself was unprecedented both in terms of numbers and the demographic mix. Everyone commented on the optimistic and buoyant mood, and many spoke of overwhelming joy at being part of a limitless throng of like-minded, peace-loving humans. On that day that was what Britain looked like, and those who took part felt they belonged to something precious with many different coloured faces. The confused American in London would have got the message had he witnessed the crowd on that day. There was one unanimous demand: No war on Iraq.

The harmful effects of the invasion and subsequent occupa-tion of Iraq on young British Muslims had been established beyond doubt but I wanted to speak to a different constituency whose political consciousness was shaped within the crucible of the anti-war movement. I was curious to find out what hap-pened to the optimism expressed on that day and how subse-quent events had affected the political mood of that generation. I had spoken to many who had taken part but it still wasn't clear how the failure to stop the invasion had affected student politics, for example, or whether it had led to greater cynicism about politics in general. I decided to call on two old friends who had just hit twenty-one, confident that they would help me gauge the longer-term effects of growing up in a country at war.

I was looking forward to seeing Jacob and Reuben again as they were young boys the last time we met. In 2003 they were both seventeen and doing their A levels. Now they were at uni-versity, and in the middle of their final year. They were quite matter-of-fact when I asked them about the big demonstration before the invasion started.

'We couldn't get a sense of numbers as we were in the mid-dle of it,' said Jacob. I had found them at their family home in north London and Reuben was making the tea. 'But I remem-ber a lot of free and easy conversation. We got chatting to a fireman's union in front of us. People were talking to each other as members of the population rather than staying with the groups they came with.'

'It was a very young demonstration,' added Reuben as he passed round the mugs. 'But the really significant thing for us was the school students coming out on the day Iraq was invaded.'

'You organised a walk-out, didn't you?' I asked. We were living in the United States then but my son happened to be in London at the time and joined the students who had left their schools in droves to converge on Parliament Square along with other outraged protestors. He told us that night how tense the atmosphere had been. Objects were flying through the air, and several demonstrators were arrested which made things even more volatile.

'Yes,' said Reuben, 'there was a conference of school students beforehand where everyone agreed to walk out if and when it happened. The day after the bombing started we turned up at the school with banners and asked everyone to come out with us.'

'Do you think that most kids went to get a day out, or did they really want to protest?'

'There was a broad spectrum,' said Jacob sagely. 'People who were not normally politicised said I'm going because I have these beliefs. It's more important for me to be there. It was no longer about stopping the war but about registering objection.'

'So, what, in your opinion, was the effect of being ignored? Do you think that it made people feel less inclined to get involved in politics after that?'

'No, not at all,' said Reuben who was studying history. When we last met he was immersed in reading about the Spanish Civil War and I knew he took a long view of things. 'A lot of people do think that having something to say about the war is part of life. The fact they even talk about being ignored is better than not having anything to say in the first place.'

'The fact is,' added Jacob, who was more of a music man, 'that our generation has remained politicised on the issue of war. Student union debates about this war are always popular – you even get science students and people who are not normally considered political or people who don't read newspapers.'

↜

'It took us five hours to walk from start to finish,' Farhana told me when I asked her about her experience of being on the historic anti-war march in 2003. 'It was freezing cold and my back was hurting but it just didn't matter. I felt if I could have saved one life it would have been worth it.'

It was lunchtime in Islamabad and we were trying to identify the non-meat dishes available in the buffet. Being vegetarian in Pakistan is a minority interest and we were considered a curiosity by some of the people we met. As we compared notes on the memorable day of global protest, Mariam, who dated her interest in International Relations from that point, remembered witnessing a slightly different occurrence.

'In Pakistan people burned cars and shops because they were angry the government was not taking a stand. Nothing comes of demonstrating peacefully. It just makes you think you are a loser. You might as well go and riot.'

'One of the problems that we face here,' she continued, 'is the influence of the Superpowers. America does not want democracy in Pakistan. They prefer dealing with one person and that's why they promote dictatorships.'

Hamza, a fellow student with Mariam, joined in. Before lunch he had acted the part of the donkey farmer with great relish. His talent for comic improvisation had allowed him to express his anger about the state of his country by playing to the gallery, but now he was utterly serious.

'I was a kid when Musharraf took over seven years ago,' he said bitterly. 'Democracy has become more of a mockery in Pakistan. People know that when we cast our votes it doesn't have any value.'

In spite of the fact that Musharraf's book was being hawked all over the subcontinent I never saw anyone actually reading a copy. It was written largely for Western eyes and involves a great deal of score-settling that has left opponents infuriated. His readiness to sign up to the US-led War on Terror in 2001 earned him the nickname 'Busharraf' among critics at home. On a visit to the United States to promote the book, however, he attempted to redress his collusion with American interests by claiming that a member of the State Department had threatened to bomb Pakistan back to the Stone Age if he didn't cooperate.

But there were other reasons why the president had alienated large sections of the country. When he seized power in 1999, on board a passenger plane circling over Karachi, he initially found a high level of support by promising to bring stability and reform in sectors such as education and land rights. When it became clear that little was going to change, a wave of cynicism engulfed the country.

'The weird thing is,' continued Hamza, 'if you have a dictatorship, then say that's what it is – but we are still told it's a democracy. It's just deceiving the world. Fine, we have freedom of speech and I can say this openly in the street. But the fundamentals of democracy are not here.

'Musharraf is not elected, he is the chief of army staff. His priority is to maintain his own role. He has more of a military approach to things. Take the Barjaur incident. I know people who when they heard about the bombing said we need to do something about it – they are turning fundamentalist.'

Just a few weeks before we met there were two events that stunned the country, giving added weight to Hamza's complaints. First, in the early hours of an October morning, a religious school in the Barjaur tribal region was attacked from the air with the result that over eighty people were killed, many of them children. Many in the opposition parties blamed the attack on American forces, and locals swore that they witnessed US drones firing hellfire missiles at the madrasa. President Musharraf, however, insisted that the attack was carried out at his command, and that the school had been targeted because it was being used as a training base for terrorists.

Nine days later, at least forty trainee soldiers were killed and twenty injured when a suicide bomber drove a car into a military base in Dargai, 100 kilometres from Peshawar. Both events were polarising, but the religious right lost some sympathy after the carnage of the second attack. The soldiers killed were, after all, the sons of peasant farmers forced by poverty to join the army.

Hamza was by no means ill-disposed towards the US, despite being critical of their prosecution of the War on Terror. He had lived in Kansas City when he was younger and speaks with an American accent. But he had had an experience that had revealed the level of corruption in politics, and this had undermined his faith in any sense of functioning democracy in Pakistan. His mother had recently and successfully stood in an election for local government and he had been shocked by attempts to manipulate the ballot.

'I saw with own eyes, I'm not exaggerating. The voting took place and the police arrived at one of the polling stations and tried to take the ballot boxes out. The votes were already scanned but they tried to sneak more ballot papers in. I have to tell this reality so that they will know.'

Mariam listened to Hamza's protest patiently. She too had an American accent but swore that she had never been there. She had earlier played the role of the smooth-talking politician.

'I have a lot of relatives there,' she told me, 'and I guess I learned to talk like them. But to go back to your question: Why don't people talk about democracy in Pakistan? First, during the ten to fifteen years we did have democracy, the leaders didn't come up to expectations. People realised that even if we have a dictatorship at least we are more likely to prosper. I think we've given up on democracy. Second, people need to accept in Western countries that each state could have their own way of governance – it could be better than what they define as democracy. Why do the superpowers insist that democracy is impossible in an Islamic state? Our problem is that our revolutionary leaders died too soon, before they could build on their ideals here. That's where we differ from India. Gandhi may have been assassinated, but Nehru was in power for twenty years and this gave them a sense of continuity.'

It was an accepted fact that Jinnah's tragic murder in 1948, and the assassination of his prime minister, Liaquat Ali Khan, in 1951, robbed the new republic of its ideological foundations. The country had to wait for almost ten years for a constitution as a result. Eqbal Ahmad, one of Pakistan's most insightful political analysts until his own untimely death in 1999, often drew attention to their vision of a secular state guided by Islamic ideals. In 1995 he reminded readers of a speech delivered by Jinnah shortly before he died when he spoke passionately about the direction he wanted the new nation to take:

'Islam and its ideals have taught us democracy. It has taught us equality of man, justice and fair play to everybody... In any

case Pakistan is not going to be a theocratic state, to be ruled
by priests with a divine mission. We have many non-Muslims
– Hindus, Christians, and Parsis – but they are all Pakistanis.
They will enjoy the same rights and privileges and will play
their rightful part in the affairs of Pakistan.'

Atif was listening to our conversation about the mixture of
confusion, anger and apathy among young people. 'There are
many other problems in civil society,' he said, 'but sometimes
you have to go outside the country to campaign for justice.' He
regularly breaks the law in his home town of Islamabad. He
never took a driving test and drives without a licence or insur-
ance. 'You must get stopped by the police a lot,' I asked him,
imagining him weaving through the traffic with a trail of flash-
ing lights behind him. 'I do,' he replied, 'but when they ask to
see my licence I tell them that I am not allowed to have one.
People with disabilities are not supposed to drive so I can't
take a test even if I want to. Anyway the police know me now
and don't bother.'

Atif is a disability activist and campaigner which means that
he is crystal clear about how society perpetuates the exclusion
of people with disabilities. 'In Pakistan there are four barriers,'
he explained, 'though this is true in other countries, as well.
First, the family: attitudes towards disability start at home.
Second, the environment is designed in a way to prevent
accessibility to all sorts of services available to everyone else,
but especially school. Third, there is the question of communication. Blind people need to learn Braille, deaf people sign language and so on. But the most important barrier to overcome
is the law. Without legislation nothing will change. In Pakistan
we have laws banning institutional discrimination, but it will
take time to implement them, especially in villages.'

The custom in rural areas where there are often informal
social-welfare networks is that women with disabilities are
taken as second wives. They tend to be treated in one of two
ways: either they are ignored or else they are worshipped as
though they have spiritual powers. But Atif had learned something important about the link between disability and environment when he was involved in a scheme to bring wheelchairs
to villages outside the city.

'We took fifty wheelchairs and made sure that people knew

how to use them. Then three months later we went back to assess what difference they had made. They had disappeared – they were nowhere to be seen. We asked what happened and they told us that they had sold them and bought donkeys instead. It was much easier to get around on donkeys because of the terrain and it suited them perfectly.'

Atif had another wheelchair story that illustrated the particular problems facing activists in Pakistan. They had arranged a series of demonstrations in Islamabad to protest about the laws banning them from holding licences. Over a hundred wheelchair-users blocked the road causing a huge traffic jam and attracting a lot of attention.

'What did the police do?' I asked. 'Did they try to move you out of the way?'

'No, they just said things like, "You should stay home, you shouldn't come out like this."'

Atif was getting ready to lobby the Minister for Social Welfare to demand that Pakistan sign up to the UN Convention on Human Rights of Persons with Disabilities for Inclusion and Integration. He was particularly hoping that the government would adopt the clause that gave people with disabilities entitlement to social benefits. His proudest achievement was the publication of a book directed at changing attitudes to disability among children. *Just like the Other Kids* was written by a team of eleven- to fifteen-year-olds and had just been published in Urdu and English.

⁓

'Poverty is one of the biggest employers, and what's more, has created some of the biggest gravy trains in history.' A Kenyan blogger called Grey Matter started a new post shortly after the Make Poverty History campaign was launched in the UK in the summer of 2005. Called 'Get Real: Poverty Eradication Education 101,' the blog ranted at length about the way that NGOs had proliferated in Kenya, thriving on a bottomless pit of funding as they competed with each other to make work out of alleviating hardship. Grey Matter's special scorn was reserved for those who came in from outside to lead the moral crusade for Africa.

'Poverty has created opportunities for everyone, no matter what field they are in. Poverty has allowed characters like Bob

Geldof, who would have otherwise faded into the yesteryear, to get his vaguely belligerent countenance on televisions around the world, and his own tele-documentary, *Geldof in Africa*, where he managed to pass through Africa with fleeting contact with technology and architecture.'

Among the many old newspaper and press cuttings lying on my floor there is one heading that winks at me regularly as if to remind me not to forget. 'Arise, Sir Bono!' it cries, 'it's a beautiful day for the singer who uses his voice to help Africa.' The article that follows explains how the Irish singer had been awarded an honorary knighthood in recognition of his humanitarian work. Handing him the award, the Prime Minister praised his efforts to organise the Live8 performance timed to coincide with the G8 summit at Gleneagles in Scotland in 2005. 'You have tirelessly used your voice to speak up for Africa,' he told him. 'I know how much these causes matter to you.'

I remembered Binyavanga's image of the starving African who wanders the refugee camp nearly naked, and waits for the benevolence of the West. And I wished I had had a pound for every sarcastic comment about Bob Geldof I had heard in Nairobi. But in this age of single-issue wristband pseudo-politics, I had trouble consigning every well-meant British gesture towards Africa as a pointless exercise in smug do-gooding. There had to be ways of harnessing young people's shame at their relative wealth and prosperity to a global politics of debt relief that didn't involve self-delusion on the one hand and a patronising, even racist, attitude towards generic Africans on the other.

The twins proved to be ideal informants because they had astute political fingers in many pies. It was heartening to hear them talk enthusiastically about their activities, just as I remembered them when they were younger. Both avid bloggers themselves, they had gone to Gleneagles to protest at the G8 summit, and they had strong views about the parallel mobilisation around the Make Poverty History campaign. They became more animated as they took turns to recall their trip to Scotland to take part in the week of protests.

'One day we went up to that place where they lock up

asylum seekers. It's basically a prison camp in the middle of nowhere.'

'The last day was Gleneagles, but that got drowned out because the day of that demo was when London got the Olympics and the day after was when the tube exploded.'

'We were camping with anarchists.'

'No, communists.'

'No, it was organised by anarchists,' continued Reuben, 'anyway Edinburgh gave us this sports field on the edge of the city – there was a massive camp of all the different sects. The council estate was called Craig Mellar. At first they were basically just attacking us as hippies and they were mad that we were using their one amenity for miles around. There were some people being really irresponsible and having raves all night. By the end of the week of action there were people, older people who didn't have much education, for economic reasons – they came to Gleneagles with us, made food for us in their houses and completely joined in the protest. It was really amazing how much that community took on what the media called "extremist politics".

'What were your demands there?' I asked. It was true that the combination of the Olympics announcement followed by the bomb attacks in London had totally obscured the events at Gleneagles.

'People were talking about shutting down the G8 – that wasn't a realistic demand. But the protest was defined against the whole G8 thing – we were basically saying this is an illegitimate meeting – we don't recognise the right of leaders there to make decisions about the world, undemocratically and behind closed doors.'

'There was a big gathering in the Meadows in Edinburgh,' said Jacob, 'and there were the anti-capitalist people – anarchist, communist activists – in the same space as Live 8. On one screen there was a big image of Bono and on another you'd see people slagging him off.'

The brothers were in agreement with Grey Matter although they had not come across his or her blog. They had not been impressed by Bono's humanitarian mission or Bob Geldof's ability to organise a concert for a global audience. They were inclined to see their efforts as self-promotion, as a bid for popularity rather than politics. But more than a personal distaste for celebrity posturing, they were critical of making such a complex subject like poverty into an 'absolute single issue'.

'Compared to the anti-war movement,' said Jacob, 'it didn't make people feel like they had agency.'

Reuben agreed wholeheartedly, 'It was a completely depoliticised event.'

'It was really very strange,' continued Jacob. 'Because they don't try to analyse what poverty means, and the fact that poverty in the Third World is also contingent on wealth in the UK and the US – they think that poverty is a thing in itself that can be wiped out by will power, by donations, even. They don't see it as part of a global economic system. That's the main difference between the people marching at Gleneagles and people who were at the concerts.'

Reuben was enthusiastic about the way that they were able to file their own reports on *Indymedia*, an independent newsgathering enterprise that had set up sites in the campground where individuals could write about their experiences, providing an instant resource for future reference. He too had thought a lot about the importance of taking a more political view of what caused and sustained inequality in a global context.

'I believe that the majority of people marching at Gleneagles were not only saying that this meeting is wrong because it makes decisions over everyone's heads. It's wrong because these are the people that are keeping the rest of the world poor. The two are not entirely disconnected.

'We are not against charities per se, but the politics of poverty needs to be explained rather than a flabby view of "poverty is bad". That just makes people upset and doesn't change anything.'

～

Most cities look grim in the rain, especially when you go to the parts where poorer people live, crammed together on every square inch of space and parted only by impatient traffic that snakes across their paths. Things can look a lot worse when the roads are not paved and the rain falls non-stop for twenty-four hours. Leaden-grey skies can drain a scene of colour, forcing the eye to seek it out in strange places. Washing lines under ledges and on balconies, rubbish thrown idly on the ground, ubiquitous kiosks selling lottery tickets and phone cards, plastic shoes and umbrellas picking their way through torrents of rushing brown water. It doesn't appear any more cheerful if you're looking out of the steamed-up window of a car, stuck in a line of vehicles trying to pluck up courage to cross the bottomless lake spreading across the street.

It was like that in Nairobi the day Hodhan offered to take us to the various community centres where she worked. The rain made everything take longer so we couldn't drive as far as we wanted. But as she explained when we passed through the exclusive enclave where the president and his ministers reside, the Third World was only on the other side of the valley. As I try to recall the day now, I struggle to describe that journey. I look at my photos, shot in my usual sneaky manner from the inside of the car and dulled even further by the condensation forming on the glass. After years of using a camera to record and express what I see around me, I have become used to a certain way of looking through my lens. Focus and composition are less important to me now than the memory of what it felt like to be there taking that picture at that moment.

I had not really had a conversation with Hodhan until that day. In the taxi we had time to learn more about each other against a soundtrack of Luther Vandross and Marvin Gaye. But I found it a bit confusing as Hodhan seemed to be doing so many things at once. She was only twenty-six years old, a single parent with two kids, aged nine and three, working part-time as a physical therapist, training to be a social worker and doing voluntary work with disabled kids and young girls at risk of going into prostitution. She was also trying to set up her own project near her home. It was not until we had completed our journey that I began to understand how all these aspects of her life came together and to glimpse what kept her going.

Hodhan's family were Somali Soju, originating in the northern part of Kenya which she described as one of the driest and dustiest places on the planet. She was born the third of ten children in Pumwani Majengo, one of Nairobi's first informal settlements populated mainly by Muslims who were connected to the Swahili-speaking coastal community. She married young to a Kikuyu man, much to the distress of her family who told her she was lost. The hostility between the two communities made intermarriage extremely hard for the young couple and they separated after a few years.

I extracted these facts from my notebook, but they do little justice as an introduction to Hodhan and the path she had chosen for herself. As we set out on our journey I had no idea where we would end up. At the age of nineteen she had begun to work as a volunteer social worker, drawn to mentoring girls between the ages of thirteen and eighteen. These were the most crucial years. Primary school had only recently been made free but secondary school required fees. It was easy for teenagers to drop out but almost impossible to make a living without putting themselves at risk. I asked Hodhan what had motivated her in particular, apart from having a hard time herself at that age.

'My aunt was a social worker,' she told me. 'I really admired her and she always said that I could do that work too, if I wanted. I remember her distributing condoms and I used to ask her about it. "The community is you and me," she used to say, "and they want you to help".'

There was a lot to learn on that day and too much to take in. As the taxi drove us from one community project to another Hodhan pointed out new maternity hospitals, affordable housing projects and other glimpses of social reconstruction. She filled us in about the National Aids Control Council, a top priority of the government established well before the current multi-ethnic coalition under President Kibaki. Funds had been made available for urgent intervention in communities like the ones we were visiting, with special attempts to reach youth in their early to mid-teens. When we passed an area of open ground she pointed out the telltale signs of cultivation by people desperate for food as well as space.

The rain eased off as the morning progressed and the streets began to fill with people. The centres we visited were quiet though staff and volunteers were on duty and happy to show us round. We began with a showcase youth club, famous because it grew from a small football team kicking a ball made of plastic bags tied with rubber bands to a league which is now famous throughout the country. MYSA, the Mathare Youth and Sports Association, now hosts a drama club and a well-stocked library opened by none other than the British High Commissioner in 2002.

Later when we visited a less prestigious youth club I noticed our guide asking Hodhan disapprovingly why she had taken us to see MYSA. I wondered if it was because it was high on the 'must-see' list of success stories offered to foreign diplomats touring Nairobi's slums. In this centre their funding for a special project aimed at young women had just been cut. The plan was to teach them skills in hairdressing and bread-making so that they could earn money, and therefore be less tempted to turn to prostitution which was an ever-present danger. This was the field of work that Hodhan cared most passionately about. She was making arrangements to take a group of fifteen girls to Mombasa for a week so that they might share the pressures and problems they experienced in their own families. The most important thing, she said, was to get them out of their environment and help them to see their world differently. When we reached her home she showed us photos of the work she had been involved in, using drama and poetry to reach young women and offer them a chance to change their lives.

I sat on the narrow bench which Hodhan's son used for a bed, drinking the Seven Up which she had sent a neighbour's child to buy for us. Her daughter, who had run to greet her mother as soon as we arrived, had followed us as far as the door and now stood watching us shyly. Just then a baby started to howl next door. As the walls did not quite reach the roof, the sound erupted through the gap, driving home the smallness of the space and proximity of the neighbours. It had not occurred to me that Hodhan might live in one room with her children, with no toilet or running water for their own private use. Her cooking utensils were neatly stacked in one corner and a washing line hung diagonally across the ceiling.

'I've applied for a one-room apartment,' said Hodhan, who was sitting on the double bed that she shared with her daughter. 'Now that my son is getting older we need more space.' As we strolled back to the waiting taxi Hodhan introduced me to the women washing clothes by the standpipe. It would be hard, she said, moving out of the area to somewhere new, where she couldn't ask her friends to look after her kids. Several of the women she introduced me to were working with her to set up a youth project in the neighbourhood mosque and Hodhan was planning to come to Europe to fundraise once she had finished her training.

Glimpsing the unspoken solidarity between Hodhan and her friends, I could imagine what motivated many young women who felt responsible for younger siblings as well as their own children. Rachel, whom I had met the previous day, grew up in Kangemi, a similar area of Nairobi where the rate of HIV infection was between twenty-one and thirty per cent. I remembered her talking about the lack of amenities there and the danger of everyday disasters caused by overcrowding. Although living in close proximity might make it safer for adults to keep an eye on children, the sheer number of people would make it easy to disappear as well.

'I am haunted,' said Rachel, 'by the idea of so much kerosene burning in people's homes, and the lack of emergency services when houses catch fire.'

In Hodhan's home I could see that the walls were constructed out of hard-packed clay and wooden beams, roofed by corrugated iron and joined to each other to make winding passageways. The community had been there for many years, unlike some of the more makeshift dwellings that were made entirely from scrap material.

'My parents separated when I was twelve years old,' Rachel told me, when I asked her about her own story of adolescence, 'and I had to start income-generating activities by cooking food for people and taking it to the factories to sell to support my brothers and sisters. We are five, three girls and two boys and I am the firstborn.'

Being the eldest meant that Rachel has had to suspend her dream to go to university until the youngest has finished school with her help. She managed to complete her own schooling by working her way through college, using her secretarial skills as well as helping out on her grandmother's farm. Their parents remarried, but her mother since died and they have no contact with their father.

'I look for a day when I will be able to join university and continue with my studies if I could get a scholarship,' she told me. 'I know I can make it but what I earn now is just for my brother and sister to educate them.'

Like Hodhan, Rachel was politicised by the environment around her. She could see the chains of unemployment, poverty and insecurity binding young people, especially women, to the effects of drug trafficking, prostitution, early marriages, dropping out of school, teenage pregnancies and violent conflicts between tenants and landlords. 'It's obvious that security is paramount for survival,' she said, 'but community solidarity appeared to be the key to development.' Her response was to try to find the creative resources to address these problems among the very people whose lives were at risk.

'We started with a young ladies' organisation, doing activities together, like playing football. This attracted young men who also wanted to take part, and then some refugees became involved as well. One thing led to another, and we decided to have a national group. A young refugee from Burundi was made chair and we raised money from General Motors, individual donors and other organisations.'

Rachel's group decided to share their vision of peace and solidarity among impoverished and marginalised communities elsewhere in Kenya. In 2004 they had the extraordinary idea of taking a camel train to more remote, rural areas of the country as a way to symbolise the slow, patient work needed to make social change. Camels were used in the dry desert regions but elsewhere they were a novelty which added to the appeal. The first caravan travelled 500 kilometres and was so successful that it has become an annual event.

'It's about starting with grass-root communities,' Rachel told me. 'It's about encouraging young people to see their own potential for making change, and becoming aware of how they can volunteer, and become more involved in taking control of their lives.'

↬

It was in Kenya that I learned about the distinction between the *wananchi* – the ordinary citizens, people who by virtue of belonging to the nation work towards the common good, and the *wenyenchi*, the fat cats, who skim the fat off the land for their individual benefit. But Hodhan had learned from her aunt that the community of *wananchi* was not an abstract concept that was hard to pin down in real life. Community began at home, and there was plenty to do if you wanted to be useful.

This put me in mind of Gosia who had given up her employment as a community worker in north London to do more effective work among new Polish arrivals whose problems she understood. It took me a while to find her mothers' and toddlers' group at the back of the Salvation Army building where they met each week. I was just about to give up and reach for her phone number when I spotted two candidates walking towards me, pushing buggies and speaking Polish. When I had established that we were headed for the same place I walked with them, my mind still back in Kenya where I had left Hodhan and Rachel and the difficulties of describing how I felt about that journey.

Today London was similarly glum, not actually raining but with heavy skies, puddles and sodden rubbish clinging to the sides of the gutter. Occasional red buses offered a cheery aspect to the street scene but otherwise it was business as usual on a damp February morning. I was eager to talk to my new Polish companions about motherhood in a strange city and began to explain my interest in coming to the group. How did they feel about London? I asked them.

'It's very dirty,' replied one.

'Don't you think that everywhere looks depressing in the rain? Surely Poland doesn't look any better on a day like this.'

I was actually thinking of Nairobi. We had just passed a line of small shops that looked uncannily like the ones I had just been visiting in my photos. They were one story high, no more than room-size, and covered with metal shutters resembling corrugated iron. A kiosk the size of a phone box was selling sweets and lottery tickets on the other side of the road, tucked into the end of another building as if to prove that no square metre must be wasted in the interests of scraping a living. Litter was strewn into gaps between buildings and some of it smelled bad.

'No, it's much cleaner in Poland,' she said. 'I don't know why London is so dirty. I think perhaps it's because there are too many nationalities.'

I wondered if this was the kind of thinking that Gosia was trying to address in her attempts to bring new arrivals together and show them the ropes. But at that moment we had arrived at the door of the centre and buggies were converging from all directions.

Inside I was happy to find Dorota, another research student working on Polish migration whom I had met through Michal earlier. She was identifying participants for her research on how individuals approach their citizenship rights, taking names and addresses of volunteers to follow up later. Mothers were an important group for her survey. They were the ones who needed services like health care, childcare and other family support. Dorota was curious about their expectations of life in the UK, and what kinds of resources they drew on as they made new lives away from home.

'They are EU citizens so they are entitled to a whole range of rights here. It's not something that other migrants can afford. I think this is a new situation, and it makes migration into a stratified experience. It's as though some migrants are better and some worse.'

Dorota had come to London for love, although she had found it in Vilnius in Lithuania. She met her Scottish partner there while they were both on holiday and after much discussion they had settled in London, although this had meant leaving a good job at a university in Warsaw. After three years of working as a researcher she went back to being a student and was enjoying her new assignment at the School of Slavonic and East European Studies. I asked her if the gathering of Polish mums and kids was making her homesick. 'No, not at all,' she said, 'and besides, since I left, Poland has come here. We can get any Polish food or drink, and the language is all around us.'

I wandered round the hall with my polystyrene cup of tea, trying not to trip over the two-year-olds playing in the centre of the room. It was a while since I had seen so many of them gathered together and I had forgotten how hilarious they were, and how solemn. What on earth would they want to be when they were old enough to vote? I tried to find mothers to talk to but the language issue was more of a problem than I had thought. I spotted a free chair and went to sit down and introduce myself to a young woman who looked up in a friendly manner and said hello. Her name was Kasia and she spoke English fluently. Although she was holding a baby with bright-blue eyes, it turned out to belong to her sister who was visiting from Kraków.

Kasia told me how long she had been in London, where she

was perfectly content, but there was a sadness about her, too. Her only problem she said was that she hated the NHS and I wondered if this was the cause of her sorrow. She recounted a horrible but familiar experience involving interminable waiting, an uncaring doctor and a sense of an impersonal and inefficient service. This all compared with the treatment she had received in Poland where she went for frequent visits. There, she said, the doctors are much better and take more care, and you still don't have to pay. Even private consultations, she mentioned, are much cheaper than in the UK.

Kasia's sister, Elzbieta, returned to pick up her baby. Her other daughter, a three-year-old with spectacles, came and went as we talked, giving me a stern look when I told her I liked her frames. She understood English, said her mother, but refused to speak it. It took me a bit longer to work out her story as I had assumed she was living here with her children but it turned out that she was only visiting. Kasia translated as her sister was not as fluent, and because their situation was more complicated, I asked if she had had her children in London.

'Oh no, I had them in Poland. I wouldn't like to have them here,' she said, alarmed. 'I've heard bad things about the hospitals here and I wanted to be at home.'

Elzbieta's husband had a reasonable job in London so it meant commuting monthly between two bases. But she preferred living in the flat they had bought together in Kraków.

'Childcare is too expensive here and I can't work now that I have two kids. At least in Poland I live in my own home.'

I asked if she would like to stay here if she could.

'Maybe if we had gone to a small town. There are too many cars in London, too many people and too much rubbish. And I don't like the way that kids are brought up. I don't like the way that if you go to a park here, you see parents playing with their kids. The children are not encouraged to play with each other.'

Another mother, expecting twins, joined our discussion which inevitably returned to the subject of the health service. Kasia translated her story of apparent neglect and vagueness which she took to imply a lack of care. Several times she mentioned her frustration that interpreters had not been on hand to intercede. The consensus remained that 'doctors are better in Poland, they care more'.

I went back to talk to Dorota before the session ended. I found it fascinating, I said, how people are talking about their experiences of the NHS as though it was a uniformly terrible institution.

'Yes, it's interesting,' she replied. 'There's definitely a different approach to health care and pregnancy in Poland. They have different expectations.'

I asked if she could draw any conclusions from her own interviews yet. I was already beginning to form mine.

'No, it's too early. But I do think that it's not helpful to talk in terms of community, as though it was a single bloc. It makes us miss what is new about this phenomenon. I think things are really changing.

'Citizenship is about rights and entitlement but it also suggests obligation towards society. Then there is the question of identity but that's largely a question of choice. People are free to choose whether they feel Polish, for example, or European, and in what situations. It can't be imposed from above. Brussels can't force them to feel more or less European just because they are EU citizens.'

I finally caught up with Gosia as the last members of the group left. I wanted to speak to her alone to get a better sense of what was behind her dynamic energy to keep this work going. She put down the paintbrushes she was washing and made a motion with her hands.

'I believe it is so important to work from the bottom up. We need to encourage these young women to learn English, to give them a sense of confidence to take risks. They need to develop so they can build their country back up again and have a better life.'

Gosia often spoke about the importance of daring to take risks and becoming more open-minded, more tolerant. I thought of this when I was talking to Kasia and her sister earlier. My revelation that I had given birth to my children at home was met with horror. Was I not worried that something might go wrong? I had definitely detected a different approach to medical expertise as well as expectations from the state. But I wanted to ask Gosia about something else.

I had spotted from the UNICEF report on the well-being of children from wealthy countries that Poland's children ended up in the lower-middle of the table. But in many ways their results were harder to assess than those of the UK. They scored highly in education but were on the lowest ranking when it came to poverty and inequality. They were second in terms of low levels of teenage drinking, drugs and sex, but right at the bottom of the unhappiness ladder along with Britain and France. This made me think of the mood I had observed in the film *Ode to Joy*. The musical backdrop of all three stories had been a rap by Peras, one of the characters. One line played over and over again was: 'Don't fuck up your life.' I remembered Michal's response when I said I thought the film was bleak: 'Poles have to import happiness or ways to express it.'

'What do you make of the report,' I asked both Gosia and Dorota before we parted. 'Why do you think that Poland came out at the bottom in the happiness dimension when it did so well in all the other categories?'

Neither of them had noticed this aspect although they had heard about the report.

'I think that parents are very keen on discipline in Poland,' said Gosia. 'They are more inclined to tell their kids, don't do this, don't do that. I don't think they give them enough freedom.'

Dorota was more sceptical. 'I think it has a lot to do with cultural traits,' she said, agreeing with Michal when I told her what he said. 'How do you measure well-being anyway?'

On my way back I ran into my friend Maki. Unlike the young women from Eastern Europe she was visibly identifiable as a foreigner and constantly asked whether she was planning to return 'home' any time soon. She had kindly planted my garlic for me a few weeks earlier as I missed the autumn window when I went on my travels. How did it feel I asked her, knowing that she had not had a garden of her own since she lived in Britain? She is an amazing cook and often talks about the Japanese herbs she grows on her windowsill. I was interested to know whether the act of digging the ground and sowing seeds for next year gave her a different sense of connection to London, and therefore to living in Britain.

'Yes, I so enjoyed the whole process,' she said, 'getting muddy, getting the soil ready for planting. I don't really care about the produce. It's such a metaphor for life, the way things sprout and grow, and wilt if you forget to water them. By the way, have you checked to see if the garlic is coming up? I would feel terrible if nothing happened, like going fishing and coming back with an empty net.'

⌒

A man kicks a ball in Liverpool and a fight breaks out in Nairobi.

'What I hate,' said David from Rwanda, 'is when everyone stands up and cheers at the same time.'

'But that's what you do when you love the game,' retorted Etonde from Cameroon. She was well up on the English Premier League along with half the people in the room.

'I can hear Arsenal from my front door,' I boasted. Actually this was only true when the wind blew in our direction and someone scored a goal. To be truthful I rather resent the way that you can't move around on a match day because of the sheer volume of fans invading the area. I can't honestly say I am a great connoisseur of the game, but I am drawn to the drama of men from different countries going through all those emotions together – and I am talking about the players not the crowds.

But the crowds too had their own history. Once you could stand in the stalls and risk hearing the most vile racist epithets hurled at the few black players, along with bananas and other hostile objects thrown on to the pitch. Two decades of campaigning inside and outside the grounds had almost eliminated racism among the spectators, of an audible kind anyway, and any expression of racist name-calling among players was dealt with harshly, as well. But the way that different nationalities talk about sport can tell you a lot about their collective state of mind. One example was the banning of national flags at Arsenal matches when Greek Cypriot supporters objected to the sight of Turkish Cypriot flags in the stadium. The decision – which was supposed to reflect the multi-national club's commitment to inclusivity – enraged other fans who were told that they could not fly any national flag, including the England flag of St George.

But as well as negotiating local disputes about national identity, sport can also open a window on the way that corporate globalisation divides up the world by determining who watches what and where.

Say 'cricket' in many parts of South Asia and you'll find yourself immersed in a heated debate about the condition of the national team. Even those who are not usually patriotic find themselves taking sides in test matches. It's a familiar pattern replicating geo-political rivalries deeply rooted in history. As the Antiguan cricket hero, Viv Richards, said, 'It's about resistance.' Pakistanis support any team playing against India except England, and Indians do likewise. It provides a strong unifying force, which naturally has divisive aspects as well. In South India football is often more popular than cricket which is increasingly identified with Bollywood celebrity culture centred in the north.

In Kenya, however, the national football team is not worth watching these days. It used to be, when games were shown regularly on KBC, but then various factors combined to turn people's attention away as the quality of playing declined. The availability of European leagues on satellite TV was one, although in practice this meant watching them in bars and hotels at a price. It also means that English football is reduced to about three teams: Arsenal, Liverpool and Manchester United. Chelsea is beginning to appear thanks to the number of African stars like Didier Drogba. The drain – some would say theft – of promising young players from African countries is another reason why national teams fail to keep up with expectations. One exception is Nigeria where football continues to be a unifying force. There is currently a billboard in the London underground advertising the Nigerian national squad. Under the name of each player is the team they represent outside the country, demonstrating that they enjoy the best of both worlds.

With the prospect of the World Cup taking place in South Africa in 2010, a new satellite company has been formed allowing people across the continent to watch in the comfort of their own homes. From the summer of 2007 viewers in at least a dozen countries including Kenya, Uganda, Namibia, Botswana, Zambia, Malawi and Sierra Leone will be able to get fifteen channels from providers such as the BBC, as well as Hollywood movies and local programmes. The price is estimated at around $20 per month, less than the existing service offered by a rival South African company.

When fifty people in Nairobi, Dhaka or Rio club together to pay for one satellite dish to watch the World Cup, they enter into the same time zone regardless of longitude and latitude. There's the love of the game wherever you are but there is always politics whether the rivalries are local or international. When fans move beyond Mexican waves to take out their hatred on others wearing the 'wrong' shirts it can be fatal. Altaf's experience of living near Ibrox Park, the home of Rangers football team, was terrifying. He didn't know that he'd moved into the heart of Scottish Protestant territory, and that football was an established means for expressing old sectarian hatreds against Catholics.

In rugby as in cricket, everyone loves to beat England. Old scores can be settled time and time again by rubbing the noses of the former imperialists in the dirt. On 24 February 2007 a new layer of history was added when the England rugby team was roundly defeated by Ireland in the Six Nations Cup. Thirty burly men wrestled over a ball in the rain at Croke Park, the home of Gaelic football and the site of the massacre which came to be called Bloody Sunday. On 21 November 1920 British paramilitary forces opened fire on the players and the crowd in retaliation for the murder of fourteen British agents in Dublin that morning. This was a defining moment in the Irish War of Independence. For many it echoed the British massacre in India the previous year when forces under General Dyer fired on a crowd in Jallianwala Bagh near Amritsar. In ten minutes 1,600 rounds were fired, and the number of slaughtered never properly counted. Some reports estimated well over 1,000 deaths. Although the incidents were different in character, they were connected by an awareness of the tyranny of British colonialism which fueled nationalist rage at that time.

The death toll in Dublin was considerably lower but the innocence of the victims shocked even the King. Seven were killed outright, including two children and a player, and scores were wounded. The blighted stadium continued to be the home of Gaelic football and a seat of memory of the struggle for Irish independence. Few ever imagined that the sound of the British national anthem would be played there without protest. I came home from the demonstration against Trident just in time to watch the build-up to the event. Commentators outdid themselves in reaching to describe the atmosphere at the ground and the mood of the crowd. The overriding sentiment seemed to be that 'it was time to shake hands and say goodbye to history'. When the first notes of 'God Save the Queen' were played by the brass band, the world turned on its axis and the Irish crowd let it pass without protest. The real victory of that day was the result of the game, a resounding thumping of the England team.

~

The last rays of the afternoon sun catch a bunch of red balloons tied to a dark green bench. A woman sits there with her hands folded in her lap in quiet contemplation. The colour of her sari perfectly matches the worn stone of the building behind her, making her almost invisible next to the gaiety of the balloons. I am still shy of taking a picture even though she's not looking at me, and I am more drawn to the colours than the subject matter. There's another reason why I am lingering at the scene, and it's not because of the sixteenth century architecture rising up in the background. Lodhi Gardens is full of Mughal tombs and monuments and much as I love the style they are all beginning to look a little similar. Just next to the bench there's a birthday picnic taking place with children in party clothes and it's reminding me of when my own kids were small.

I was walking laps of the park in an attempt to recover the use of my legs after being driven everywhere for a week in Dhaka, and it was on my third time past that the party began to break up and drift on to my path. As I looked nostalgically at the balloons a young woman approached me, sent by the fates to waylay me and point me in a new direction.

'Can my son speak to you?' She asked. The boy was about seven and he was immediately overcome by shyness. But at last he managed to whisper, 'What is your name?'

Jayasingh, his mother, introduced herself when the conversation faltered and asked what I was doing in Delhi. When I told her I was talking to young people about national identity her face lit up. 'I work in education,' she told me, 'and I find this all very interesting. I'm based at the National Council of Educational Research and Training at the moment.'

We began to discuss the problems that each country shared and how they could be addressed in schools. Literacy levels had risen consistently: according to the CIA World Factbook it was officially sixty to seventy per cent for men and under fifty per cent for women in 2004. When Britain left India in 1947 the level of literacy was as low as seven per cent in some states. Just then Binay, a friend and fellow party guest, joined us with his own son of a similar age. It turned out that he worked as an educational consultant and had been involved in drafting the country's national curriculum guidelines published the previous year. The document offered a framework for elementary education, he explained, rather than a formal plan leading to standardised tests and measurable learning outcomes. It was produced in consultation with different types of schools, from rural to private right across the country, dealing with every subject including arts and crafts, science, and the importance of the midday meal.

The next day I was still marvelling at this providential encounter. I had decided that the red balloons must have been the magic sign placed there to get my attention. I had quickly followed the trail, using Jayasingh's instructions, and found the national curriculum framework online. Phrases like 'creative spirit' and 'generous joy' leapt off my screen, drawing me into a utopian world where education is inspired by a child's desire to make sense of the world around her. The document begins with a quotation from Rabindranath Tagore which sets the tone for the child-centred recommendations that follow.

> When I was a child I had the freedom to make my own toys out of trifles and create my own games from imagination. In my happiness my playmates had their full share; in fact the complete enjoyment of my games depended on their taking part in them.

Tagore goes on to say that one day this childhood paradise was spoiled. One of his playmates was given an English toy by an adult, and this allowed him to boast of his better fortune and superior possessions. It created discord in the group because he kept the toy to himself and no longer wanted to play with them. The temptation offered by this expensive toy ran counter to the children's creative spirit, devaluing the innocent joy of their imaginative games.

Later I tracked down the source of this extract and found

that it was taken out of context. But Tagore's wisdom worked here to emphasise the precious resource of children's natural curiosity and openness, stressing the importance of encouraging children to question and communicate as well as to express themselves in numerous different ways. It paints a very different picture of the place of children in society than the image that emerges from the UNICEF report on child welfare.

Using Tagore's name also helped to underline the way that education was essential to the national project of creating a peaceful secular, egalitarian and pluralistic society, in line with India's constitution. In all areas of the country, the framework stated, the local community stands to benefit from involvement in children's education. It was crucial in managing environmental resources as well as developing democratic structures on the ground.

I knew I could have access to the document long after I left the country but was troubled by the lack of time to explore how these ideals were being put into practice in India, particularly in rural areas. The closest I was going to get to a village was 30,000 feet overhead. I had seen a bigger picture as I flew to Delhi from Bangladesh, although it was little more than a cursory glance. On my way I had read a newspaper article that explored how far the country had come in living up to Mahatma Gandhi's dreams for the new republic. Written by an Indian diplomat shortly after the centenary of the non-violent resistance movement called satyagraha, initiated by Gandhi in South Africa in 1906, it looked at the nationalist leader's vision for an India freed from colonial rule. In 1931 Gandhi had spoken of a country where all communities would live in perfect harmony, where there would be no room for the curse of untouchability and where women would enjoy the same rights as men.

Today, the writer concluded, India is certainly making progress in various realms, and is considered a potential world power. Yet the intractable problems that Mahatma Gandhi identified in 1931 were still blighting the vast majority of the population, condemning them either to leave the country in search of work or struggle for bare survival at home. Policies to eradicate poverty and caste hierarchy were frequently manipulated by power-hungry politicians and corrupt bureaucrats.

Although India was proud of its rich cultural diversity and secular identity, the fact was that communal clashes were likely to take place at the slightest provocation, and tension and mutual suspicion between the communities was being 'fuelled by religious zealots and political leaders who have their own agenda.'

The only index of development that came near to matching Gandhi's conviction was equality between men and women. 'It is a matter of great satisfaction,' wrote the author, 'that Indian women do enjoy the same rights as men in government, Parliament, civil service, science and technology and every realm of society. This aspect is a saving grace.'

As I pondered over the idealism of the document that Jayasingh had directed me to, I reread this opinion piece with fresh eyes. Articulating the shared goals of a society can be as important for showing up its failures as for measuring its success. This time I was struck by the argument in the last paragraph. The government clearly had a huge responsibility for addressing the problems outlined, but it could not and should not deal with them alone. 'Every organ of society,' it insisted, 'educational institutions, NGOs, civil societies, every organised group or movement, and individuals should play an effective role to create a modern India of the Mahatma's dreams.'

Fine words and noble values help to define the way we all speak about political ideals but as in the UK, the Indian media are generally far more interested in the stories that sell. Earlier that day I had met a journalist from a national paper based in Kolkata. She was an experienced writer with a special interest in issues of social and cultural conflict, but she complained to me that she was continuously being pulled away from serious articles to report on trivia instead. The latest example, she told me, was that she had to rush to a press conference to cover a story about Miss Universe fainting when she made a tour of one of the city's slums. The obsession with celebrity gossip and the superficial glamour of the new Indian wealth was making an impact on how the country was represented to itself as well as how it was seen in the outside world. Our conversation later helped me to put the outcry about Shilpa Shetty and Jade Goody in sharper perspective.

But it was a very different kind of female status symbol

that had become famous over the months before my visit. The media had become fascinated by the case of Imrana, the wife of a rickshaw-puller and part-time brick-kiln worker in northern India, who was raped by her father-in-law when her husband was away at work. The crime had become public knowledge when her brothers beat up the culprit, and the families went to the village *panchayat* (a council of elders) for arbitration. Local religious authorities attending the meeting ruled that Imrana's marriage was now illegal according to the Shariat, and that she should return to her parents' village. The logic of this decision was that as she had sexual relations with the father, even though they were under coercion, she could only be her husband's mother.

I was hoping Urvashi could help me out as I was meeting her the next day. When we sat down to enjoy our Earl Grey tea in the outdoor cafe in Delhi I couldn't wait to ask her about Imrana's case. I partly wanted to understand how the story related to the government's attempts to develop the complicated structure of grass-roots democracy. But I was also aware that the media attention itself was a significant factor in revealing the most sensational issues dividing the country.

As I predicted, Urvashi knew all about the importance of the controversial ruling because it touched the gelignite that so often separates entrenched religious values and civil, secular codes of behaviour. 'Yes, it has indeed been a cause célèbre for women's organisations and NGOs throughout the country,' she said. 'It's also complicated because religious leaders across the country have been pronouncing on Imrana's case, not just the ones in her village. That's how it started. It's basically about the clash that is coming up again and again in India between what are seen as so-called "traditional structures of power" and the actual secular structures of governance, if you like.'

'What has happened to Imrana herself?' I asked, since the poor woman was evidently under a burden no single person could possibly bear.

'There's this strange situation where Imrana's husband is saying he wants her to be with him because they are, after all, married, but the religious leaders are saying she can't go back to the husband. She really has nowhere to go. She can't abandon her children but there is no space for her. How to survive, what will she live on – all those questions need to be answered still. This case makes you question the notion of justice and the kind of power that community leaders have and how they become the only arbiters of morality. The *panchayat* is not necessarily a religious body, it's a village authority structure. It just so happens that they often can be of a higher caste, but not always. Also they have had nothing to say about the father-in-law at all. It all comes back to the woman.'

As we talked further about the implications of this case, Urvashi helped me get my head round the *panchayats*. The sound of the birds singing in Lodhi Gardens next door reminded me of my magical encounter there with Jayasingh the day before. I could see that the emphasis on the role of education in revitalising local democratic participation was a lot more complicated than I had thought from my initial reading of the summarised national curriculum guidelines. The move to bridge the gap between school and community mirrored similar debates in the UK about the importance of citizenship education at an early age, but I was grateful to Urvashi for filling in some of the background details that put Imrana's story into broader perspective.

'The irony is that there has been an attempt in recent years to revive and strengthen the *panchayats*,' she said, pouring us another round of tea. 'There is actually a kind of broader filtering of democracy so that people who are away from the centre and who are in, let's say, rural India can actually have a hand in the structures of power and governance and decisions that are taken about them. Strengthening the *panchayats* has been overall a very good thing, very interesting. Also it is a process which has brought so many women into power. The reservation of one third of elected posts for women has made a huge difference to that structure. Since 1992, we have over a million women in positions of power at that level. So in itself it's a really fantastic and fascinating thing, but there are instances in which it turns upon its head and takes these decisions, which are almost always anti-women.'

Since we were talking about the way that the media grabbed hold of particular events and used them to highlight controversial topics, I asked Urvashi as a matter of interest what she had thought about Jack Straw's infamous outburst against the niqab. The ensuing media frenzy had certainly reached Bangladesh, judging from conversations I had had there before arriving in India.

'I did read about it – I think I don't really know whether I have a clear view as so many things enter the picture. First of all, Straw saying that at that moment was widely understood to be a political move to gain popularity and reinvent himself in a certain way. I don't know how much importance we should give to something like that. On other hand, he is a political leader, having been seen as a friend of Muslims so far, so we can't discount it. Then I think that it's a dangerous argument to make, to say this is not part of our society. What is? Who decides? The veil for women is something that has been forced on them even though a small number may voluntarily take it up. But by and large women have been pushed into being veiled and in an ideal situation you want a way for them to be able to emerge out of this which is not another coercion – not another decision taken on their behalf by someone else for another reason. Like Jack Straw saying, "We've decided what's good for you…"'

✎

'So, Altaf, do you think that Britain has a chance to show the rest of the world how a diverse society can function?' I asked him as we walked back over the river. We had met in the Tate Modern as he was in London for a few days and I was enjoying hearing more about his adventures in Sheffield. I had a soft spot for him from the start because of the way he spoke about his mother when I met him in Mumbai. 'I always carry a picture of her,' he said, 'although photographs are forbidden in my household and my mother refuses to have hers taken. This is the only one that exists, as far as I know.'

'My family practices an Indian version of Wahabism, called the Deobandi sect,' he told me, soon after we first met.

This immediately rang a bell. It was the Deobandi school that pronounced on Imrana's case, declaring a fatwa that she should leave her husband and return to her parents. Altaf explained that a fatwa would be issued in relation to religious affairs and codes of conduct in daily life, if you asked for it. Whether you chose to practice it or not, that was an individual's prerogative. But a fatwa in India, or in the global context, is almost looked on as a final word of God.

'There's a lot of religious indoctrination, and every decision has to be based on Islamic principles,' Altaf continued. 'We never had a TV in the house, for example. You can imagine how jaws dropped when I said I wanted to work in the media. But I am making slow inroads into the way my family think, though. They have the Internet at home now. My mother listens to BBC Urdu online. I feel so proud of her.'

Altaf was encouraged to work in the media by an uncle who was a heart surgeon in the United States. He belonged to the American Federation of Muslims of Indian Origin, an expatriate organisation that raised funds specifically to address poverty and deprivation among Indian Muslims. The majority of their support went to educational projects, and Altaf had been inspired by his uncle's philanthropic work in the villages in Gujarat not far from his family home.

'Though my Islamic identity is the core of who I am and that will not change, I have managed to integrate into the wider world with greater acceptance of what "the other" means. But I always wanted to break from the ordinary scheme of things, explore new ideas and I am always up for a new adventure,' he had told me. 'And at twenty-six, I am still exploring my path, while most of my cousins are contemplating marriage or are already married.'

That was how he ended up near Glasgow hiding from drunken football supporters on Saturday afternoons. He went to work with an organisation called Global Exchange, running a YMCA for asylum seekers. Since then he had returned to the UK for another period of voluntary work. He was enjoying being outside India and making plans about what to do next.

When I threw him the trick question about Britain's ability to cope with diversity, he was ready with a perceptive answer.

'Yes, I do think so,' he began, 'I've found that it's mainly a problem of ignorance here. But if you explain something to people they seem to accept it. As an Indian, though,' he added, 'I would happily live in London, but I am not sure I could live anywhere else in the country.'

Most people find out what nationality means to them by leaving their country of citizenship and becoming a foreigner somewhere else. Even Reuben, who had talked to me about his sense of global citizenship, was prepared to admit that he had discovered on a trip to Bulgaria how British he really was. Before that he placed his intellectual development within an explicitly Jewish but secular, radical tradition.

'I'm probably more British than I'd like to be. I know there's a disjuncture between how I'd like to be seen and how others see me. Britishness structures my life opportunities – it becomes clear when you travel.'

Gordon Brown, one of the main cheerleaders for Britishness as a strategy to unite the country, has consistently placed a great emphasis on what he calls British youth national community service. He believes that young people should be encouraged, and supported financially if necessary, to do community work as part of their preparation for adult life. At times the phrase 'national service' sounds dangerously like compulsory community work, the very opposite of volunteering, in fact, which suggests motives of unselfishness and giving that are supposed to make it attractive. But the idea that young people should express their commitment to their country of citizenship by donating their labour for free, either in the country or in far-flung communities elsewhere, was something that needed to be discussed. I asked Jacob and Reuben about this, too.

Although the twins were not identical and they studied different subjects, they took care to listen to each other's point of view and had clearly developed similar outlooks. It was quite tricky afterwards remembering who had said what. They were both quite disdainful of the idea that defining Britishness was going to be a panacea for the country's problems, particularly if it demanded loyalty to the nation.

'For those of us who don't believe in borders we have a large problem with saying, "I believe in this country,"' said Jacob. 'I think it's more important that people feel loyalty to fellow citizens of the world.'

They both started laughing at the prospect of buying things that taste British, something that they had heard Tory leader David Cameron talking about on the radio. I wondered what they'd make of the British Shoppe.

'But if your country is going to the dogs,' I ventured, 'do you have responsibility to do something about that?'

'Yes,' said Reuben thoughtfully.

'In the sense that we do have a material stake here,' added Jacob, 'and I suppose we have influence and agency here though we believe it's divided up arbitrarily.'

'Basically we do our activism where it works, that's a reflection on political reality.'

We had gone on to talk about what was happening in east London where the BNP had done so well in the local elections a few months earlier. They told me about a demonstration they had been on recently to counter the BNP rally which underlined their commitment to working for justice at home as well as in the stratosphere of anti-globalisation politics. I was beginning to see the connection. Having started off with an idea that young people in Britain were a bit too quick to claim global citizenship in a world which was virtually their oyster, I could see that there were ways in which a growing number, like the twins, understood that their rights, entitlements and responsibilities came down to one course of action: *Do what works*. But the crucial element that gave them their sense of agency was an ability to analyse the links between power and oppression.

For the young activists I had been fortunate to meet, whether in the UK or in each country I visited, the idea of community service is not an abstract notion that they decided to fit in between school and university. Their life experience, whether as members of minorities or through difficult material circumstances, has given them added incentive to use their influence and agency where they feel it matters most. At the same time they are able to operate within a much more extensive world of transnational politics that involves networking, fundraising, information gathering and dialogue with like-minded people. The line between local and global citizenship is imaginary but no less significant because of that.

In any case, for young Brits it has become obligatory at least to consider taking a year off between school and university, even if the idea of doing voluntary work does not appeal. Students are encouraged to reflect on their readiness to enter university after years of schooling, to think of their self-development if not their CVs and future employment prospects. Foreign travel is promoted as an end in itself, but the opportunity to work as a volunteer is advertised as a guaranteed way to give something to others less fortunate and to immerse oneself in local cultures at the same time.

The shelves of guidebooks at any decent bookshop are only one indication of the way that tourism has opened up the world to younger generations of travellers. There is a dedicated industry in protective equipment for the individual explorer ready to cope with polluted water, mosquitoes, starvation, and all forms of physical discomfort. Racks and racks offer competing brands of document holders, neck pillows, sleeping sacks, first-aid kits, water bottles and whistles, all to be carried in state-of-the-art backpacks and ingenious safety pockets. Most of these items are indeed valuable and often essential, but they also underline the mental adjustment necessary before embarking on a journey to countries outside Europe.

However, as Shamser pointed out, for many people the idea of a gap-year expedition is a passport to enjoy the same kind of hedonistic lifestyles they might practice at home, only in warmer and more exotic surroundings. Not all are motivated by altruism or the desire to immerse themselves in different cultures. Many of the organisations that cater for would-be volunteers seeking placements in different parts of the world issue guidelines about how not to be a cultural conquistador, for example. But they are relatively powerless to curb the racist or purely ignorant attitudes that travellers from wealthy countries often bring with them. In some locations, the sheer numbers of American and European itinerants have led to an alternative economy of 'Westernised' bars, restaurants and hostels. This means that they have relatively little contact with local people outside their assignment, although their presence can benefit the tourist economy and their record of foreign service can still look good on a CV.

Regardless of how well or badly the volunteers behave, the interactions with their host families or the institutions where they work inevitably reflect on their countries of origin. In this sense they can act as ambassadors. It's important to remember too that they are not the only ones changed by inter-cultural encounters. Hodhan had been impressed by two young Danish women who had come to stay in her community for a few weeks. They had gone to great lengths to share the same conditions as everyone else, even to the extent of refusing to wear sunscreen.

I had many talks with Farhana about volunteering abroad as her own experience had had a profound effect on her career. She studied marketing at university and planned to become a Marketing Director by the age of thirty, but after her sister came home from a two-week trip to Palestine in June 2002, and told her about the terrible injustices she had seen, Farhana was inspired to travel back there with her to learn more about life in the West Bank and the Gaza Strip.

After seeing the situation for herself, Farhana decided to return as a volunteer. The following summer she joined an Israeli/Palestinian peace group called ICAHD (Israeli Committee Against House Demolitions) whose main task is rebuilding family homes that have been demolished by Israeli security forces. There was one incident that caused her to question her own values and priorities.

'We were visiting a family whose house happened to be in the way of the Israeli security wall,' she told me. 'The army wanted to demolish it but the peace groups had managed to keep them away for several weeks. The family had been given an ultimatum on that day but they insisted on cooking us lunch while we all sat down and listened to stories about what they had been though. After about ten minutes the soldiers arrived and told us: "We'll arrest you if you don't leave." We all decided to leave because we didn't want to get the family into trouble. Just as they finished cooking the food, the husband was dragged away. But the women passed us food over the fence that marked the border. They still gave us lunch! They passed us cucumbers with a knife saying, "We are sorry that we haven't made any salad." This made me realise that simple things are important. And it made me want to do different things with my life rather than work on my own career.'

⤲

'You know, there's a beautiful cathedral in Blackburn,' said Amar, 'but you'll rarely find Muslims going in even to have a look.' I had tracked him down on his BlackBerry to ask him how he had got on in Northern Ireland after taking a party of young people there under the auspices of an inter-faith project.

'When we went to Belfast we took the group to a lovely old monastery and the Muslims lit candles along with everyone else. If they did that in Blackburn they'd be accused of converting.'

You don't have to go very far to experience the benefits of being in a difference environment where your identity can mean something very different. Amar was struck by the example of a young Protestant from Northern Ireland who refused to be seen engaging with Catholics on his home patch.

'When we visited a Catholic project, even though he was well-disposed to them he made sure to stand physically with us. He said that if word went round that he was soft on Catholics he would get retribution. But when he came to Blackburn on a return visit he had many opportunities to talk to Catholics and there were no problems at all. It's like you can be more honest when you are outside your community.'

Amar was busy developing plans to make the most of the exchange on a more sustainable basis. The aim was to train the small number of participants to act as mentors so that they could work with groups of young people over the age of sixteen. He was delighted that two local radio stations had jointly commissioned a documentary that would follow the project over a period of twelve months. It was an opportunity to learn how neglected topics like political literacy and basic citizenship might be taught outside the classroom among young adults often bequeathed a harsh and divided world by their parents' generation.

Citizenship education has been included in the English school curriculum for some time now, but in practice it largely depends on teachers' availability and space in the time table. In Northern Ireland, however, it has been developed as an urgent strategy to bring divided communities together. The results are being closely observed in England and Wales, as well as in Scotland where the national curriculum is being comprehensively reviewed.

'Citizenship here is different from England,' said Anne-Marie Poyner, when I reached her by phone. 'It's not about voting here, but about multiple identities.'

Anne-Marie is based at a teachers' centre in Derry where she writes materials for teaching diversity and inclusiveness to eleven-year-olds. She explained some of the background details that led to the programme.

'In Northern Ireland during the Troubles, teachers saw schools as an oasis of calm. The thinking was in both communities that a child should be able to get away from horrible things, like if a brother was taken in the night or there was a raid on their homes. These things were not discussed or debated in school.'

A survey in Northern Ireland found that teachers were avoiding issues of sectarianism and racism locally because they didn't feel able to deal with it. Educational reform had tried to address the legacy of sectarianism but it wasn't until recently that schools began to introduce the topic of Local and Global Citizenship as a compulsory subject.

'We started by looking at group identity rather than personal identity,' said Anne-Marie, 'presenting children with the idea that behaviour can change according to the group they're in.'

'What sort of things did you do?' I asked.

'We used picture cards, for example, using symbols associated with nationalists and Protestants. Kids regrouped them in clusters but not always along predictable sectarian lines. One card, for instance, had a picture of the big drum used in Orange marches, and another showed the boron, the small drum used in Irish traditional music. The kids would put them together as musical instruments, rather than immediately seeing them as symbols belonging to opposing communities.'

But as Anne-Marie stressed, the project of integrating schools was not just a problem of division between the two communities. The question of racism and the exclusion of other categories of people was a central issue to be addressed in schools, raising issues for teachers who were not trained in dealing with conflict.

'It's important to look at groups of people who are marginalised, like the travelling community. They have been part of Ireland for as long as anyone can remember. Also kids from the Philippines. They tend to be spotlighted. I know of one case where the teacher was doing something on Travellers and asked kids what associations they had. Of course they were all negative and racist and it was distressing for the one Traveller kid, and the teacher didn't know how to deal with this. There's a problem training teachers and giving them time to think about their own identities. It's also hard to get them to see that tokenism has to be avoided. It's not about celebrating Polish festivals to make one Polish kid fit in.'

One of the government's immediate responses to the 7 July bomb attacks in London was to commission an investigation into the teaching of British values in schools. When the report on Diversity and Citizenship was published it began with a quote from Mahatma Gandhi. 'The ability to reach unity in diversity will be the beauty and the test of our civilisation,' he said, although he was probably not thinking about the British national curriculum at the time.

Sir Keith Ajegbo, who led the review, explained how this related to schools. 'We passionately believe that it is the duty of all schools to address issues of "how we live together" and "dealing with difference", however controversial and difficult they might sometimes seem.' He was a former head teacher at a successful south London school, one of the three examples that Pratap had used in his documentary on multilingual education.

One of the striking conclusions that Sir Keith Ajegbo had stressed in his report was the potential neglect of white British children in the interests of reaching out to minorities:

'Nor is there any advantage in creating confidence in minority ethnic pupils if it leaves white pupils feeling disenfranchised and resentful,' he wrote. 'Many indigenous white pupils have negative perceptions of their own identity. White children in areas where the ethnic composition is mixed can often suffer labelling and discrimination. They can feel beleaguered and marginalised, finding their own identities under threat as much as minority ethnic children might not have theirs recognised.'

Anne-Marie was confident that there were ways to bring everyone into the debates about citizenship in Northern Ireland.

'We said to the schools, you can always start with global issues and move into local ones. Get kids to look at global issues that are contentious and make links. In Enniskillen one chap showed films that he had made in Nepal and Kenya, based on the lives of young people. They were looking at issues they might share here. He also made a documentary about two Polish families in Enniskillen and traced where they had come from.'

She continued: 'There was one positive experience that really stands out. A chap came from Israel, who had worked with Palestinian and Israeli peace groups. He told the kids from both communities: "Bring in something from home that is important in your families. Tell a story about it." The exercise included parents and grandparents. The kids brought things in like family Bibles, symbols that might normally be contentious because they were related to religion. It was a lovely way to talk about things that would normally be divisive. And it was a way to include everyone. If you are hearing a Filipino child's story, why not ask everybody?'

I heard a clock strike six as I wove my way down through the city streets towards Trafalgar Square. It was the evening of 21 March, the first day of spring, and four years and a day after the bombs began to fall over Baghdad.

That day in 2003 had seen plenty of global protests as well, but they were mixed with rage and sorrow rather than the optimism of the previous month. In New York it had rained ceaselessly, and we had got drenched as we stood helplessly among hundreds of tearful people uncertain how to register their fury or contain their shame.

As I walked, head down to avoid the bitter wind that swept round the corners of narrow side streets, I remembered what Martin had said about teaching citizenship in schools.

'The difficulty with politicians,' he had told me, 'when they talk about teaching citizenship, or using history to teach Britishness, is that they are trying to get people to think like they do. The reality of Britishness is that it is not a single narrative, a single view of who we are.'

I had agreed heartily with him at the time, but since then the public debates about national identity have become even more dominated by experts eager to offer their authoritative views on belonging, integration and social cohesion. The government was said to be drafting a 'core script' of British values that could be taught alongside citizenship. Meanwhile more statistics were appearing that showed schools were failing to equip students with basic literacy skills, let alone a grounding in ethical behaviour.

I had heard someone from the army recruiting office say that they were seeing applicants aged twenty with the reading age of a five-year-old. It was only when they were encouraged to read the wording on their weapons, he said, that they could see the point of making the effort.

Nor is this the legacy of a previous decade of poor standards. In some areas of the country a high proportion of children are leaving primary schools every year without basic skills. According to *The Scotsman*, a report in 2005 showed that the worst performing area in Britain was Glasgow where in half of the primary schools, most children leave without reaching level D in reading and writing. In a third of the city's schools, most pupils were failing to reach basic levels of numeracy.

It bothered me too that so many of the educational reforms were aimed at eleven- to fourteen-year-olds. This coincides with adolescence, the difficult passage from childhood to the start of more independent teenage years. In the wealthier countries, among all classes, this is the age when children are targeted as consumers, made to feel insecure about their looks, their bodies, their tastes and their friendships. It is the age when the concept of loyalty is tested to the core, when loneliness and confusion can take root in a child's growing consciousness. Education can offer the solution to these growing pains, but can also become the source of individual and societal problems. Schools reflect social, economic and cultural divisions: segregation, poverty, wealth, sectarianism, privilege, despair. However exceptional the school, the students still go back to their families at the end of the day, but even with a supportive home life, a child at this age can be unsettled by the stress of peer-group conflict and uncaring teachers.

I had almost reached my destination and was waiting to cross the street by the National Portrait Gallery on Charing Cross Road. I could see a small number of women, all dressed in black, standing silently around the base of Edith Cavell's statue. Some held placards, while others stared straight ahead. As I walked over to join them I suddenly became mindful of the millions of people who had gathered in this square mile over previous centuries, sometimes in silence but more often in loud and angry revolt against all manner of injustice. I had read that the army barracks were once stationed next to Trafalgar Square, behind the National Portrait Gallery, so that they could be on hand to quell angry crowds. In the distance I could see South Africa House which had seen years of demonstrations outside in solidarity with the global movement against apartheid. I felt overwhelmed by the thought of all the children, women and men who had lost parents, partners, friends, sons and daughters in many parts of the world, making their way to the square to bear witness to crimes against humanity, clamouring for justice and solidarity.

The monument to Edith Cavell just a little north of the square has become a favoured place for anti-war protestors because of the inscription on the base of the statue. *Patriotism is not enough. I must have no hatred or bitterness for anyone.* I found it slightly ironic that I had learned about her in infant school, along with Florence Nightingale, Grace Darling and other British heroines who had stood for something, and who, like Cavell, had been prepared to die for their beliefs. I remembered a banner I had seen in an anti-globalisation march in New York: 'Sharing: a value we learned in kindergarten.' And now a government that had taken the country to war on the basis of a lie was advocating the teaching of British values in schools, values that they defined such as Liberty, Fair Play and Equality of Opportunity.

The excerpt from Tagore's story that I had read in the Indian national curriculum guidelines was not really about children at all. It was taken from a lecture he had given in China in 1924 called Civilisation and Progress. In his meditation on the progress that mankind had made in different parts of the world he recounted something he had read in the American journal, *The Nation*.

A group of British airmen was bombing a rural area of Afghanistan during the Anglo-Afghan War in 1919 when one plane crash-landed in the middle of a village. The crew escaped unhurt only to find themselves surrounded by a party of old women armed with knives. To cut the story short, the visitors were treated with customary hospitality, even though their compatriots were still dropping bombs over the village, until they could be guided to safety, disguised as villagers. Tagore used this verified account to speculate on the human costs borne by the Europeans who felt it necessary to proclaim their superiority by mechanical warfare, in contrast with the 'uncivilised' peoples whom they were attacking.

> Those people who went to bomb the Mahsud villages measured their civilisation by the perfect effectiveness of their instruments which were their latest scientific toys. So strongly do they realise the value of these things that they are ready to tax to the utmost limit of endurance their own people, as well as those others who may occasionally have the chance to taste in their own persons the deadly perfection of these machines.

Tagore himself had attended school in London where his grandfather was buried, as I was informed in Kolkata. In 1915 he was awarded a knighthood from the British government which he subsequently returned in protest at its policies in India and elsewhere. His lecture, written when aerial bombing was a new phenomenon, reminded me of the opening words of 'The Lion and the Unicorn', George Orwell's famous essay on English national identity: 'As I write highly civilised human beings are flying overhead, trying to kill me.' Orwell's plea for a socialist revolution that recognised the positive benefits of patriotism was published in 1941, the year that Tagore died. It was composed after the Battle of Britain had taken place but before the process of decolonisation was truly underway. The impetus for writing was the prospect that England, like other European countries, might follow a totalitarian path in response to Hitler's onslaught. In response he argued for an intelligent patriotism that swept away all that was anachronistic and unequal in favour of an egalitarian England – by which he admitted he meant Great Britain as a whole – that remained true to itself.

'By revolution,' he wrote, 'we become more ourselves, not less. There is no question of stopping short, striking a compromise, salvaging "democracy", standing still. Nothing ever stands still. We must add to our heritage or lose it, we must grow greater or grow less, we must go forward or backward.'

The unseasonably cold wind of that early spring day tugged

and pulled at the placards held up for passers-by. Four years ago I had joined a small group of American students who had met in a public place to scream their fury at what was happening in their name in Iraq. It was eerie to hear such a sound emanating from our own safe bodies, but at the time it felt like an utterly human response to a cataclysm taking place in another part of the world. Orwell's words have retained their power to stir despite the world having moved on inexorably since he wrote them. The question remains, who are the 'we', whose is the 'our' and for what kind of revolution must a new generation of global citizens make their plans?

Acknowledgements

This book is the result of an extraordinary journey. In the course of my research I encountered many remarkable individuals whose words, ideas and insights have shaped the outcome. It is impossible to thank everyone by name, but every individual who took part in our discussions should know that their contribution added to the mix and enriched the whole. I hope that this work is itself an acknowledgement of the positive vibes of creativity, intelligence and resistance that course throughout our beleaguered planet.

First and foremost, however, my thanks go to Nick Wadham-Smith who gave me the opportunity to carry out this project and the freedom to develop it in my own way. The same goes for the rest of team: Bob Ness, Christine Melia, Martin Rose, and especially Ginny Marriott and Farhana Ahmad, who accompanied me on different parts of the trip and encouraged me throughout. Thanks also to the British Council staff in Dhaka, Chittagong, New Delhi, Kolkata, Mumbai, Karachi, Lahore, Islamabad, Dublin, Nairobi and Warsaw for their brilliant planning and tireless organising.

I could not have managed this book without the energy and wisdom of particular individuals I met along the way. I want to express my gratitude to Leyla Hussein, Shamser Sinha and Michal Garapich who gave freely of their time and expertise and who each supplied moments of clarity that unlocked difficult questions. Gratitude and respect also go to Amar Abass, Altaf Mohammed Abid, Abdia Hodhan Hussein, Gosia Shannon, Sabreena Ahmad, Mohammed Sheikh Atif, Nazmun Choudhury, Madhumita Bhattacharyya, Elaine Nesbitt, Mariam Zaidi, Bano Murtuja, Roxana Buitrago, Dorota Osipovic, Peray Ahmet, Felicity Tyson, Huda Jawad, Muhamed Mesic, Helen Tse, Omar Said Abasheikh, Rachel Kung'u, Parselelo Kantai, Jacob Bard-Rosenberg, Reuben Bard-Rosenberg. Thanks to Suja Khaled for his vision and for providing the setting for conviviality. Conversations with Bokani Tshidzu, Rajay Naik, Christina Papatheodorou, Joyce Nyairo, Omar El-Khairi, George Kolankiewicz, Nelson Kraybill, Anne-Marie Poynor,

Piaras Jackson, Richard Cull, Robert Macintosh, Erik Salholm, Tareque Masud, Catherine Masud, Monabina Gupta, Gillian Hamill, Colette Kinsella, Claire Cromie and Ian Walsh were all appreciated. Special thanks to Maki Kimura for the garlic which grew in abundance.

I am indebted to Mahmud who gave up his time to show me around Dhaka and set my feet on the ground. I am grateful to Shafayatul, Nazma, and Ashraf for their unforgettable hospitality. Sara Hossain and Farah Kabir provided warmth and solidarity at an early, critical time. Thanks to Nazzina Mohsin and Riffat Jahan for making things happen despite the curfews and emergencies; to Mariya Afzal for kindness and care, and to Rukhsana Ashfaq for the shopping trip. I appreciated the hospitality of Les Dangerfield, June Rollinson, Kalpana Das, on the road, and especially the convivial evening at Kewpies in Kolkata. Special thanks to Sujarta Sen and Samarjit Guha for advice and personal commitment to this project and for setting things up in India. Meeting Phase Five in Mumbai was an inspiration, and thanks to Manjula Rao for bringing them in.

Thanks to Carrie Ndoka and Eva Kiiru for their brilliant powers of organisation and to Binyavanga Wainaina and Yvonne Owuor for running the show, and for a warm congenial evening at The Cedars. James Muriuki and Myriam provided tea and restorative hospitality. Zarina Patel, Zahed Rajan, Urvashi Butalia and Martin Spafford went out of their way to make time to talk, and their experience and political insights were invaluable. It was a pleasure to work with Pratap Rughani and I am indebted to him for sharing his creativity and for his genius at putting people at their ease.

I am indebted to old friends Georgie Wemyss, Max Farrar, Patrick Wright, Roger Hewitt and Manzu Islam for insights, contacts and advice.

Sheila Kazcmarek, Gritli Rabin, Eugenia Barton, Gail Friedland, Yola Maryanska, Christine Schloss, Hazel Carby, Wendy Pamer and Linda Anderson kept the faith in CT. Thanks to Gary Younge for professional tips and the example of his succinct writing style.

Les Back, Vikki Bell, Tricia Bohn, Helen Crowley, Hoda Elsadda, Catherine Hall, Stuart Hall, Cora Kaplan, Jill Lewis, Angela McRobbie, Sarah Nuttall, Bridget Orr, Emmanuel

Raymundo, Flemming Rogilds, Mandy Rose, Greta Slobin, Mark Slobin, Inger Sjoerslev, Rebecca Smith, Ed Vulliamy and Honor Ware all encouraged, inquired, inspired and understood from their different perspectives. My mother, Elizabeth Ware, waited patiently for me to finish.

After moving between different countries over the past decade I am finally figuring out how to think about home. They say that once you've left you can never come back, but that's not the whole story. Travelling back and forth across the Atlantic I learned with and from my family to comprehend how identifications work across, against, beyond, within and in spite of national borders. While I was writing this book, Marcus Gilroy Ware made time to read sections and offer indispensable advice. Cora Gilroy Ware set high literary standards and gave me courage. Paul Gilroy was always there, keeping the tea flowing and the fire burning.

Bibliography

Books

Akhtar, Shaheen, *The Search* translated by Ella Datta, New Delhi: Zubaan, 2007.

Alagiah, George, *A Home from Home: From Immigrant Boy to English Man*, London: Little, Brown, 2006.

Anand, Mulk Raj, *The Road*, New Delhi: Sterling Publishers, 1974.

Anderson, David, *Histories of the Hanged: Britain's Dirty War in Kenya and the End of Empire*, London: Weidenfield & Nicolson, 2004

Bayly, Christopher & Tim Harper, *Forgotten Armies: Britain's Asian Empire & the War With Japan*, London, Penguin, 2005.

Beetham, David, *Transport and Turbans: A Comparative Study in Local Politics*, London: Oxford University Press, 1970

Bengelsdorf, Carollee, Margaret Cerullo, & Yogesh Chandrani, Eds. *The Selected Writings of Eqbal Ahmad*, New York: Columbia, 2006.

Bragg, Billy, *The Progressive Patriot: A Search for Belonging*, London: Bantam Press, 2006.

Butalia, Urvashi, *The Other Side of Silence: Voices from the Partition of India*, London: Hurst & Co. 2000.

Butalia, Urvashi, Ed., *A Sense of the Past: Women's Writings on Partition*, New Delhi: Zubaan, 2007.

Dalrymple, William, *The Last Mughal: The Fall of a Dynasty, Delhi, 1857*, London: Bloomsbury, 2006.

Danziger, Nick, *Danziger's Britain: A Journey to the Edge*, London: Flamingo, 1997.

Das, Bina, *Bina Das: A Memoir*, translated by Dhira Dhar. New Delhi: Zubaan, 2007.

Davis, Mike, *Planet of Slums*, London: Verso, 2006.

Elkins. Caroline, *Imperial Reckonings: The Untold Story of Britain's Gulag in Kenya*, New York: Henry Holt, 2005.

Gilroy, Paul, *After Empire: Multiculture or Melancholia?* London: Routledge, 2004.

Gross, Jan T., *Neighbours: The Destruction of the Jewish*

Community in Jedwabne, Poland Princeton: University of Princeton Press, 2001.

Gross, Jan T., *Fear: Anti-Semitism in Poland After Auschwitz. An Essay in Historical Interpretation,* New York: Random House, 2006.

Hewitt, Roger, *White Backlash and the Politics of Multiculturalism,* Cambridge: Cambridge University Press, 2005.

International Bank for Reconstruction and Development, *Just Like the Other Kids,* Pakistan: Oxford University Press, 2006.

Mahmud, *Our World: Women in Bangladesh,* Dhaka: Map/ Matri Productions, 2005.

Islam, Manzu, *Burrow,* Leeds: Peepal Tree, 2004.

Jones, John P., *India: Its Life and Thought,* New York: Macmillan, 1908.

Koch, Connie, Ed., *2/15 The Day the World Said No to War,* New York: Hello (NYC) 2003.

Lentin, Ronit and Robbie McVeigh, *After Optimism? Ireland, Racism and Globalisation,* Dublin: Metro Éireann Publications, 2006.

Malkani, Gautam, *Londonstani,* London: Fourth Estate, 2006.

Mutah,Wahome, *How to Be a Kenyan,* Nairobi: Kenway Publications, 2002.

Muter, Mrs, *My Recollection of the Sepoy Revolt,* London: John Long Ltd, 1911.

Narrain, Arvind & Gautam Bhan, Eds, *Because I Have a Voice: Queer Politics in India,* New Delhi: Yoda Press, 2005.

Nasson, Bill, *Britannia's Empire: Making a British World,* Stroud: Tempus, 2004.

Newsinger, John, *The Blood Never Dried: A People's History of the British Empire,* London: Bookmarks Publications, 2006.

Nunneley, John, *Tales From the King's African Rifles,* London: Cassell & Co. 2000.

Nussbaum, Martha C., *For Love of Country? In a New Democracy Forum on the Limits of Patriotism,* Boston: Beacon Press, 2002.

Omar, Rageh, *Only Half of Me: Being a Muslim in Britain,* London, Viking, 2006.

Orwell, George, *The Collected Essays, Journalism and letters: Volume 2*, London: Penguin, 1970.

Patel, Zarina, *Alibhai Mulla Jeevanjee*, East Lansing: Michigan State University Press, 2002.

Patel, Zarina, *Jeevanjee, Rebel of the Empire*, Nairobi: Sasa Sema Publications, 2002.

Patel, Zarina, *Unquiet: The Life and Times of Makhan Singh*, Nairobi: Zand Graphics, 2002.

Pillai, Paramesvara G., *London and Paris through Indian Spectacles*, Madras: Vaijayanti Press, 1897.

Runnymede Trust, The, *The Future of Multi-Ethnic Britain: The Parekh Report*, London: Profile Books, 2000.

Sardar, Ziauddin, *Desperately Seeking Paradise: Journeys of a Sceptical Muslim*, London: Granta Books, 2004.

Schivelbusch, Wolfgang, *The Culture of Defeat: On National Trauma, Mourning, and Recovery*, London: Granta Books, 2003.

Sen, Amartya, *The Argumentative Indian: Writings on Indian Culture, History and Identity*, London: Penguin, 2005.

Sen, Amartya, *Identity and Violence: The Illusion of Destiny*, London: Penguin, 2006.

Stanley, Peter, *British Military Culture in India 1825-1875*, London: Hurst & Co., 1998.

Tagore, Rabindranath, *Selected Short Stories*, London: Penguin, 2005.

Tse, Helen, *Sweet Mandarin: the courageous true story of three generations of Chinese women and their journey from East to West*, Ebury Press, 2007.

Wainaina, Binyavanga, 'How to Write About Africa' in *The View From Africa*, Granta 92, winter 2005.

Wild, Anthony, *The East India Company: Trade and Conquest from 1600*, New York: Lyons Press, 2000.

Woolf, Virginia, *Three Guineas*, Oxford: Oxford UP, 1992.

X, Malcolm, *The Autobiography of Malcolm X*, London: Penguin, 2001.

Younge, Gary, *No Place Like Home: A Black Briton's Journey Through the American South*, London: Picador, 1999.

Younge, Gary, *Stranger in a Strange Land: Encounters in the Disunited States* New York: The Guardian, 2006.

Journals
Kwani?: Nairobi, Kenya.
Awaaz: Voices from the South Asian Diaspora.

British Council Publications
Britain & Ireland: Lives Entwined, British Council Ireland, 2005.
Britain & Ireland: Lives Entwined II, British Council Ireland, 2006.
Maps and Metaphors: Writings by Young Writers from Bangladesh and United Kingdom, Dhaka: British Council, 2006.

Online resources
http://www.awaazsaw.org/
http://bulletsandhoney.blogspot.com/
http://www.citizenshipfoundation.org.uk/
http://www.counterpoint-online.org/
http://www.drishtipat.org/
http://londynek.net/
http://www.thinkersroom.com/blog/
http://www.peace-caravan.org/
http://www.phasefive.org/
http://www.youthactionnetwork.org.uk/

Index

Kimathi, Dedan, 126, 136
Kolkata, 59, 117, 124
Kwani?, 169, 170, 174

Lahore, 38, 39, 151
Language, 15, 174
    and mobile phones, 173
    as cultural barrier, 40
    and cultural difference, 60
    bilingual education, 28
Lawrence, Stephen, 100
Leeds, 38
Leyton, 7, 98, 133
Leytonstone, 7
Literacy
    in British schools, 225
    in India, 209
Live Aid, 136, 169
Live8, 193
Liverpool dockers' strike, 183
London, 4, 147, 216
    surveillance in, 147
London bombings, 28, 66, 88, 112, 167, 223
London School of Economics, 120, 155
Londonstani. See Malkani, Gautam
loneliness, 149
Ludmer, Maurice, 95

McDonald's, 43
Make Poverty History, 192
Malaysia, 85
Malcolm X, 163
Malkani, Gautam, 56
Manchester, 82, 90
Medicins du Monde, 42
migration, 24
minorities, 65–6, 73–4
    perspectives of, 57
mobile phones, 68, 147,173
Mohaiemen, Naeem, 54
Moi, Daniel Arap, 121
Mru, 52
multiculturalism, 14, 33
    and well-being of children, 176;
    in London, 5

history of, 88–94
Mumbai, 29
Musharraf, Pervez, 110, 188
music, 23, 145, 176–9, 180
    as soundtrack, 196
    in Bangladesh, 171
Muter, Mrs, 129

Nairobi, 118, 125, 132, 196
names, 35, 58
national curriculum
    in India, 210
    in Northern Ireland, 221
    in Scotland, 221
    in UK, 133–5, 223
National Front, 17, 95
national identity
    and history, 139
    and minorities, 65
    and music, 145
    in Northern Ireland, 165
    in relation to other identities, 142
    and media, 35
    in Ireland, 36
national narratives, 2, 114, 140, 168
nationalism, 28, 32
    and British far right, 97
    persecution of minorities, 55
Naz Foundation, 73
neo-liberalism, 50, 69
New Delhi, 108, 209
NHS, 41, 204
Northern Ireland, 4, 32, 35, 165
    and Europe, 115
    and inter-faith projects, 220
    and teaching history, 138
    migrant workers in, 166

Ode to Joy, 21, 205
Olympics, 8, 100, 194
Orwell, George, 4, 227

Pakistan
    and democracy, 188
    and identity, 67, 68, 72
    migrants from, 44
Palestine, 220